Mometrix
TEST PREPARATION

TExES

Physical Science 6-12 (237) Exam Secrets Study Guide

DEAR FUTURE EXAM SUCCESS STORY

First of all, **THANK YOU** for purchasing Mometrix study materials!

Second, congratulations! You are one of the few determined test-takers who are committed to doing whatever it takes to excel on your exam. **You have come to the right place.** We developed these study materials with one goal in mind: to deliver you the information you need in a format that's concise and easy to use.

In addition to optimizing your guide for the content of the test, we've outlined our recommended steps for breaking down the preparation process into small, attainable goals so you can make sure you stay on track.

We've also analyzed the entire test-taking process, identifying the most common pitfalls and showing how you can overcome them and be ready for any curveball the test throws you.

Standardized testing is one of the biggest obstacles on your road to success, which only increases the importance of doing well in the high-pressure, high-stakes environment of test day. Your results on this test could have a significant impact on your future, and this guide provides the information and practical advice to help you achieve your full potential on test day.

Your success is our success

We would love to hear from you! If you would like to share the story of your exam success or if you have any questions or comments in regard to our products, please contact us at **800-673-8175** or **support@mometrix.com**.

Thanks again for your business and we wish you continued success!

Sincerely,
The Mometrix Test Preparation Team

Need more help? Check out our flashcards at:
http://MometrixFlashcards.com/TExES

TABLE OF CONTENTS

Introduction

Thank you for purchasing this resource! You have made the choice to prepare yourself for a test that could have a huge impact on your future, and this guide is designed to help you be fully ready for test day. Obviously, it's important to have a solid understanding of the test material, but you also need to be prepared for the unique environment and stressors of the test, so that you can perform to the best of your abilities.

For this purpose, the first section that appears in this guide is the **Secret Keys**. We've devoted countless hours to meticulously researching what works and what doesn't, and we've boiled down our findings to the five most impactful steps you can take to improve your performance on the test. We start at the beginning with study planning and move through the preparation process, all the way to the testing strategies that will help you get the most out of what you know when you're finally sitting in front of the test.

We recommend that you start preparing for your test as far in advance as possible. However, if you've bought this guide as a last-minute study resource and only have a few days before your test, we recommend that you skip over the first two Secret Keys since they address a long-term study plan.

If you struggle with **test anxiety**, we strongly encourage you to check out our recommendations for how you can overcome it. Test anxiety is a formidable foe, but it can be beaten, and we want to make sure you have the tools you need to defeat it.

Secret Key #1 – Plan Big, Study Small

There's a lot riding on your performance. If you want to ace this test, you're going to need to keep your skills sharp and the material fresh in your mind. You need a plan that lets you review everything you need to know while still fitting in your schedule. We'll break this strategy down into three categories.

Information Organization

Start with the information you already have: the official test outline. From this, you can make a complete list of all the concepts you need to cover before the test. Organize these concepts into groups that can be studied together, and create a list of any related vocabulary you need to learn so you can brush up on any difficult terms. You'll want to keep this vocabulary list handy once you actually start studying since you may need to add to it along the way.

Time Management

Once you have your set of study concepts, decide how to spread them out over the time you have left before the test. Break your study plan into small, clear goals so you have a manageable task for each day and know exactly what you're doing. Then just focus on one small step at a time. When you manage your time this way, you don't need to spend hours at a time studying. Studying a small block of content for a short period each day helps you retain information better and avoid stressing over how much you have left to do. You can relax knowing that you have a plan to cover everything in time. In order for this strategy to be effective though, you have to start studying early and stick to your schedule. Avoid the exhaustion and futility that comes from last-minute cramming!

Study Environment

The environment you study in has a big impact on your learning. Studying in a coffee shop, while probably more enjoyable, is not likely to be as fruitful as studying in a quiet room. It's important to keep distractions to a minimum. You're only planning to study for a short block of time, so make the most of it. Don't pause to check your phone or get up to find a snack. It's also important to **avoid multitasking**. Research has consistently shown that multitasking will make your studying dramatically less effective. Your study area should also be comfortable and well-lit so you don't have the distraction of straining your eyes or sitting on an uncomfortable chair.

The time of day you study is also important. You want to be rested and alert. Don't wait until just before bedtime. Study when you'll be most likely to comprehend and remember. Even better, if you know what time of day your test will be, set that time aside for study. That way your brain will be used to working on that subject at that specific time and you'll have a better chance of recalling information.

Finally, it can be helpful to team up with others who are studying for the same test. Your actual studying should be done in as isolated an environment as possible, but the work of organizing the information and setting up the study plan can be divided up. In between study sessions, you can discuss with your teammates the concepts that you're all studying and quiz each other on the details. Just be sure that your teammates are as serious about the test as you are. If you find that your study time is being replaced with social time, you might need to find a new team.

Secret Key #2 – Make Your Studying Count

You're devoting a lot of time and effort to preparing for this test, so you want to be absolutely certain it will pay off. This means doing more than just reading the content and hoping you can remember it on test day. It's important to make every minute of study count. There are two main areas you can focus on to make your studying count.

Retention

It doesn't matter how much time you study if you can't remember the material. You need to make sure you are retaining the concepts. To check your retention of the information you're learning, try recalling it at later times with minimal prompting. Try carrying around flashcards and glance at one or two from time to time or ask a friend who's also studying for the test to quiz you.

To enhance your retention, look for ways to put the information into practice so that you can apply it rather than simply recalling it. If you're using the information in practical ways, it will be much easier to remember. Similarly, it helps to solidify a concept in your mind if you're not only reading it to yourself but also explaining it to someone else. Ask a friend to let you teach them about a concept you're a little shaky on (or speak aloud to an imaginary audience if necessary). As you try to summarize, define, give examples, and answer your friend's questions, you'll understand the concepts better and they will stay with you longer. Finally, step back for a big picture view and ask yourself how each piece of information fits with the whole subject. When you link the different concepts together and see them working together as a whole, it's easier to remember the individual components.

Finally, practice showing your work on any multi-step problems, even if you're just studying. Writing out each step you take to solve a problem will help solidify the process in your mind, and you'll be more likely to remember it during the test.

Modality

Modality simply refers to the means or method by which you study. Choosing a study modality that fits your own individual learning style is crucial. No two people learn best in exactly the same way, so it's important to know your strengths and use them to your advantage.

For example, if you learn best by visualization, focus on visualizing a concept in your mind and draw an image or a diagram. Try color-coding your notes, illustrating them, or creating symbols that will trigger your mind to recall a learned concept. If you learn best by hearing or discussing information, find a study partner who learns the same way or read aloud to yourself. Think about how to put the information in your own words. Imagine that you are giving a lecture on the topic and record yourself so you can listen to it later.

For any learning style, flashcards can be helpful. Organize the information so you can take advantage of spare moments to review. Underline key words or phrases. Use different colors for different categories. Mnemonic devices (such as creating a short list in which every item starts with the same letter) can also help with retention. Find what works best for you and use it to store the information in your mind most effectively and easily.

Secret Key #3 – Practice the Right Way

Your success on test day depends not only on how many hours you put into preparing, but also on whether you prepared the right way. It's good to check along the way to see if your studying is paying off. One of the most effective ways to do this is by taking practice tests to evaluate your progress. Practice tests are useful because they show exactly where you need to improve. Every time you take a practice test, pay special attention to these three groups of questions:

- The questions you got wrong
- The questions you had to guess on, even if you guessed right
- The questions you found difficult or slow to work through

This will show you exactly what your weak areas are, and where you need to devote more study time. Ask yourself why each of these questions gave you trouble. Was it because you didn't understand the material? Was it because you didn't remember the vocabulary? Do you need more repetitions on this type of question to build speed and confidence? Dig into those questions and figure out how you can strengthen your weak areas as you go back to review the material.

Additionally, many practice tests have a section explaining the answer choices. It can be tempting to read the explanation and think that you now have a good understanding of the concept. However, an explanation likely only covers part of the question's broader context. Even if the explanation makes perfect sense, **go back and investigate** every concept related to the question until you're positive you have a thorough understanding.

As you go along, keep in mind that the practice test is just that: practice. Memorizing these questions and answers will not be very helpful on the actual test because it is unlikely to have any of the same exact questions. If you only know the right answers to the sample questions, you won't be prepared for the real thing. **Study the concepts** until you understand them fully, and then you'll be able to answer any question that shows up on the test.

It's important to wait on the practice tests until you're ready. If you take a test on your first day of study, you may be overwhelmed by the amount of material covered and how much you need to learn. Work up to it gradually.

On test day, you'll need to be prepared for answering questions, managing your time, and using the test-taking strategies you've learned. It's a lot to balance, like a mental marathon that will have a big impact on your future. Like training for a marathon, you'll need to start slowly and work your way up. When test day arrives, you'll be ready.

Start with the strategies you've read in the first two Secret Keys—plan your course and study in the way that works best for you. If you have time, consider using multiple study resources to get different approaches to the same concepts. It can be helpful to see difficult concepts from more than one angle. Then find a good source for practice tests. Many times, the test website will suggest potential study resources or provide sample tests.

Practice Test Strategy

If you're able to find at least three practice tests, we recommend this strategy:

Untimed and Open-Book Practice

Take the first test with no time constraints and with your notes and study guide handy. Take your time and focus on applying the strategies you've learned.

Timed and Open-Book Practice

Take the second practice test open-book as well, but set a timer and practice pacing yourself to finish in time.

Timed and Closed-Book Practice

Take any other practice tests as if it were test day. Set a timer and put away your study materials. Sit at a table or desk in a quiet room, imagine yourself at the testing center, and answer questions as quickly and accurately as possible.

Keep repeating timed and closed-book tests on a regular basis until you run out of practice tests or it's time for the actual test. Your mind will be ready for the schedule and stress of test day, and you'll be able to focus on recalling the material you've learned.

Secret Key #4 – Pace Yourself

Once you're fully prepared for the material on the test, your biggest challenge on test day will be managing your time. Just knowing that the clock is ticking can make you panic even if you have plenty of time left. Work on pacing yourself so you can build confidence against the time constraints of the exam. Pacing is a difficult skill to master, especially in a high-pressure environment, so **practice is vital**.

Set time expectations for your pace based on how much time is available. For example, if a section has 60 questions and the time limit is 30 minutes, you know you have to average 30 seconds or less per question in order to answer them all. Although 30 seconds is the hard limit, set 25 seconds per question as your goal, so you reserve extra time to spend on harder questions. When you budget extra time for the harder questions, you no longer have any reason to stress when those questions take longer to answer.

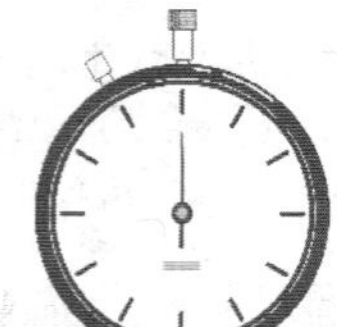

Don't let this time expectation distract you from working through the test at a calm, steady pace, but keep it in mind so you don't spend too much time on any one question. Recognize that taking extra time on one question you don't understand may keep you from answering two that you do understand later in the test. If your time limit for a question is up and you're still not sure of the answer, mark it and move on, and come back to it later if the time and the test format allow. If the testing format doesn't allow you to return to earlier questions, just make an educated guess; then put it out of your mind and move on.

On the easier questions, be careful not to rush. It may seem wise to hurry through them so you have more time for the challenging ones, but it's not worth missing one if you know the concept and just didn't take the time to read the question fully. Work efficiently but make sure you understand the question and have looked at all of the answer choices, since more than one may seem right at first.

Even if you're paying attention to the time, you may find yourself a little behind at some point. You should speed up to get back on track, but do so wisely. Don't panic; just take a few seconds less on each question until you're caught up. Don't guess without thinking, but do look through the answer choices and eliminate any you know are wrong. If you can get down to two choices, it is often worthwhile to guess from those. Once you've chosen an answer, move on and don't dwell on any that you skipped or had to hurry through. If a question was taking too long, chances are it was one of the harder ones, so you weren't as likely to get it right anyway.

On the other hand, if you find yourself getting ahead of schedule, it may be beneficial to slow down a little. The more quickly you work, the more likely you are to make a careless mistake that will affect your score. You've budgeted time for each question, so don't be afraid to spend that time. Practice an efficient but careful pace to get the most out of the time you have.

Secret Key #5 – Have a Plan for Guessing

When you're taking the test, you may find yourself stuck on a question. Some of the answer choices seem better than others, but you don't see the one answer choice that is obviously correct. What do you do?

The scenario described above is very common, yet most test takers have not effectively prepared for it. Developing and practicing a plan for guessing may be one of the single most effective uses of your time as you get ready for the exam.

In developing your plan for guessing, there are three questions to address:

- When should you start the guessing process?
- How should you narrow down the choices?
- Which answer should you choose?

When to Start the Guessing Process

Unless your plan for guessing is to select C every time (which, despite its merits, is not what we recommend), you need to leave yourself enough time to apply your answer elimination strategies. Since you have a limited amount of time for each question, that means that if you're going to give yourself the best shot at guessing correctly, you have to decide quickly whether or not you will guess.

Of course, the best-case scenario is that you don't have to guess at all, so first, see if you can answer the question based on your knowledge of the subject and basic reasoning skills. Focus on the key words in the question and try to jog your memory of related topics. Give yourself a chance to bring the knowledge to mind, but once you realize that you don't have (or you can't access) the knowledge you need to answer the question, it's time to start the guessing process.

It's almost always better to start the guessing process too early than too late. It only takes a few seconds to remember something and answer the question from knowledge. Carefully eliminating wrong answer choices takes longer. Plus, going through the process of eliminating answer choices can actually help jog your memory.

Summary: Start the guessing process as soon as you decide that you can't answer the question based on your knowledge.

How to Narrow Down the Choices

The next chapter in this book (**Test-Taking Strategies**) includes a wide range of strategies for how to approach questions and how to look for answer choices to eliminate. You will definitely want to read those carefully, practice them, and figure out which ones work best for you. Here though, we're going to address a mindset rather than a particular strategy.

Your odds of guessing an answer correctly depend on how many options you are choosing from.

Number of options left	5	4	3	2	1
Odds of guessing correctly	20%	25%	33%	50%	100%

You can see from this chart just how valuable it is to be able to eliminate incorrect answers and make an educated guess, but there are two things that many test takers do that cause them to miss out on the benefits of guessing:

- Accidentally eliminating the correct answer
- Selecting an answer based on an impression

We'll look at the first one here, and the second one in the next section.

To avoid accidentally eliminating the correct answer, we recommend a thought exercise called **the $5 challenge**. In this challenge, you only eliminate an answer choice from contention if you are willing to bet $5 on it being wrong. Why $5? Five dollars is a small but not insignificant amount of money. It's an amount you could afford to lose but wouldn't want to throw away. And while losing $5 once might not hurt too much, doing it twenty times will set you back $100. In the same way, each small decision you make—eliminating a choice here, guessing on a question there—won't by itself impact your score very much, but when you put them all together, they can make a big difference. By holding each answer choice elimination decision to a higher standard, you can reduce the risk of accidentally eliminating the correct answer.

The $5 challenge can also be applied in a positive sense: If you are willing to bet $5 that an answer choice *is* correct, go ahead and mark it as correct.

Summary: Only eliminate an answer choice if you are willing to bet $5 that it is wrong.

Which Answer to Choose

You're taking the test. You've run into a hard question and decided you'll have to guess. You've eliminated all the answer choices you're willing to bet $5 on. Now you have to pick an answer. Why do we even need to talk about this? Why can't you just pick whichever one you feel like when the time comes?

The answer to these questions is that if you don't come into the test with a plan, you'll rely on your impression to select an answer choice, and if you do that, you risk falling into a trap. The test writers know that everyone who takes their test will be guessing on some of the questions, so they intentionally write wrong answer choices to seem plausible. You still have to pick an answer though, and if the wrong answer choices are designed to look right, how can you ever be sure that you're not falling for their trap? The best solution we've found to this dilemma is to take the decision out of your hands entirely. Here is the process we recommend:

Once you've eliminated any choices that you are confident (willing to bet $5) are wrong, select the first remaining choice as your answer.

Whether you choose to select the first remaining choice, the second, or the last, the important thing is that you use some preselected standard. Using this approach guarantees that you will not be enticed into selecting an answer choice that looks right, because you are not basing your decision on how the answer choices look.

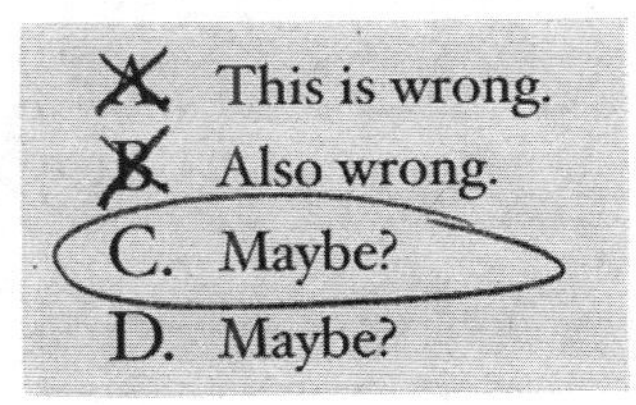

This is not meant to make you question your knowledge. Instead, it is to help you recognize the difference between your knowledge and your impressions. There's a huge difference between thinking an answer is right because of what you know, and thinking an answer is right because it looks or sounds like it should be right.

Summary: To ensure that your selection is appropriately random, make a predetermined selection from among all answer choices you have not eliminated.

Test-Taking Strategies

This section contains a list of test-taking strategies that you may find helpful as you work through the test. By taking what you know and applying logical thought, you can maximize your chances of answering any question correctly!

It is very important to realize that every question is different and every person is different: no single strategy will work on every question, and no single strategy will work for every person. That's why we've included all of them here, so you can try them out and determine which ones work best for different types of questions and which ones work best for you.

Question Strategies

☑ Read Carefully

Read the question and the answer choices carefully. Don't miss the question because you misread the terms. You have plenty of time to read each question thoroughly and make sure you understand what is being asked. Yet a happy medium must be attained, so don't waste too much time. You must read carefully and efficiently.

☑ Contextual Clues

Look for contextual clues. If the question includes a word you are not familiar with, look at the immediate context for some indication of what the word might mean. Contextual clues can often give you all the information you need to decipher the meaning of an unfamiliar word. Even if you can't determine the meaning, you may be able to narrow down the possibilities enough to make a solid guess at the answer to the question.

☑ Prefixes

If you're having trouble with a word in the question or answer choices, try dissecting it. Take advantage of every clue that the word might include. Prefixes can be a huge help. Usually, they allow you to determine a basic meaning. *Pre-* means before, *post-* means after, *pro-* is positive, *de-* is negative. From prefixes, you can get an idea of the general meaning of the word and try to put it into context.

☑ Hedge Words

Watch out for critical hedge words, such as *likely, may, can, often, almost, mostly, usually, generally, rarely*, and *sometimes*. Question writers insert these hedge phrases to cover every possibility. Often an answer choice will be wrong simply because it leaves no room for exception. Be on guard for answer choices that have definitive words such as *exactly* and *always*.

☑ Switchback Words

Stay alert for *switchbacks*. These are the words and phrases frequently used to alert you to shifts in thought. The most common switchback words are *but, although*, and *however*. Others include *nevertheless, on the other hand, even though, while, in spite of, despite*, and *regardless of*. Switchback words are important to catch because they can change the direction of the question or an answer choice.

☑ Face Value

When in doubt, use common sense. Accept the situation in the problem at face value. Don't read too much into it. These problems will not require you to make wild assumptions. If you have to go beyond creativity and warp time or space in order to have an answer choice fit the question, then you should move on and consider the other answer choices. These are normal problems rooted in reality. The applicable relationship or explanation may not be readily apparent, but it is there for you to figure out. Use your common sense to interpret anything that isn't clear.

Answer Choice Strategies

✅ ANSWER SELECTION

The most thorough way to pick an answer choice is to identify and eliminate wrong answers until only one is left, then confirm it is the correct answer. Sometimes an answer choice may immediately seem right, but be careful. The test writers will usually put more than one reasonable answer choice on each question, so take a second to read all of them and make sure that the other choices are not equally obvious. As long as you have time left, it is better to read every answer choice than to pick the first one that looks right without checking the others.

✅ ANSWER CHOICE FAMILIES

An answer choice family consists of two (in rare cases, three) answer choices that are very similar in construction and cannot all be true at the same time. If you see two answer choices that are direct opposites or parallels, one of them is usually the correct answer. For instance, if one answer choice says that quantity *x* increases and another either says that quantity *x* decreases (opposite) or says that quantity *y* increases (parallel), then those answer choices would fall into the same family. An answer choice that doesn't match the construction of the answer choice family is more likely to be incorrect. Most questions will not have answer choice families, but when they do appear, you should be prepared to recognize them.

✅ ELIMINATE ANSWERS

Eliminate answer choices as soon as you realize they are wrong, but make sure you consider all possibilities. If you are eliminating answer choices and realize that the last one you are left with is also wrong, don't panic. Start over and consider each choice again. There may be something you missed the first time that you will realize on the second pass.

✅ AVOID FACT TRAPS

Don't be distracted by an answer choice that is factually true but doesn't answer the question. You are looking for the choice that answers the question. Stay focused on what the question is asking for so you don't accidentally pick an answer that is true but incorrect. Always go back to the question and make sure the answer choice you've selected actually answers the question and is not merely a true statement.

✅ EXTREME STATEMENTS

In general, you should avoid answers that put forth extreme actions as standard practice or proclaim controversial ideas as established fact. An answer choice that states the "process should be used in certain situations, if..." is much more likely to be correct than one that states the "process should be discontinued completely." The first is a calm rational statement and doesn't even make a definitive, uncompromising stance, using a hedge word *if* to provide wiggle room, whereas the second choice is far more extreme.

✅ BENCHMARK

As you read through the answer choices and you come across one that seems to answer the question well, mentally select that answer choice. This is not your final answer, but it's the one that will help you evaluate the other answer choices. The one that you selected is your benchmark or standard for judging each of the other answer choices. Every other answer choice must be compared to your benchmark. That choice is correct until proven otherwise by another answer choice beating it. If you find a better answer, then that one becomes your new benchmark. Once you've decided that no other choice answers the question as well as your benchmark, you have your final answer.

☑ PREDICT THE ANSWER

Before you even start looking at the answer choices, it is often best to try to predict the answer. When you come up with the answer on your own, it is easier to avoid distractions and traps because you will know exactly what to look for. The right answer choice is unlikely to be word-for-word what you came up with, but it should be a close match. Even if you are confident that you have the right answer, you should still take the time to read each option before moving on.

General Strategies

☑ TOUGH QUESTIONS

If you are stumped on a problem or it appears too hard or too difficult, don't waste time. Move on! Remember though, if you can quickly check for obviously incorrect answer choices, your chances of guessing correctly are greatly improved. Before you completely give up, at least try to knock out a couple of possible answers. Eliminate what you can and then guess at the remaining answer choices before moving on.

☑ CHECK YOUR WORK

Since you will probably not know every term listed and the answer to every question, it is important that you get credit for the ones that you do know. Don't miss any questions through careless mistakes. If at all possible, try to take a second to look back over your answer selection and make sure you've selected the correct answer choice and haven't made a costly careless mistake (such as marking an answer choice that you didn't mean to mark). This quick double check should more than pay for itself in caught mistakes for the time it costs.

☑ PACE YOURSELF

It's easy to be overwhelmed when you're looking at a page full of questions; your mind is confused and full of random thoughts, and the clock is ticking down faster than you would like. Calm down and maintain the pace that you have set for yourself. Especially as you get down to the last few minutes of the test, don't let the small numbers on the clock make you panic. As long as you are on track by monitoring your pace, you are guaranteed to have time for each question.

☑ DON'T RUSH

It is very easy to make errors when you are in a hurry. Maintaining a fast pace in answering questions is pointless if it makes you miss questions that you would have gotten right otherwise. Test writers like to include distracting information and wrong answers that seem right. Taking a little extra time to avoid careless mistakes can make all the difference in your test score. Find a pace that allows you to be confident in the answers that you select.

☑ KEEP MOVING

Panicking will not help you pass the test, so do your best to stay calm and keep moving. Taking deep breaths and going through the answer elimination steps you practiced can help to break through a stress barrier and keep your pace.

Final Notes

The combination of a solid foundation of content knowledge and the confidence that comes from practicing your plan for applying that knowledge is the key to maximizing your performance on test day. As your foundation of content knowledge is built up and strengthened, you'll find that the strategies included in this chapter become more and more effective in helping you quickly sift through the distractions and traps of the test to isolate the correct answer.

Now that you're preparing to move forward into the test content chapters of this book, be sure to keep your goal in mind. As you read, think about how you will be able to apply this information on the test. If you've already seen sample questions for the test and you have an idea of the question format and style, try to come up with questions of your own that you can answer based on what you're reading. This will give you valuable practice applying your knowledge in the same ways you can expect to on test day.

Good luck and good studying!

Scientific Inquiry and Processes

Safety and Equipment

Laboratory Accidents

Any spills or accidents should be **reported** to the teacher so that the teacher can determine the safest clean-up method. The student should start to wash off a **chemical** spilled on the skin while reporting the incident. Some spills may require removal of contaminated clothing and use of the **safety shower**. Broken glass should be disposed of in a designated container. If someone's clothing catches fire they should walk to the safety shower and use it to extinguish the flames. A fire blanket may be used to smother a **lab fire**. A fire extinguisher, phone, spill neutralizers, and a first aid box are other types of **safety equipment** found in the lab. Students should be familiar with **routes** out of the room and the building in case of fire. Students should use the **eye wash station** if a chemical gets in the eyes.

Safety Procedures

Students should wear a **lab apron** and **safety goggles**. Loose or dangling clothing and jewelry, necklaces, and earrings should not be worn. Those with long hair should tie it back. Care should always be taken not to splash chemicals. Open-toed shoes such as sandals and flip-flops should not be worn, nor should wrist watches. Glasses are preferable to contact lenses since the latter carry a risk of chemicals getting caught between the lens and the eye. Students should always be supervised. The area where the experiment is taking place and the surrounding floor should be free of clutter. Only the lab book and the items necessary for the experiment should be present. Smoking, eating, and chewing gum are not permitted in the lab. Cords should not be allowed to dangle from work stations. There should be no rough-housing in the lab. Hands should be washed after the lab is complete.

Fume Hoods

Because of the potential safety hazards associated with chemistry lab experiments, such as fire from vapors and the inhalation of toxic fumes, a **fume hood** should be used in many instances. A fume hood carries away vapors from reagents or reactions. Equipment or reactions are placed as far back in the hood as practical to help enhance the collection of the fumes. The **glass safety shield** automatically closes to the appropriate height, and it should be low enough to protect the face and body. The safety shield should only be raised to move equipment in and out of the hood. One should not climb inside a hood or stick one's head inside. All spills should be wiped up immediately, and the glass should be cleaned if a splash occurs.

Common Safety Hazards

Some specific safety hazards possible in a chemistry lab include:

- **Fire**: Fire can be caused by volatile solvents such as ether, acetone, or benzene being kept in an open beaker or Erlenmeyer flask. Vapors can creep along the table and ignite if they reach a flame or spark. Solvents should be heated in a hood with a steam bath, not on a hot plate.
- **Explosion**: Heating or creating a reaction in a closed system can cause an explosion, resulting in flying glass and chemical splashes. The system should be vented to prevent this.
- **Chemical and thermal burns**: Many chemicals are corrosive to the skin and eyes.
- **Inhalation of toxic fumes**: Some compounds severely irritate membranes in the eyes, nose, throat, and lungs.
- **Absorption** of toxic chemicals such as dimethyl sulfoxide (DMSO) and nitrobenzene through the skin.
- **Ingestion** of toxic chemicals.

Safety Gloves

There are many types of **gloves** available to help protect the skin from cuts, burns, and chemical splashes. There are many considerations when choosing a glove. For example, gloves that are highly protective may limit dexterity. Some gloves may not offer appropriate protection against a specific chemical. Other considerations include degradation rating, which indicates how effective a glove is when exposed to chemicals; breakthrough time, which indicates how quickly a chemical can break through the surface of the glove; and permeation rate, which indicates how quickly chemicals seep through after the initial breakthrough. Disposable latex, vinyl, or nitrile gloves are usually appropriate for most circumstances, and offer protection from incidental splashes and contact. Other types of gloves include butyl, neoprene, PVC, PVA, Viton, Silver Shield, and natural rubber. Each offers its own type of protection but may have drawbacks as well.

Proper Handling and Storage of Chemicals

Students should take care when **carrying chemicals** from one place to another. Chemicals should never be taken from the room, tasted, or touched with bare hands. **Safety gloves** should be worn when appropriate and glove/chemical interactions and glove deterioration should be considered. Hands should always be **washed** thoroughly after a lab. Potentially hazardous materials intended for use in chemistry, biology, or other science labs should be secured in a safe area where relevant **Safety Data Sheets (SDS)** can be accessed. Chemicals and solutions should be used as directed and labels should be read before handling solutions and chemicals. Extra chemicals should not be returned to their original containers, but should be disposed of as directed by the school district's rules or local ordinances. Local municipalities often have hazardous waste disposal programs. Acids should be stored separately from other chemicals. Flammable liquids should be stored away from acids, bases, and oxidizers.

Bunsen Burners

When using a **Bunsen burner**, loose clothing should be tucked in, long hair should be tied back, and safety goggles and aprons should be worn. Students should know what to do in case of a fire or accident. When lighting the burner, strikers should always be used instead of matches. Do not touch the hot barrel. Tongs (never fingers) should be used to hold the material in the flame. To heat liquid, a flask may be set upon wire gauze on a tripod and secured with an iron ring or clamp on a stand. The flame is extinguished by turning off the gas at the source.

Safety Procedures Related to Animals

Animals to be used for **dissections** should be obtained from a company that provides animals for this purpose. Road kill or decaying animals that a student brings in should not be used. It is possible that such an animal may have a pathogen or a virus, such as rabies, which can be transmitted via the saliva of even a dead animal. Students should use gloves and should not participate if they have open sores or moral objections to dissections. It is generally accepted that biological experiments may be performed on lower-order life forms and invertebrates, but not on mammalian vertebrates and birds. No animals should be harmed physiologically. Experimental animals should be kept, cared for, and handled in a safe manner and with compassion. Pathogenic (anything able to cause a disease) substances should not be used in lab experiments.

Lab Notebooks

A **lab notebook** is a record of all pre-lab work and lab work. It differs from a lab report, which is prepared after lab work is completed. A lab notebook is a formal record of lab preparations and what was done. **Observational recordings** should not be altered, erased, or whited-out to make corrections. Drawing a single line through an entry is sufficient to make changes. Pages should be numbered and should not be torn out. Entries should be made neatly, but don't necessarily have to be complete sentences. **Entries** should provide detailed information and be recorded in such a way that another person could use them to replicate the experiment. **Quantitative data** may be recorded in tabular form, and may include calculations made during an experiment. Lab book entries can also include references and research performed before the experiment.

Entries may also consist of information about a lab experiment, including the objective or purpose, the procedures, data collected, and the results.

Lab Reports

A **lab report** is an item developed after an experiment that is intended to present the results of a lab experiment. Generally, it should be prepared using a word processor, not hand-written or recorded in a notebook. A lab report should be formally presented. It is intended to persuade others to accept or reject a hypothesis. It should include a brief but descriptive **title** and an **abstract**. The abstract is a summary of the report. It should include a purpose that states the problem that was explored or the question that was answered. It should also include a **hypothesis** that describes the anticipated results of the experiment. The experiment should include a **control** and one **variable** to ensure that the results can be interpreted correctly. Observations and results can be presented using written narratives, tables, graphs, and illustrations. The report should also include a **summation** or **conclusion** explaining whether the results supported the hypothesis.

Types of Laboratory Glassware

Two types of flasks are Erlenmeyer flasks and volumetric flasks. **Volumetric flasks** are used to accurately prepare a specific volume and concentration of a solution. **Erlenmeyer flasks** can be used for mixing, transporting, and reacting, but are not appropriate for accurate measurements.

A **pipette** can be used to accurately measure small amounts of liquid. Liquid is drawn into the pipette through a bulb. The liquid measurement is read at the **meniscus**. There are also plastic disposable pipettes. A **repipette** is a hand-operated pump that dispenses solutions.

Beakers can be used to measure mass or dissolve a solvent into a solute. They do not measure volume as accurately as a volumetric flask, pipette, graduated cylinder, or burette.

Graduated cylinders are used for precise measurements and are considered more accurate than Erlenmeyer flasks or beakers. To read a graduated cylinder, it should be placed on a flat surface and read at eye level. The surface of a liquid in a graduated cylinder forms a lens-shaped curve. The measurement should be taken from the bottom of the curve. A ring may be placed at the top of tall, narrow cylinders to help avoid breakage if they are tipped over.

A **burette**, or buret, is a piece of lab glassware used to accurately dispense liquid. It looks similar to a narrow graduated cylinder, but it includes a stopcock and tip. It may be filled with a funnel or pipette.

Microscopes

There are different kinds of microscopes, but **optical** or **light microscopes** are the most commonly used in lab settings. Light and lenses are used to magnify and view samples. A specimen or sample is placed on a slide, and the slide is placed on a stage with a hole in it. Light passes through the hole and illuminates the sample. The sample is magnified by lenses and viewed through the eyepiece. A simple microscope has one lens, while a typical compound microscope has three lenses. The light source can be room light redirected by a mirror, or the microscope can have its own independent light source that passes through a condenser. In this case, there are diaphragms and filters to allow light intensity to be controlled. Optical microscopes also have coarse and fine adjustment knobs.

Other types of microscopes include **digital microscopes**, which use a camera and a monitor to allow viewing of the sample. **Scanning electron microscopes (SEMs)** provide greater detail in terms of a sample's surface topography and can produce magnifications much greater than those possible with optical microscopes. The technology of an SEM is quite different from an optical microscope in that it does not rely on lenses to magnify objects, but uses samples placed in a chamber. In one type of SEM, a beam of electrons from an electron gun scans and actually interacts with the sample to produce an image.

Wet mount slides designed for use with a light microscope typically require a thin portion of the specimen to be placed on a standard glass slide. A drop of water is added, and a cover slip or cover glass is placed on top. Air bubbles and fingerprints can make viewing difficult. Placing the cover slip at a 45-degree angle and allowing it to drop into place can help avoid the problem of air bubbles. A **cover slip** should always be used when viewing wet mount slides. The viewer should start with the objective in its lowest position and then fine-focus. The microscope should be carried with two hands and stored with the low-power objective in the down position. **Lenses** should be cleaned with lens paper only. A **graticule slide** is marked with a grid line, and is useful for counting or estimating a quantity.

Balances

Balances such as triple-beam balances, spring balances, and electronic balances measure mass and force. An **electronic balance** is the most accurate, followed by a **triple-beam balance** and then a **spring balance**. One part of a **triple-beam balance** is the plate, which is where the item to be weighed is placed. There are also three beams, which have hash marks indicating amounts and which hold the weights that rest in the notches. The front beam measures weights between 0 and 10 grams, the middle beam measures weights in 100-gram increments, and the far beam measures weights in 10-gram increments. The sum of the weight of each beam is the total weight of the object. A triple beam balance also includes a set screw to calibrate the equipment, as well as a mark indicating that the object and counterweights are in balance.

Chromatography

Chromatography refers to a set of laboratory techniques used to separate or analyze **mixtures**. Mixtures are dissolved in their mobile phases. In the stationary or bonded phase, the desired component is separated from other molecules in the mixture. In chromatography, the analyte is the substance to be separated. **Preparative chromatography** refers to the type of chromatography that involves purifying a substance for further use rather than further analysis. **Analytical chromatography** involves analyzing the isolated substance. Other types of chromatography include column, planar, paper, thin layer, displacement, supercritical fluid, affinity, ion exchange, and size exclusion chromatography. Reversed phase, two-dimensional, simulated moving bed, pyrolysis, fast protein, counter current, and chiral are also types of chromatography. **Gas chromatography** refers to the separation technique in which the mobile phase of a substance is in gas form.

Review Video: Paper Chromatography
Visit mometrix.com/academy and enter code: 543963

Reagents and Reactants

A **reagent** or **reactant** is a chemical agent for use in chemical reactions. When preparing for a lab, it should be confirmed that glassware and other equipment have been cleaned and/or sterilized. There should be enough materials, reagents, or other solutions needed for the lab for every group of students completing the experiment. Distilled water should be used instead of tap water when performing lab experiments because distilled water has most of its impurities removed. Other needed apparatus such as funnels, filter paper, balances, Bunsen burners, ring stands, and/or microscopes should also be set up. After the lab, it should be confirmed that sinks, workstations, and any equipment used have been cleaned. If chemicals or specimens need to be kept at a certain temperature by refrigerating them or using another storage method, the temperature should be checked periodically to ensure the sample does not spoil.

Diluting Acids

When preparing a solution of **dilute acid**, always add the concentrated acid solution to water, not water to concentrated acid. Start by adding approximately $\frac{2}{3}$ of the total volume of water to the graduated cylinder or volumetric flask. Next, add the concentrated acid to the water. Add additional water to the diluted acid to bring the solution to the final desired volume.

Cleaning After Acid Spills

In the event of an **acid spill**, any clothes that have come into contact with the acid should be removed and any skin contacted with acid must be rinsed with clean water. To the extent a window can be opened or a fume hood can be turned on, do so. Do not try to force air circulation, such as by adding a fan, as acid fumes can be harmful if spread.

Next, pour one of the following over the spill area: sodium bicarbonate, baking soda, soda ash, or cat litter. Start from the outside of the spill and then move towards the center, in order to prevent splashing. When the clumps have thoroughly dried, sweep up the clumps and dispose of them as chemical waste.

Centrifuges

A centrifuge is used to separate the components of a heterogeneous mixture (consisting of two or more compounds) by spinning it. The solid precipitate settles in the bottom of the container, and the liquid component of the solution, called the **centrifugate**, is at the top. A well-known application of this process is using a centrifuge to separate blood cells and plasma. The heavier cells settle on the bottom of the test tube, and the lighter plasma stays on top. Another example is using a salad spinner to help dry lettuce.

Electrophoresis, Calorimetry, and Titration

- **Electrophoresis** is the separation of molecules based on electrical charge. This is possible because particles dispersed in a fluid usually carry electric charges on their surfaces. Molecules are pulled through the fluid toward the positive end if the molecules have a negative charge and are pulled through the fluid toward the negative end if the molecules have a positive charge.
- **Calorimetry** is used to determine the heat released or absorbed in a chemical reaction.
- **Titration** helps determine the precise endpoint of a reaction. With this information, the precise quantity of reactant in the titration flask can be determined. A burette is used to deliver the second reactant to the flask and an indicator or pH meter is used to detect the endpoint of the reaction.

Field Studies and Research Projects

Field studies may facilitate scientific inquiry in a manner similar to indoor lab experiments. Field studies can be interdisciplinary in nature and can help students learn and apply scientific concepts and processes. **Research projects** can be conducted in any number of locations, including school campuses, local parks, national parks, beaches, or mountains. Students can practice the general techniques of observation, data collection, collaborative planning, and analysis of experiments. Field studies give students the chance to learn through hands-on applications of scientific processes, such as map making in geography, observation of stratification in geology, observation of life cycles of plants and animals, and analysis of water quality.

Students should watch out for obvious outdoor **hazards**. These include poisonous flora and fauna such as poison ivy, poison oak, and sumac. Depending on the region of the United States in which the field study is being conducted, hazards may also include rattlesnakes and black widow or brown recluse spiders. Students should also be made aware of potentially hazardous situations specific to **geographic locales** and the possibility of coming into contact with **pathogens**.

Field studies allow for great flexibility in the use of traditional and technological methods for **making observations** and **collecting data**. For example, a nature study could consist of a simple survey of bird species within a given area. Information could be recorded using still photography or a video camera. This type of activity gives students the chance to use technologies other than computers. Computers could still be used to create a slide show of transferred images or a digital lab report. If a quantitative study of birds was being performed, the simple technique of using a pencil and paper to tabulate the number of birds counted in the field could also be used. Other techniques used during field studies could include collecting specimens for lab study, observing coastal ecosystems and tides, and collecting weather data such as temperature, precipitation amounts, and air pressure in a particular locale.

Scientific Inquiry and Reasoning

Scientific Inquiry

The concept of **scientific inquiry** refers to the idea of how one thinks and asks questions in a logical way to gain trustworthy information. The underlying motivation of science is to try to understand the natural world. Much of human thought is based on assumptions about how things work that may or may not be true. The goal of scientific inquiry is to test those assumptions to gain a greater understanding of the world with good questions and objective tests, and then re-use what was learned to ask better questions. The more we understand about the natural world, the better the questions we can ask, and that is the general idea behind scientific inquiry. The applied practice of scientific inquiry is to ask questions in a systematic method, called the scientific method.

Scientific Knowledge

Scientific knowledge refers to any topic that is studied **empirically**, meaning that it is based on observation of a **phenomenon** in an objective way. The body of **scientific knowledge** is often broken down into several domains including biology, ecology, Earth science, space science, physics, and chemistry. These each have further subdomains and are overlapping in many ways. For instance, ecology is the study of ecosystems, which are made up of biological factors and geological factors, so it contains elements of both biology and Earth science. Each of these domains is subject to the concepts of scientific inquiry, such as the scientific method, scientific facts, hypotheses, and scientific laws.

Important Terminology

- A **phenomenon** is an event or effect that is observed.
- A **scientific fact** is considered an objective and verifiable observation. Usually, a fact can be repeated or demonstrated to others.
- A **scientific theory** is a proposition explaining why or how something happens and is built on scientific facts and laws. Scientific theories can be tested, but are not fully proven. If new evidence is found that disproves the theory, it is no longer considered true.
- A **hypothesis** is an educated guess that is not yet proven. It is used to predict the outcome of an experiment in an attempt to solve a problem or answer a question.
- A **law** is an explanation of events that always leads to the same outcome. It is a fact that an object falls. The law of gravity explains why an object falls. The theory of relativity, although generally accepted, has been neither proven nor disproved.
- A **model** is used to explain something on a smaller scale or in simpler terms to provide an example. It is a representation of an idea that can be used to explain events or applied to new situations to predict outcomes or determine results.

History of Scientific Knowledge

When one examines the history of **scientific knowledge**, it is clear that it is constantly **evolving**. The body of facts, models, theories, and laws grows and changes over time. In other words, one scientific discovery leads to the next. Some advances in science and technology have important and long-lasting effects on science and society. Some discoveries were so alien to the accepted beliefs of the time that not only were they rejected as wrong, but were also considered outright blasphemy. Today, however, many beliefs once considered incorrect have become an ingrained part of scientific knowledge, and have also been the basis of new advances. Examples of advances include: Copernicus's heliocentric view of the universe, Newton's laws of motion and planetary orbits, relativity, geologic time scale, plate tectonics, atomic theory, nuclear physics, biological evolution, germ theory, industrial revolution, molecular biology, information and communication, quantum theory, galactic universe, and medical and health technology.

Scientific Inquiry and Scientific Method

Scientists use a number of generally accepted techniques collectively known as the **scientific method**. The scientific method generally involves carrying out the following steps:

- Identifying a problem or posing a question
- Formulating a hypothesis or an educated guess
- Conducting experiments or tests that will provide a basis to solve the problem or answer the question
- Observing the results of the test
- Drawing conclusions

An important part of the scientific method is using acceptable experimental techniques. Objectivity is also important if valid results are to be obtained. Another important part of the scientific method is peer review. It is essential that experiments be performed and data be recorded in such a way that experiments can be reproduced to verify results. Historically, the scientific method has been taught with a more linear approach, but it is important to recognize that the scientific method should be a cyclical or **recursive process**. This means that as hypotheses are tested and more is learned, the questions should continue to change to reflect the changing body of knowledge. One cycle of experimentation is not enough.

Review Video: The Scientific Method
Visit mometrix.com/academy and enter code: 191386

Metric and International System of Units

The **metric system** is the accepted standard of measurement in the scientific community. The **International System of Units (SI)** is a set of measurements (including the metric system) that is almost globally accepted. The United States, Liberia, and Myanmar have not accepted this system. **Standardization** is important because it allows the results of experiments to be compared and reproduced without the need to laboriously convert measurements. The SI is based partially on the **meter-kilogram-second (MKS) system** rather than the **centimeter-gram-second (CGS) system**. The MKS system considers meters, kilograms, and seconds to be the basic units of measurement, while the CGS system considers centimeters, grams, and seconds to be the basic units of measurement. Under the MKS system, the length of an object would be expressed as 1 meter instead of 100 centimeters, which is how it would be described under the CGS system.

Review Video: Metric System Conversions
Visit mometrix.com/academy and enter code: 163709

Basic Units of Measurement

Using the **metric system** is generally accepted as the preferred method for taking measurements. Having a **universal standard** allows individuals to interpret measurements more easily, regardless of where they are located. The basic units of measurement are: the **meter**, which measures length; the **liter**, which measures volume; and the **gram**, which measures mass. The metric system starts with a base unit and increases or decreases in units of 10. The prefix and the base unit combined are used to indicate an amount. For example, deka- is 10 times the base unit. A dekameter is 10 meters; a dekaliter is 10 liters; and a dekagram is 10 grams. The prefix hecto- refers to 100 times the base amount; kilo- is 1,000 times the base amount. The prefixes that indicate a fraction of the base unit are deci-, which is $\frac{1}{10}$ of the base unit; centi-, which is $\frac{1}{100}$ of the base unit; and milli-, which is $\frac{1}{1,000}$ of the base unit.

Common Prefixes

The prefixes for multiples are as follows:

Deka	(da)	**10^1** (deka is the American spelling, but deca is also used)
Hecto	(h)	10^2
Kilo	(k)	10^3
Mega	(M)	10^6
Giga	(G)	10^9
Tera	(T)	10^{12}

The prefixes for subdivisions are as follows:

Deci	(d)	**10^{-1}**
Centi	(c)	10^{-2}
Milli	(m)	10^{-3}
Micro	(μ)	10^{-6}
Nano	(n)	10^{-9}
Pico	(p)	10^{-12}

The rule of thumb is that prefixes greater than 10^3 are capitalized when abbreviating. Abbreviations do not need a period after them. A decimeter (dm) is a tenth of a meter, a deciliter (dL) is a tenth of a liter, and a decigram (dg) is a tenth of a gram. Pluralization is understood. For example, when referring to 5 mL of water, no "s" needs to be added to the abbreviation.

Basic SI Units of Measurement

SI uses **second(s)** to measure time. Fractions of seconds are usually measured in metric terms using prefixes such as millisecond ($\frac{1}{1,000}$ of a second) or nanosecond ($\frac{1}{1,000,000,000}$ of a second). Increments of time larger than a second are measured in **minutes** and **hours**, which are multiples of 60 and 24. An example of this is a swimmer's time in the 800-meter freestyle being described as 7:32.67, meaning 7 minutes, 32 seconds, and 67 one-hundredths of a second. One second is equal to $\frac{1}{60}$ of a minute, $\frac{1}{3,600}$ of an hour, and $\frac{1}{86,400}$ of a day. Other SI base units are the **ampere** (A) (used to measure electric current), the **kelvin** (K) (used to measure thermodynamic temperature), the **candela** (cd) (used to measure luminous intensity), and the **mole** (mol) (used to measure the amount of a substance at a molecular level). **Meter** (m) is used to measure length and **kilogram** (kg) is used to measure mass.

Significant Figures

The mathematical concept of **significant figures** or **significant digits** is often used to determine the accuracy of measurements or the level of confidence one has in a specific measurement. The significant figures of a measurement include all the digits known with certainty plus one estimated or uncertain digit. There are a number of rules for determining which digits are considered "important" or "interesting." They are:

- All non-zero digits are *significant.*
- Zeros between digits are *significant.*
- Leading and trailing zeros are *not significant* unless they appear to the right of the non-zero digits in a decimal.

For example, in 0.01230, the significant digits are 1230, and this number would be said to be accurate to the hundred-thousandths place. The zero indicates that the amount has actually been measured as 0. Other zeros are considered placeholders and are not important. A decimal point may be placed after zeros to indicate their importance (in "100." for example).

Graphs and Charts

Graphs and charts are effective ways to present scientific data such as observations, statistical analyses, and comparisons between dependent variables and independent variables. On a line chart, the **independent variable** (the one that is being manipulated for the experiment) is represented on the horizontal axis (the x-axis). Any **dependent variables** (the ones that may change as the independent variable changes) are represented on the y-axis. An **XY** or **scatter plot** is often used to plot many points. A "best fit" line is drawn, which allows outliers to be identified more easily. Charts and their axes should have titles. The x and y interval units should be evenly spaced and labeled. Other types of charts are **bar charts** and **histograms**, which can be used to compare differences between the data collected for two variables. A **pie chart** can graphically show the relation of parts to a whole.

Review Video: Identifying Variables
Visit mometrix.com/academy and enter code: 627181

Review Video: Data Interpretation of Graphs
Visit mometrix.com/academy and enter code: 200439

Data Presentation

Data collected during a science lab can be organized and **presented** in any number of ways. While **straight narrative** is a suitable method for presenting some lab results, it is not a suitable way to present numbers and quantitative measurements. These types of observations can often be better presented with **tables** and **graphs**. Data that is presented in tables and organized in rows and columns may also be used to make graphs quite easily. Other methods of presenting data include illustrations, photographs, video, and even audio formats. In a **formal report**, tables and figures are labeled and referred to by their labels. For example, a picture of a bubbly solution might be labeled Figure 1, Bubbly Solution. It would be referred to in the text in the following way: "The reaction created bubbles 10 mm in size, as shown in Figure 1, Bubbly Solution." Graphs are also labeled as figures. Tables are labeled in a different way. Examples include: Table 1, Results of Statistical Analysis, or Table 2, Data from Lab 2.

Statistical Precision and Errors

Errors that occur during an experiment can be classified into two categories: random errors and systematic errors. **Random errors** can result in collected data that is wildly different from the rest of the data, or they may result in data that is indistinguishable from the rest. Random errors are not consistent across the data set. In large data sets, random errors may contribute to the variability of data, but they will not affect the average. Random errors are sometimes referred to as noise. They may be caused by a student's inability to take the same measurement in exactly the same way or by outside factors that are not considered variables, but influence the data. A **systematic error** will show up consistently across a sample or data set, and may be the result of a flaw in the experimental design. This type of error affects the average, and is also known as bias.

Scientific Notation

Scientific notation is used because values in science can be very large or very small, which makes them unwieldy. A number in **decimal notation** is 93,000,000. In **scientific notation**, it is 9.3×10^7. The first number, 9.3, is the **coefficient**. It is always greater than or equal to 1 and less than 10. This number is followed by a multiplication sign. The base is always 10 in scientific notation. If the number is greater than ten, the exponent is positive. If the number is between zero and one, the exponent is negative. The first digit of the number is followed by a decimal point and then the rest of the number. In this case, the number is 9.3, and the decimal point was moved seven places to the right from the end of the number to get 93,000,000. The number of places moved, seven, is the exponent.

STATISTICAL TERMINOLOGY

- **Mean**—The average, found by taking the sum of a set of numbers and dividing by the number of numbers in the set.
- **Median**—The middle number in a set of numbers sorted from least to greatest. If the set has an even number of entries, the median is the average of the two in the middle.
- **Mode**—The value that appears most frequently in a data set. There may be more than one mode. If no value appears more than once, there is no mode.
- **Range**—The difference between the highest and lowest numbers in a data set.
- **Standard deviation**—Measures the dispersion of a data set, or how far from the mean a single data point is likely to be.
- **Regression analysis**—A method of analyzing sets of data and sets of variables. It involves studying how the typical value of the dependent variable changes when any one of the independent variables is varied and the other independent variables remain fixed.

Review Video: Mean, Median, and Mode
Visit mometrix.com/academy and enter code: 286207

Review Video: Standard Deviation
Visit mometrix.com/academy and enter code: 419469

Chapter Quiz

Ready to see how well you retained what you just read? Scan the QR code to go directly to the chapter quiz interface for this study guide. If you're using a computer, simply visit the online resources page at **mometrix.com/resources719/texesphysc6-12** and click the Chapter Quizzes link.

Physics

Thermodynamics

TEMPERATURE, SCALES, HEAT, AND HEAT CAPACITY

TEMPERATURE SCALES

Empirical or relative temperature scales, like Celsius (°C) and Fahrenheit (°F), can have a corresponding **absolute temperature scale**, which in this case would be Kelvin (K) and Rankine (R), respectively. A temperature of 0 K or 0 R is known as **absolute zero**, at which point atomic motion and thermal energy are, theoretically, at a minimum. Kelvins and degrees Celsius are related by the equation, $T_K = T_C + 273.15$. Similarly, Rankines and degrees Fahrenheit are related as $T_R = T_F + 459.67$. From these relations, we can see that within both individual pairs of temperature scales, the magnitude of the unit is the same; that is, an increase of 1 °C is the same an increase of 1 K, while an increase of 1 °F equals an increase of 1 R. Converting from Fahrenheit to Celsius is slightly more complicated: $T_C = \frac{5}{9}(T_F - 32)$, or in reverse, $T_F = \frac{9}{5}T_C + 32$. From these equations, we can see that a change of 1 °C is greater than a change of 1 °F .

RELATIONSHIP BETWEEN HEAT AND TEMPERATURE

It is often useful to know how much heat is required to cause a certain amount of material to reach a desired temperature. Each material has a property called specific heat, which allows this calculation. To bring about a temperature increase ΔT to a mass m made of a material with specific heat c, the required heat input is found by the equation $Q = mc\Delta T$. This equation can also be used to calculate the amount of heat absorbed during a given temperature increase. The amount of heat required to raise the temperature of 1 gram of water by 1 degree Celsius, or 1 Kelvin, is 1 calorie or 4.184 joules. Thus, the specific heat of water is 1 $\frac{\text{cal}}{\text{g K}}$ or 4.184 $\frac{\text{J}}{\text{g K}}$.

Note that since Kelvin and Celsius scales use the same unit size and the heat equation uses *change* in temperature, it is equally valid to use units of $\frac{\text{J}}{\text{g K}}$ or $\frac{\text{J}}{\text{g °C}}$.

LATENT HEAT AND SPECIFIC HEAT

Suppose we wish to convert ice initially at -5 °C to water at 5 °C. We must provide heat to accomplish this. The amount of heat energy required to raise the temperature of a given quantity of a material is a property known as **specific heat**. This is most often given on a mass basis, with units of $\frac{\text{J}}{\text{g K}}$, but may also be given as a molar property as $\frac{\text{J}}{\text{mol K}}$. If the given quantity of material and the given specific heat are not unit compatible, it will be necessary to multiply or divide by the molar weight of the material to achieve compatibility. Returning to the problem at hand, in order for ice initially at -5 °C to reach 5 °C, it must undergo a phase change from a solid to a liquid. When the ice is heated, it does not simply become water when it reaches 0 °C. In order for the ice to become water, additional heat must be added to break the bonds of the solid. This heat is called the **latent heat of fusion** and, like the specific heat, may be given on a mass or a molar basis, with common units of kJ/g or kJ/mol, respectively. This heat input for the phase change occurs while the material remains at a constant temperature. Once the phase change has been completed, the water temperature will begin to rise again with heat input, though the specific heat of liquid water will be different from that of ice. If the water need be heated above 100 °C, it will have to undergo a second phase change, overcoming the **latent heat of vaporization**, and its temperature will subsequently be governed by a third specific heat, that of the gas phase.

THERMAL EXPANSION AND CONTRACTION

When the temperature of most materials changes, they will undergo some amount of size change called **thermal expansion**. Though generally quite small, it is important to know how much of an impact thermal expansion might have on the size of an object. Each material has a linear coefficient of thermal expansion α, generally having units of °C^{-1} or °F^{-1}, that relates the change in length to the original length. The percentage change in length is found by the equation $\frac{\Delta L}{L_0} = \alpha \Delta T$, and the absolute change is found by a rearrangement of that equation, $\Delta L = L_0 \alpha \Delta T$. Negative thermal expansion means that either ΔT is negative (i.e., getting colder) or the material has a negative α (some materials in specific conditions have this property).

Assuming that the material is able to expand in all directions, there will similarly be a change in **areas** and **volumes**. The change in an area A_0 will be $\Delta A = 2\alpha A_0 \Delta T + \alpha^2 \Delta T^2$. Because α is generally much less than 1, $\alpha^2 \Delta T^2$ will most often be negligible. Thus, the change in area becomes $\Delta A = 2\alpha A_0 \Delta T$. From this we can see that the area coefficient of thermal expansion is $\gamma = 2\alpha$, and $\Delta A = \gamma A_0 \Delta T$. By making similar assumptions with the equation for change in volume, we find that the volume coefficient of thermal expansion is $\beta = 3\alpha$ and that $\Delta V = \beta V_0 \Delta T$.

Various Sample Temperature Conversions

Convert 200.0 Degrees Fahrenheit to the Celsius Scale.

To convert from 200.0 °F to °C, use the equation $T_C = \frac{5}{9}(T_F - 32)$. Substituting 200.0 in for T_F yields $T_C = \frac{5}{9}(200.0 - 32) = \frac{5}{9}(168.0) = 93.33$ °C.

Convert 24.0 Degrees Celsius to the Fahrenheit Scale.

To convert from 24.0 °C to °F, use the equation $T_F = \frac{9}{5}T_C + 32$. Substituting 24.0 in for T_C yields $T_F = \frac{9}{5}(24.0) + 32 = 43.2 + 32 = 75.2$ °F

Convert 21.5 Degrees Celsius to the Kelvin Scale.

To convert from 21.5 °C to K, use the equation $T_K = T_C + 273.15$. Substituting 21.5 in for T_C yields $T_K = 21.5 + 273.15 = 294.65$ K.

Thermal Energy

Thermal energy is part of a system's **total internal energy**, which consists of potential and kinetic energy. Thermal energy is the total internal kinetic energy of a system due to the random motions of the particles. The thermal energy of a system is measured by its temperature, which is the average kinetic energy of the particles in that system. The flow of thermal energy is referred to as heat. Appropriate units for thermal energy include the joule (J), British thermal unit (Btu), calorie (cal), and kilocalorie (kcal).

$$1 \text{ Btu} = 1{,}055 \text{ J}$$
$$1 \text{ cal} = 4.184 \text{ J}$$
$$1{,}000 \text{ cal} = 1 \text{ kcal}$$

Heat Capacity and Specific Heat

Heat capacity is the amount of heat required to raise a sample of matter by 1 °C. Heat capacity is an extensive property and varies with the amount of matter in the sample. The greater the mass of the sample, the higher the heat capacity of the sample. This means that a specific type of matter will have different heat capacities depending on the size of the sample. Heat capacity may be represented by the formula $C = \frac{Q}{\Delta T}$, where Q is the heat in joules and ΔT is the change in temperature in degrees Celsius. Specific heat is the amount of heat required to raise the temperature of a unit mass by 1 °C. The formula for specific heat is $c = \frac{Q}{m\Delta T}$, where Q is the heat in joules, ΔT is the change in temperature in degrees Celsius, and m is the mass of the sample. Because the specific heat formula incorporates the mass of the sample, a specific type of substance will have a constant specific heat, making specific heat an intensive property.

Review Video: Specific Heat Capacity
Visit mometrix.com/academy and enter code: 736791

Explain How to Calculate the Amount of Heat Lost By a Piece of Copper with a Mass of 100.0 g When It Cools from 100.0°C to 20.0°C. The Specific Heat of Copper Is 0.380 J/(g·°C).

To calculate the amount of heat lost by a piece of copper with a mass of 100.0 g when it cools from 100.0 °C to 20.0 °C, use the equation $Q = mc\Delta T$, where Q is the amount of heat lost in joules, m is the mass of the copper in grams, c is the specific heat of copper, and ΔT is the change in temperature $(T_2 - T_1)$ in degrees Celsius. Substituting these known values yields:

$$Q = (100.0\text{ g})\left(0.380\ \frac{\text{J}}{\text{g °C}}\right)\left((20.0°\text{C}) - (100.0°\text{C})\right) = -3{,}040\text{ J}$$

The negative value confirms that heat was lost as the copper cooled.

Finding the Specific Heat of a Substance with a Calorimeter

The specific heat of a substance can be determined using a calorimeter. A known amount of the substance is heated to a known temperature. In the classroom setting, this can be accomplished by placing the metal in a loosely stoppered test tube and then placing the test tube in boiling water. The calorimeter is prepared by placing water of a known amount and temperature in the calorimeter. The heated metal is carefully placed into the water in the calorimeter. The temperature of the water is carefully monitored until it stops rising. The final temperature of the metal will be equal to the final temperature of the water. The heat lost by the metal equals the heat gained by the water:

$$-Q_{\text{metal}} = Q_{\text{water}}$$

$$-m_{\text{metal}}c_{\text{metal}}\Delta T_{\text{metal}} = m_{\text{water}}c_{\text{water}}\Delta T_{\text{water}}$$

In these equations, Q is the amount of heat lost or gained in joules, m is the mass in grams, c is the specific heat, and ΔT is the change in temperature $T_2 - T_1$ in degrees Celsius.

Review Video: Using a Calorimeter
Visit mometrix.com/academy and enter code: 703935

Calculating the Specific Heat of an Unknown Metal:

- In a calorimetry experiment, the specific heat of an unknown metal dropped 20.0 °C.
- The mass of the unknown metal is 100.0 g.
- The temperature of the water with a mass of 100.0 g in the calorimeter increased 1.00 °C.
- The specific heat of water is 4.184 $\frac{\text{J}}{\text{g °C}}$.

The heat lost by the metal must equal the heat gained by the water, as shown in the equation $Q_{lost\ by\ metal} = Q_{gained\ by\ the\ water}$, where Q is the amount of heat lost or gained in joules. To calculate the specific heat of the metal, use $-m_{metal}c_{metal}\Delta T_{metal} = m_{water}c_{water}\Delta T_{water}$, where m is the mass of the metal or water in grams, c is the specific heat of the metal or water, and ΔT is the change in temperature $(T_2 - T_1)$ in degrees Celsius in the metal or water. Solving the equation for c_{metal} results in:

$$c_{metal} = -\frac{m_{water}c_{water}\Delta T_{water}}{m_{metal}\Delta T_{metal}}$$

Substituting in the given information yields:

$$c_{\text{metal}} = -\frac{(100.0\text{ g})\left(4.184\ \frac{\text{J}}{\text{g °C}}\right)(1.00\text{ °C})}{(100.0\text{ g})(-20.0\text{ °C})} = 0.209\ \frac{\text{J}}{\text{g °C}}$$

HEAT TRANSFER

Heat transfer is the flow of thermal energy, which is measured by temperature. Heat will flow from warmer objects to cooler objects until an **equilibrium** is reached in which both objects are at the same temperature. Because the particles of warmer objects possess a higher kinetic energy than the particles of cooler objects, the particles of the warmer objects are vibrating more quickly and collide more often, transferring energy to the cooler objects in which the particles have less kinetic energy and are moving more slowly. Heat may be transferred by conduction, convection, or radiation. In **conduction**, heat is transferred by direct contact between two objects. In **convection**, heat is transferred by moving currents. In **radiation**, heat is transferred by electromagnetic waves.

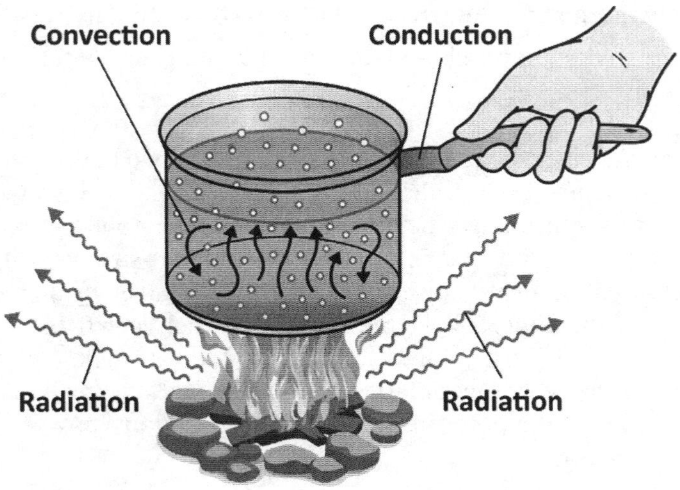

Review Video: Heat Transfer at the Molecular Level
Visit mometrix.com/academy and enter code: 451646

CONVECTION

Heat always flows from a region of higher temperature to a region of lower temperature. If two regions are at the same temperature, there is a thermal equilibrium between them and there will be no net heat transfer between them. Convection is a mode of heat transfer in which a surface in contact with a fluid experiences a heat flow. The heat rate for convection is given as $q = hA\Delta T$, where h is the convection coefficient, and q is the heat transferred per unit of time. The convection coefficient is dependent on a number of factors, including the configuration of the surface and the nature and velocity of the fluid. For complicated configurations, it often has to be determined experimentally.

Convection may be classified as either free or forced. In free convection, when a surface transfers heat to the surrounding air, the heated air becomes less dense and rises, allowing cooler air to descend and come into contact with the surface. Free convection may also be called natural convection. Forced convection in this example would involve forcibly cycling the air: for instance, with a fan. While this does generally require an additional input of work, the convection coefficient is always greater for forced convection.

CONDUCTION

Conduction is a form of heat transfer that requires contact. Since heat is a measure of kinetic energy, most commonly vibration, at the atomic level, it may be transferred from one location to another or one object to another by contact. The rate at which heat is transferred is proportional to the material's thermal conductivity k, cross-sectional area A, and temperature gradient $\frac{\Delta T}{\Delta x}$:

$$q = kA\left(\frac{\Delta T}{\Delta x}\right)$$

If two ends of a rod are each held at a constant temperature, the heat transfer through the rod will be given as $q = k\text{A}\left(\frac{T_H - T_L}{d}\right)$, where d is the length of the rod. The heat will flow from the hot end to the cold end. The thermal conductivity is generally given in units of $\frac{\text{W}}{\text{m K}}$. Metals are some of the best conductors, many having a thermal conductivity around 400 $\frac{\text{W}}{\text{m K}}$. The thermal conductivity of wood is very small, generally less than 0.5 $\frac{\text{W}}{\text{m K}}$. Diamond is extremely thermally conductive and may have a conductivity of over 2,000 $\frac{\text{W}}{\text{m K}}$. Although fluids also have thermal conductivity, they will tend to transfer heat primarily through convection.

Radiation

Radiation heat transfer occurs via electromagnetic radiation between two bodies. Unlike conduction and convection, radiation requires no medium in which to take place. Indeed, the heat we receive from the sun is entirely radiation since it must pass through a vacuum to reach us. Every body at a temperature above absolute zero emits heat radiation at a rate of $q = e\sigma AT^4$, where e is the surface emissivity and σ is the Stefan-Boltzmann constant. The net radiation heat-transfer rate for a body is given by $q = e\sigma A(T^4 - T_0^4)$, where T_0 is the temperature of the surroundings. Emissivity, which has a value between 0 and 1, is a measure of how well a surface absorbs and emits radiation. Dark-colored surfaces tend to have high emissivity, while shiny or reflective surfaces have low emissivity. In the radiation heat-rate equation, it is important to remember to use absolute temperature units, since the temperature value is being raised to a power.

Types of Energy

Chemical, Electrical, Electromagnetic, Nuclear, and Thermal Energy

Different types of energy may be associated with systems:

- **Chemical energy** is the energy that is stored in chemical bonds and intermolecular forces.
- **Electrical energy** is the energy associated with the movement of electrons or ions through a material.
- **Electromagnetic energy** is the energy of electromagnetic waves of several frequencies including radio waves, microwaves, infrared light, visible light, ultraviolet light, x-rays, and gamma rays.
- **Nuclear energy** is the binding energy that is stored within an atom's nucleus.
- **Thermal energy** is the total internal kinetic energy of a system due to the random motions of the particles.

Phase Transitions

States of Matter

The four states of matter are solid, liquid, gas, and plasma. **Solids** have a definite shape and a definite volume. Because solid particles are held in fairly rigid positions, solids are the least compressible of the four states of matter. **Liquids** have definite volumes but no definite shapes. Because their particles are free to slip and slide over each other, liquids take the shape of their containers, but they still remain fairly incompressible by natural means. **Gases** have no definite shape or volume. Because gas particles are free to move, they move away from each other to fill their containers. Gases are compressible. **Plasmas** are high-temperature, ionized gases that exist only under very high temperatures at which electrons are stripped away from their atoms.

Review Video: States of Matter
Visit mometrix.com/academy and enter code: 742449

Review Video: Properties of Liquids
Visit mometrix.com/academy and enter code: 802024

Review Video: States of Matter [Advanced]
Visit mometrix.com/academy and enter code: 298130

The following table shows similarities and differences between solids, liquids, and gases:

	Solid	**Liquid**	**Gas**
Shape	Fixed shape	No fixed shape (assumes shape of container)	No fixed shape (assumes shape of container)
Volume	Fixed	Fixed	Changes to assume volume of container
Fluidity	Does not flow easily	Flows easily	Flows easily
Compressibility	Hard to compress	Hard to compress	Compresses

Six Different Types of Phase Change

A substance that is undergoing a change from a solid to a liquid is said to be melting. If this change occurs in the opposite direction, from liquid to solid, this change is called freezing. A liquid which is being converted to a gas is undergoing vaporization. The reverse of this process is known as condensation. Direct transitions from gas to solid and solid to gas are much less common in everyday life, but they can occur given the proper conditions. Solid to gas conversion is known as sublimation, while the reverse is called deposition.

Review Video: Chemical and Physical Properties of Matter
Visit mometrix.com/academy and enter code: 717349

Phase Diagram and Critical Point

A **phase diagram** is a graph or chart of pressure versus temperature that represents the solid, liquid, and gaseous phases of a substance and the transitions between these phases. Typically, **pressure** is located on the vertical axis, and temperature is located along the horizontal axis. The curves drawn on the graph represent points at which different phases are in an equilibrium state. These curves indicate at which pressure and temperature the phase changes of sublimation, melting, and boiling occur. Specifically, the curve between the liquid and gas phases indicates the pressures and temperatures at which the liquid and gas phases are in equilibrium. The curve between the solid and liquid phases indicates the temperatures and pressures at which the solid and liquid phases are in equilibrium. The open spaces on the graph represent the distinct phases solid, liquid, and gas. The point at which the solid–liquid, solid–gas, and liquid–gas phase boundaries intersect is called the triple point. At the triple point, the solid, liquid, and gas phases all exist in equilibrium. The critical point, by contrast, is the endpoint of the liquid–gas coexistence curve, where the liquid and gas phases become indistinguishable and form a supercritical fluid.

Lettered Regions of a Phase Diagram

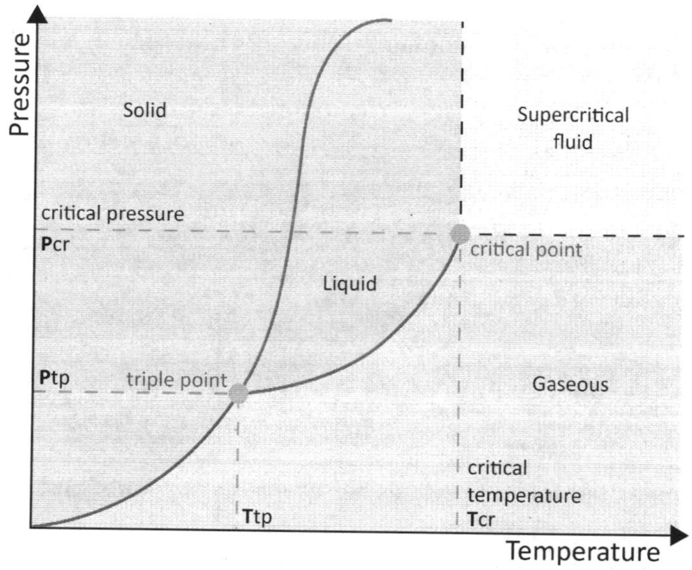

A—**Solid phase**: This is a region of high pressure and low temperature where the substance always exists as a solid.

B—**Liquid phase**: This is a region of pressure and temperature where the substance is in the liquid phase.

C—**Gas phase**: This is a region of pressure and temperature where the substance is in the gaseous phase.

D—**Sublimation point**: The portion of the curve that contains point D shows all the combinations of pressure and temperature at which the solid phase is in equilibrium with the gaseous phase.

E—**Triple point**: The point at which the solid, liquid, and gaseous phases are all in equilibrium.

F—**Boiling point**: The line that contains point F indicates all the combinations of pressure and temperature at which the liquid phase and gas phase are in equilibrium.

Calculating Phase Transitions

Heating Curve of Water from −40 °C to 140 °C

In the first portion of the curve, the graph slants up and to the right as the ice is a solid that is increasing in temperature from −40 °C to 0 °C. In the second portion of the curve, the graph remains horizontal during the phase change from solid to liquid as the temperature remains constant at 0 °C. In the third portion of the curve, the graph slants up and to the right as the water now is in the liquid state and is increasing in temperature from 0 °C to 100 °C. In the fourth portion of the curve, the graph remains horizontal during the phase change from liquid to gas as the temperature remains at 100 °C. In the last portion of the curve, the graph slants up and to the right as water now is in the gaseous state and the steam is increasing in temperature from 100 °C to 140 °C

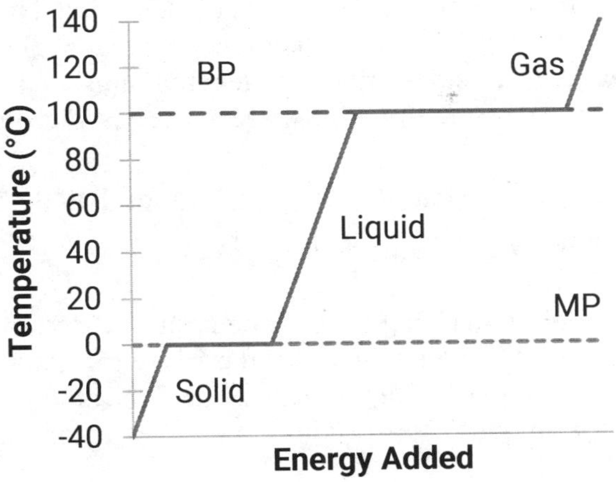

Calculating the Amount of Heat Corresponding to Each Portion of a Heating Curve

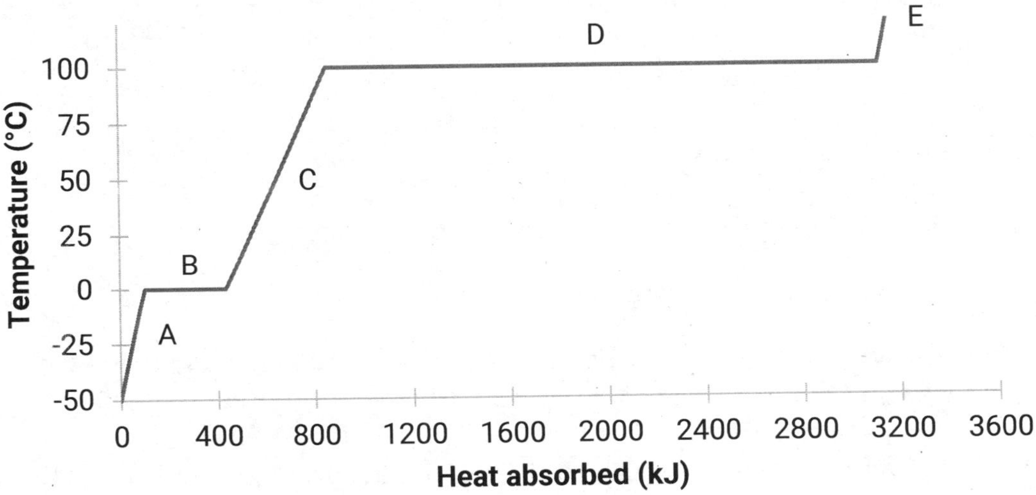

For portion A, $Q = mc_{ice}\Delta T$, where Q is the amount of heat gained in joules, m is the mass of the ice in grams, c_{ice} is the specific heat of ice, and ΔT is the temperature change in degrees Celsius.

For portion B, $Q = m\Delta H_{fus}$, where Q is the amount of heat gained in joules, m is the mass of the ice/water in grams, and ΔH_{fus} is the heat of fusion for water in joules per gram, $\frac{J}{g}$.

For portion C, $Q = mc_{water}\Delta T$, where Q is the amount of heat gained in joules, m is the mass of the water in grams, c_{water} is the specific heat of water, and ΔT is the temperature change in degrees Celsius.

For portion D, $Q = m\Delta H_{vap}$, where Q is the amount of heat gained in joules, m is the mass of the water/steam in grams, and ΔH_{vap} is the heat of vaporization for water in joules per gram, $\frac{J}{g}$.

For portion E, $Q = mc_{steam}\Delta T$, where Q is the amount of heat gained in joules, m is the mass of the steam in grams, c_{steam} is the specific heat of steam, and ΔT is the temperature change in degrees Celsius.

Heat of Vaporization, Heat of Fusion, and Heat of Sublimation

- The **heat of vaporization** (ΔH_{vap}) is the amount of heat that must be added to one mole of a substance to change the substance from the liquid phase to the gaseous phase.

- The **heat of fusion** (ΔH_{fus}) is the amount of heat that must be added to one mole of a substance to change the substance from the solid phase to the liquid phase.
- The **heat of sublimation** (ΔH_{sub}) is the amount of heat that must be added to one mole of a substance to change the substance directly from the solid phase to the gaseous phase without passing through the liquid phase.

Explain How to Calculate the Amount of Heat Required to Change 100.0 g of Ice at –10.0 °C to Water at 10.0 °C. $\left[\Delta H_{fus} = 334\ \frac{J}{g}; c_{water} = 4.18\ \frac{J}{g\,°C}, c_{ice} = 2.06\ \frac{J}{g\,°C}\right]$.

To calculate the amount of heat required to change 100.0 g of ice at −10.0 °C to water at 10.0 °C, it is necessary to calculate the heat required for each step along the way. Step 1 is to calculate the heat required to raise the temperature of the ice from −10.0 °C to 0.0 °C. Step 2 is to calculate the amount of heat required to melt the ice. Finally, step 3 is to calculate the amount of heat required to raise the temperature of the water from 0.0 °C to 10.0 °C.

For steps 1 and 3, the required equation is $Q = mc\Delta T$.

Because step 2 is a phase change, the required equation is $Q = m\Delta H_{fus}$.

For step 1: $Q_1 = (100.0\text{ g})\left(2.06\ \frac{J}{g\,°C}\right)(0.0°C - (-10.0°C)) = 2{,}060\text{ J}$.

For step 2: $Q_2 = m\Delta H_{fus} = (100.0\text{ g})\left(334\ \frac{J}{g}\right) = 33{,}400\text{ J}$.

For step 3: $Q_3 = (100.0\text{ g})\left(4.18\ \frac{J}{g\,°C}\right)(10.0\ °C - 0.0\ °C) = 4{,}180\text{ J}$.

Adding $Q_1 + Q_2 + Q_3 = 2{,}060\text{ J} + 33{,}400\text{ J} + 4{,}180\text{ J} = 39{,}640\text{ J}$.

Explain How to Calculate the Amount of Heat Required to Change 100.0 g of Water at 90.0 °C to Steam at 110.0 °C. $\left[\Delta H_{vap} = 2{,}260\ \frac{J}{g}; c_{steam} = 1.86\ \frac{J}{g\,°C}, c_{water} = 4.18\ \frac{J}{g\,°C}\right]$.

To calculate the amount of heat required to change 100.0 g of water at 90.0 °C to steam at 110.0 °C, it is necessary to calculate the heat required at each step along the way. Step 1 is to calculate the heat required to raise the temperature of the water from 90.0 °C to 100.0 °C. Step 2 is to calculate the amount of heat required to change the water to steam. Finally, step 3 is to calculate the amount of heat required to raise the temperature of the steam from 100.0 °C to 110.0 °C.

For steps 1 and 3, the required equation is $Q = mc\Delta T$.

Because Step 2 is a phase change, the required equation is $Q = m\Delta H_{vap}$.

For step 1: $Q_1 = (100.0\text{ g})\left(4.18\ \frac{J}{g\,°C}\right)(100.0\ °C - 90.0\ °C) = 4{,}180\text{ J}$.

For step 2: $Q_2 = m\Delta H_{vap} = (100.0\text{ g})\left(2{,}260\ \frac{J}{g}\right) = 226{,}000\text{ J}$.

For step 3: $Q_1 = (100.0\text{ g})\left(1.86\ \frac{J}{g\,°C}\right)(110.0°C - 100.0°C) = 1{,}860\text{ J}$.

Adding $Q_1 + Q_2 + Q_3 = 4{,}180\text{ J} + 226{,}000\text{ J} + 1{,}860\text{ J} = 232{,}040\text{ J}$.

Gas Laws

Kinetic Molecular Theory

The **kinetic molecular theory of gases** states that the pressure exerted by a gas is due to numerous collisions of molecules with one another and with container walls. This assertion led to the development of what is now known as the ideal gas law: $PV = nRT$, where P is **pressure**, V is **volume**, T is **temperature**, n is the number of moles of gas present, and R is the universal gas constant. Different aspects of this law have different names, but there are many simple relations that may be derived from it. For instance, if an ideal gas is contained such that no molecules can escape, then it may be said that $\frac{P_1V_1}{T_1} = \frac{P_2V_2}{T_2}$, where the subscripts indicate distinct sets of conditions. Generally, one of the three variables will be held constant while the other two change. If an ideal gas in a container with a constant volume is heated, the effect this has on the pressure can be determined both analytically and numerically. Additional energy imparted to the gas particles will cause them to move faster, and, according to the kinetic molecular theory, faster particles mean more collisions and a higher resulting pressure. This can be expressed numerically as $\frac{P_1}{T_1} = \frac{P_2}{T_2}$. This means that if T_2 is higher than T_1, then P_2 must be equivalently higher than P_1 to maintain the same ratio.

Other derivations from the ideal gas law include calculating molarity or moles per unit volume $\left(\frac{n}{V} = \frac{P}{RT}\right)$, gas density if the molecular weight (M) is known $\left(\rho = \frac{PM}{RT}\right)$, or molecular weight if the density is known $\left(M = \frac{\rho RT}{P}\right)$.

Ideal Gases

An **ideal gas** is a hypothetical or theoretical gas. Ideal gases are assumed to be a set of randomly moving point particles that do not interact with each other. The collisions of ideal gases are assumed to be completely elastic, and the intermolecular forces are assumed to be zero. Real gases show far more complex behaviors. The ideal gas laws tend to fail at low temperatures and high pressures when the effects of the particle size and intermolecular forces are more apparent. Also, the ideal gas assumptions do not account for phase transitions.

Avogadro's Law

Avogadro's law describes the relationship between the **volume** and **number of moles** of an ideal gas at a constant pressure and temperature. For an ideal gas, the volume and the number of moles are directly related. If the volume increases, the number of moles would have to increase in order to maintain the pressure and temperature. If the number of moles in the container increases, the volume will also need to increase to maintain the same pressure and temperature. The relationship between volume and the number of moles of a gas is represented by $V \propto n$, $V = kn$, or $\frac{V}{n} = k$. Because the quotient of the volume and the number of moles is a constant, Avogadro's law can be stated as:

$$\frac{V_i}{n_i} = \frac{V_f}{n_f}$$

Review Video: Avogadro's Hypothesis
Visit mometrix.com/academy and enter code: 968309

Boyle's Law

Boyle's law describes the relationship between the **volume** and **pressure** of an ideal gas at a constant temperature for a given amount of gas. For an ideal gas, volume and pressure are inversely related. Because gases are compressible, if the pressure of a gas sample is increased, the volume will decrease. If the pressure of a gas sample is decreased, the volume will increase. Conversely, if the volume of a gas sample is increased, the pressure will decrease. If the volume of a gas sample is decreased, the pressure will increase. For example, if the pressure of a gas sample is doubled, the volume decreases to one-half of the original volume. If the pressure of a gas sample is tripled, the volume decreases to one-third of the original volume. The relationship between volume and pressure is represented by $V \propto \frac{1}{P}$, $V = k\frac{1}{P}$, or $PV = k$. Because the product of the pressure and the volume is a constant, Boyle's law can be stated as $P_iV_i = P_fV_f$.

Review Video: Boyle's Law
Visit mometrix.com/academy and enter code: 115757

CHARLES'S LAW

Charles's law describes the relationship between the **volume** and **temperature** of an ideal gas at a constant pressure for a given amount of gas. For an ideal gas, volume and temperature are directly related. Because the kinetic energy of a gas is directly proportional to the absolute temperature, if the temperature increases, the average kinetic energy of the gas molecules increases. As the molecules move faster, they will spread farther apart as long as the pressure remains constant, which increases the volume. If the volume of the container were to increase, the temperature would also have to increase if it were to maintain a constant pressure, since the molecules must move faster to strike the container as often. The relationship between volume and temperature is represented by $V \propto T$, $V = kT$, or $\frac{V}{T} = k$. Because the quotient of the volume and the temperature is a constant, Charles's law can be stated as $\frac{V_i}{T_i} = \frac{V_f}{T_f}$, where the temperature is stated in Kelvin.

COMBINED GAS LAW

The **combined gas law** combines Boyle's law and Charles's law. According to Boyle's law, **volume** and **pressure** are inversely related, or $V \propto \frac{1}{P}$. According to Charles's law, **volume** and **temperature** are directly related, or $V \propto T$. Combining these relationships into one yields $V \propto \frac{T}{P}$ or $V = k\frac{T}{P}$. Solving for k yields $\frac{PV}{T}$. Because $k = \frac{P_1V_1}{T_1}$ and $k = \frac{P_2V_2}{T_2}$, the combined gas law can be written as:

$$\frac{P_1V_1}{T_1} = \frac{P_2V_2}{T_2}$$

For situations in which $V_1 = V_2$, the combined gas law yields a relationship of $P \propto T$, indicating that for a constant volume, the pressure and temperature are directly related.

IDEAL GAS LAW

The **ideal gas law** combines Boyle's law, Charles's law, and Avogadro's law. According to Boyle's law, $V \propto \frac{1}{P}$. According to Charles's law, $V \propto T$. According to Avogadro's law, $V \propto n$. Combining these three relationships into one relationship yields $V \propto \frac{nT}{P}$. Multiplying through by P yields $PV \propto nT$, or $PV = nRT$, where R is the ideal gas constant of $0.0821\ \frac{\text{L atm}}{\text{K mol}}$, P is the pressure in atmospheres, V is the volume in liters, n is the number of moles, and T is the temperature in Kelvin.

BEHAVIOR OF REAL GASES

Although assuming that gases are ideal is appropriate for many situations, **real gases** behave differently than **ideal gases**. The collisions of real gases are not elastic. Real gases do have attractive and repulsive forces. Real gases have **mass**, whereas ideal gases do not. The atoms or molecules of real gases are not point particles, and they do interact with each other, especially under high pressures and low temperatures. Under the right conditions of pressure and temperature, real gases will undergo phase transitions and become liquids. The pressure of real gases is less than those of ideal gases due to the small attractive forces between the particles in the gases.

Review Video: Ideal Gas vs Real Gas
Visit mometrix.com/academy and enter code: 619477

A 5.0 L GAS SAMPLE HAS A PRESSURE OF 1.0 STANDARD ATMOSPHERE (ATM). IF THE PRESSURE IS INCREASED TO 2.0 ATM, FIND THE NEW VOLUME. ASSUME THAT THE TEMPERATURE IS CONSTANT.

To find the new volume, use the equation associated with Boyle's law, $P_iV_i = P_fV_f$. Solving the equation for the unknown V_f yields $V_f = \frac{P_iV_i}{P_f}$. Substituting the given values, $P_i = 1.0$ atm, $V_i = 5.0$ L, and $P_f = 2.0$ atm, into the equation yields $V_f = \frac{(1.0\text{ atm})(5.0\text{ L})}{(2.0\text{ atm})} = 2.5$ L. This checks out because the pressure increased and the volume decreased. More specifically, because the pressure was doubled, the volume was reduced to one-half of the original volume.

A GAS SAMPLE HAS A VOLUME OF 10.0 L AT 200.0 K. FIND ITS VOLUME IF THE TEMPERATURE IS INCREASED TO 300.0 K.

To find the new volume, use the equation associated with Charles's law, $\frac{V_i}{T_i} = \frac{V_f}{T_f}$. Solving the equation for the unknown V_f yields $V_f = \frac{T_fV_i}{T_i}$. Substituting the given values, $V_i = 10.0$ L, $T_i = 200.0$ K, and $T_f = 300.0$ K, into the equation yields $V_f = \frac{(300.0\text{ K})(10.0\text{ L})}{(200.0\text{ K})} = 15.0$ L. This checks out because the temperature increased and the volume increased. Also, note that if the temperature had not been stated in Kelvin, it would have to be converted to Kelvin before substituting the values into the equation.

EXPLAIN HOW TO FIND THE PRESSURE THAT 0.500 MOL OF H_2 (G) WILL EXERT ON A 500.0 ML FLASK AT 300.0 K.

To calculate the pressure that 0.500 mol of $H_2(g)$ will exert on a 500.0 mL flask at 300.0 K, use the ideal gas equation $PV = nRT$, where R is the ideal gas constant of $0.0821\ \frac{\text{L atm}}{\text{K mol}}$, P is the pressure in atmospheres, V is the volume in liters, n is the number of moles, and T is the temperature in Kelvin. Solving the ideal gas equation for P yields $P = \frac{nRT}{V}$. First, convert the 500.0 mL to 0.500 L. Substituting in $n = 0.500$ mol, $V = 0.500$ L, $T = 300.0$ K, and $R = 0.0821\frac{\text{L atm}}{\text{K mol}}$ yields:

$$P = \frac{(0.500\text{ mol})\left(0.0821\ \frac{\text{L atm}}{\text{K mol}}\right)(300.0\text{ K})}{(0.500\text{ L})} = 24.6\text{ atm}$$

THERMODYNAMIC PROCESSES OF GASES

In discussing thermodynamic processes applied to gases, it is important to understand what is meant by some of the different types of processes that can take place. Most real processes do not strictly hold to one of these types, but most can be reasonably approximated by one of them. A process in which the pressure remains constant is known as an isobaric process. In this type of process, the volume-to-absolute-temperature ratio remains constant. In an isothermal process, the temperature remains constant, as does the product of the pressure and volume. For isothermal processes, the internal energy of the gas is constant, and, according to the first law of thermodynamics, the heat added is equal to the work done by the gas. An adiabatic process is one in which no heat is transferred between the gas or its surroundings. This does not mean that the temperature of the gas remains the same; rather, any temperature changes are due to changes in pressure or volume. According to the first law of thermodynamics, the change in internal energy of the gas is equal to the amount of work done on the gas by its surroundings.

Review Video: What is the Difference between Heat and Temperature?
Visit mometrix.com/academy and enter code: 879095

HEAT ENGINES AND THE CARNOT CYCLE

A **heat engine** is a mechanical device that **takes in heat energy** (Q_H) from a high-temperature region and uses that energy to **produce work** (W). It then **expels heat** (Q_C) to a lower-temperature region. When the machine is operating at a steady state, such that it does not change temperature, the first law of thermodynamics tells us that the net heat input is equal to the work achieved:

$$Q_H - Q_C = W$$

We can define the efficiency of a heat engine as the work received divided by the work put in, or $\eta = \frac{W}{Q_H}$. The rejected heat Q_C is not considered work received because it is not usable for work. The efficiency may also be calculated as $\eta = 1 - \frac{Q_C}{Q_H}$. From this, we can see that 100% efficiency can only be achieved if $Q_C = 0$; however, constructing a heat engine that expels no heat is impossible.

A **Carnot engine** is a heat engine that operates on the Carnot cycle, an ideal reversible gas cycle that consists of the following processes: high-temperature isothermal expansion, adiabatic expansion, low-temperature isothermal compression, and adiabatic compression. The efficiency of this ideal engine is given as $\eta = 1 - \frac{T_C}{T_H}$, where T_C and T_H are the low and high temperatures of the gas during the cycle. Carnot's theorem states that no heat engine operating between T_C and T_H can have a higher efficiency than that of the Carnot engine.

LAWS OF THERMODYNAMICS

FIRST LAW

The **first law of thermodynamics** states that energy cannot be **created** or **destroyed**, but only **converted** from one form to another. It is generally applied as $Q = \Delta U + W$, where Q is the net heat energy added to a system, ΔU is the change in internal energy of the system, and W is the work done by the system. For any input of heat energy to a system, that energy must be either converted to internal energy through a temperature increase or expended in doing work. For a system that gives off heat, either the temperature of the system must decrease or work must be done on the system by its surroundings. By convention, work done by the system is positive while work done on the system is negative.

For instance, suppose a gas is compressed by a piston while the gas temperature remains constant. If we consider the gas to be the system, the work is negative, since the work is being performed on the gas. Since the temperature remains constant, $\Delta U = 0$. Thus, Q must be a negative quantity, indicating that heat is lost by the gas. Conversely, if the gas does positive work on the piston while remaining at a constant temperature, the gas must be receiving heat input from the surroundings.

SECOND LAW

The **second law of thermodynamics** is primarily a statement of the natural tendency of all things toward disorder rather than order. It deals with a quantity called **entropy**, which is an inverse measure of the remaining useful energy in a system. If we take a system of a pot of hot water and an ice cube, the system entropy initially has a value of s_1. After the ice cube melts in the water and the system reaches an equilibrium temperature, the system has larger entropy value s_2, which is the maximum entropy for the system. The system cannot return to its initial state without work put into the system to refreeze the ice cube and reheat the water. If this is done and the system returns to a state with entropy s_1, then the entropy of the surroundings must at the same time increase by more than $s_2 - s_1$, since the net entropy from any process is always greater than zero. Reversible processes are those that may be accomplished in reverse without requiring additional work input. These processes do not exist in the real world, but can be useful for approximating some situations. All real processes are irreversible, meaning they require additional work input to accomplish in reverse. Another important concept is that of spontaneity, the ability of a process to occur without instigation. An ice cube located in an environment at a temperature above the freezing point will spontaneously melt. Although some processes can decrease system entropy at a cost to the entropy of the surroundings, all spontaneous processes involve an increase in the total entropy of the universe.

THIRD AND ZEROTH LAWS

The **third law of thermodynamics** regards the behavior of systems as they **approach absolute zero temperature**. Actually reaching a state of absolute zero is impossible. According to this law, all activity disappears as molecules slow to a standstill near absolute zero, and the system achieves a perfect crystal structure while the system entropy approaches its minimum value. For most systems, this would in fact be a value of zero entropy. Note that this does not violate the second law since causing a system to approach absolute zero would require an immense increase in the entropy of the surroundings, resulting in a positive net entropy. This law is used to determine the value of a material's standard entropy, which is its entropy at the standard temperature of 25 °C.

The **zeroth law of thermodynamics** deals with thermal equilibrium between two systems. It states that if two systems are both in thermal equilibrium with a third system, then they are in thermal equilibrium with each other. This may seem intuitive, but it is an important basis for the other thermodynamic laws.

Review Video: Laws of Thermodynamics
Visit mometrix.com/academy and enter code: 253607

ENTROPY

Entropy (S) is the amount of **disorder** or **randomness of a system**. According to the second law of thermodynamics, systems tend toward a state of greater entropy. The second law of thermodynamics can also be stated as $\Delta S > 0$. Processes with positive changes in entropy tend to be spontaneous. For example, melting is a process with a positive ΔS. When a solid changes into a liquid state, the substance becomes more disordered; therefore, entropy increases. Entropy also will increase in a reaction in which the number of moles of gases increases due to the amount of disorder increasing. Entropy increases when a solute dissolves into a solvent due to the increase in the number of particles. Entropy increases when a system is heated due to the particles moving faster and the amount of disorder increasing.

SPONTANEOUS / REVERSIBLE PROCESSES

Some chemical processes are **spontaneous**. According to the second law of thermodynamics, systems or processes always **tend to a state of greater entropy** or lower potential energy. Some exothermic chemical systems are spontaneous because they can increase their stability by reaching a lower potential energy. If processes or reactions have products at a lower potential energy, these processes tend to be spontaneous. Spontaneous reactions have only one direction as given by the second law of thermodynamics. Spontaneous processes go in the direction of greater entropy and lower potential energy. To be reversible, a reaction or process has to be able to go back and forth between two states. A spontaneous process is irreversible.

CONCEPT OF CHANGE IN ENTHALPY

All chemical processes involve either the release or the absorption of heat. Enthalpy is this heat energy. **Enthalpy** is a state function that is equivalent to the amount of heat a system exchanges with its surroundings. For **exothermic processes**, which release heat, the change in enthalpy (ΔH) is negative because the final enthalpy is less than the initial enthalpy. For **endothermic processes**, which absorb heat, the change in enthalpy (ΔH) is positive because the final enthalpy is greater than the initial enthalpy.

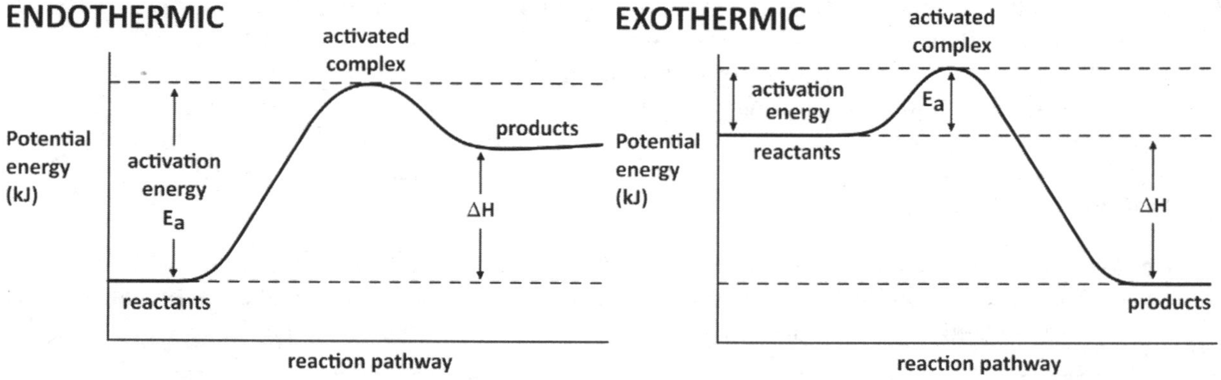

Review Video: Enthalpy
Visit mometrix.com/academy and enter code: 233315

Gibbs Energy

Gibbs energy (G), also known as Gibbs free energy, is the energy of the system that is available to do work. Gibbs energy determines the **spontaneity** of chemical and physical processes. Some processes are spontaneous because $\Delta H < 0$ or because $\Delta S > 0$. If one of the conditions is favorable but the other condition is not favorable, Gibbs energy can be used to determine if a process is spontaneous. Gibbs energy is given by $G = H - TS$. For processes that occur at constant temperature, $\Delta G = \Delta H - T\Delta S$. If ΔG is equal to zero, then the reaction is at equilibrium and neither the forward nor the reverse reaction is spontaneous. If ΔG is less than zero, then the forward reaction is spontaneous. If ΔG is greater than zero, then the reverse reaction is spontaneous.

Mechanics

Work, Energy, and Power

Basic Equation for Work

The equation for **work** (W) is $W = \boldsymbol{Fd}$, where $\boldsymbol{F}$ is the force exerted and $\boldsymbol{d}$ is the displacement of the object on which the force is exerted. For the simplest case, when the vectors of force and displacement have the same direction, the work done is equal to the product of the magnitudes of the force and displacement. If this is not the case, then the work may be calculated as $W = \boldsymbol{Fd}\cos\theta$, where θ is the angle between the force and displacement vectors. If force and displacement have the same direction, then work is positive; if they are in opposite directions, however, work is negative; and if they are perpendicular, the work done by the force is zero.

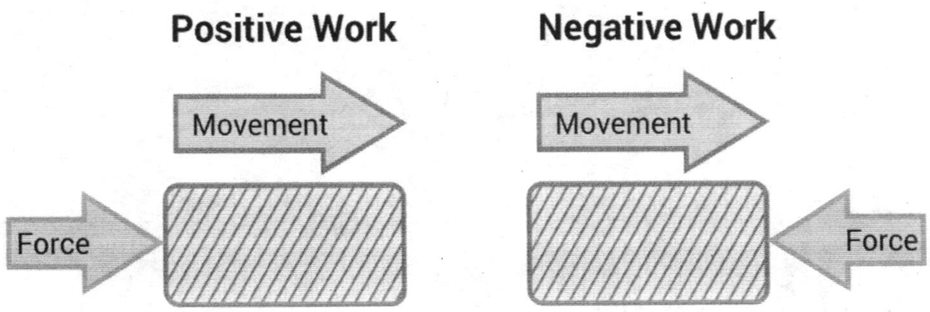

Review Video: Work
Visit mometrix.com/academy and enter code: 681834

For example, if a man pushes a block horizontally across a surface with a constant force of 10 N for a distance of 20 m, the work done by the man is 200 N-m or 200 J. If instead the block is sliding and the man tries to **slow its progress** by pushing against it, his work done is –200 J, since he is pushing in the direction opposite the motion. Also, if the man pushes vertically downward on the block while it slides, his work done is zero, since his force vector is perpendicular to the displacement vector of the block. It is important to note in each of these cases that neither the mass of the block nor the elapsed time is considered when calculating the amount of work done by the man.

Review Video: Push and Pull Forces
Visit mometrix.com/academy and enter code: 104731

Power

Put simply, **power** is the **rate at which work is done**. Power, like work, is a scalar quantity. If we know the amount of work, W, that has been performed in a given amount of time, Δt, then we may find average power, $P_{avg} = \frac{W}{\Delta t}$. If we are instead looking for the instantaneous power, there are two possibilities. If the force on an object is constant, and the object is moving at a constant velocity, then the instantaneous power is the same as the average power. If either the force or the velocity is varying, the instantaneous power should be computed by the equation $P = \boldsymbol{Fv}$, where $\boldsymbol{F}$ and $\boldsymbol{v}$ are the instantaneous force and velocity, respectively. This equation may also be used to compute average power if the force and velocity are constant. Power is typically expressed in joules per second, or watts.

Simple Machines

Simple machines include the pulley, lever, wheel and axle, wedge, inclined plane, and screw. These simple machines have no internal source of energy. More complex or compound machines can be formed from them.

Simple machines provide a mechanical advantage and make it easier to accomplish a task. Single or double pulleys allow for easier direction of force. A lever enables a multiplication of force. The wheel and axle allows for movement with less resistance. The inclined plane enables a force less than an object's weight to be used to push it to a greater height. The wedge and screw are forms of the inclined plane. A wedge turns a smaller force working over a greater distance into a larger force. The screw is similar to an incline that is wrapped around a shaft.

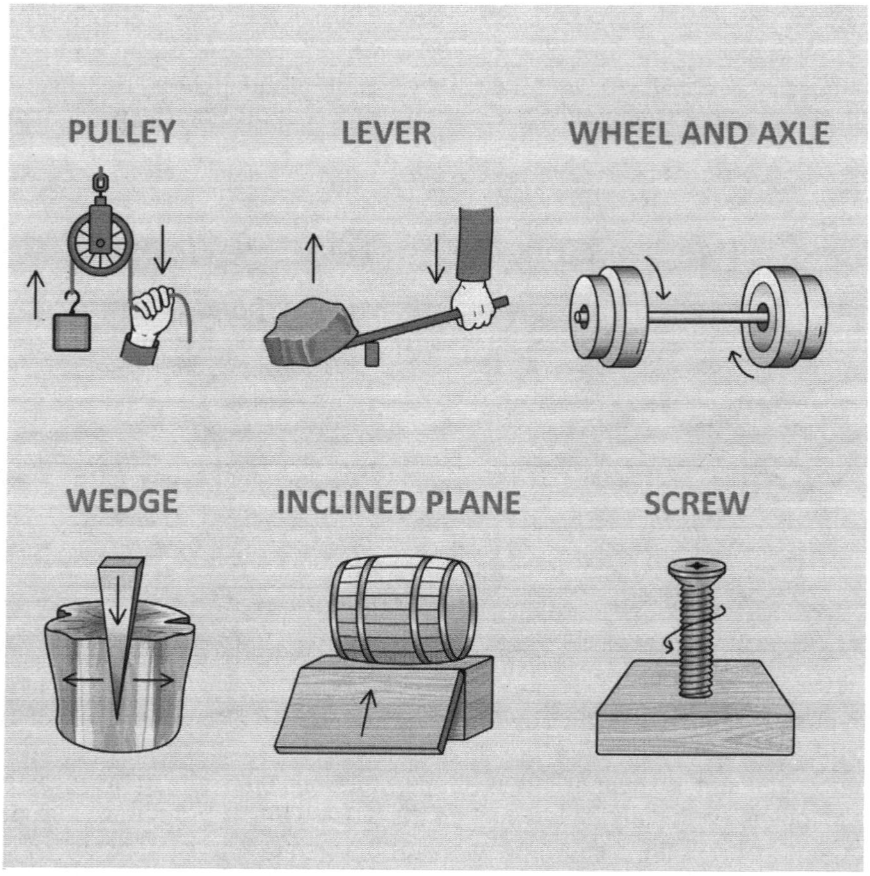

Review Video: Simple Machines
Visit mometrix.com/academy and enter code: 950789

Mechanical Advantage

There is a certain amount of **work** required to move an object that cannot be reduced. However, using one or more simple machines can increase either the distance or force needed. Since work is defined as a force multiplied by a distance, force and distance are inversely proportional.

$$\mathbf{Work_{input} = Work_{output}}$$

$$\mathbf{force_{input} \times distance_{input} = force_{output} \times distance_{output}}$$

Simple machines can either reduce the amount of input force needed by increasing the input distance or they can reduce the input distance needed by increasing the required input force. The ratio of the output force over the input force is a measure of the **mechanical advantage** of a machine. Due to the inverse relationship between force and distance for these machines, mechanical advantage can also be expressed as the ratio of input distance over the output distance.

$$\textbf{Mechanical Advantage} = \frac{\textbf{force}_{\textbf{output}}}{\textbf{force}_{\textbf{input}}} = \frac{\textbf{distance}_{\textbf{input}}}{\textbf{distance}_{\textbf{output}}}$$

LEVERS

The **lever** is the most common kind of simple machine. See-saws, shovels, and baseball bats are all examples of levers. There are three classes of levers which are differentiated by the relative orientations of the fulcrum, resistance, and effort. The **fulcrum** is the point at which the lever rotates, the **effort** is the point on the lever where force is applied, and the **resistance** is the part of the lever that acts in response to the effort.

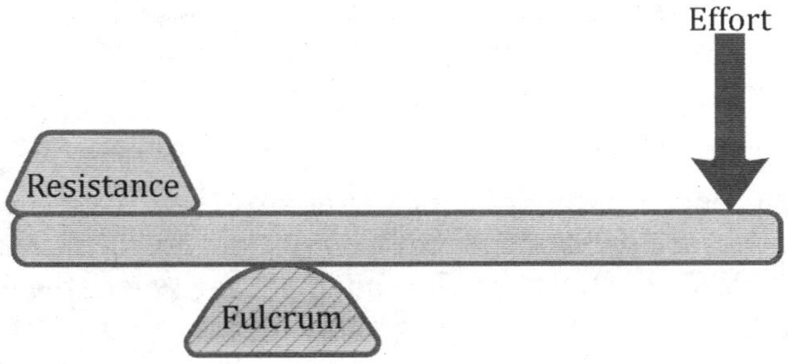

The mechanical advantage of a lever depends on the distances of the effort and resistance from the fulcrum.

$$\textbf{Mechanical Advantage} = \frac{\textbf{effort distance}}{\textbf{resistance distance}}$$

In a **first-class lever**, the fulcrum is between the effort and the resistance. A seesaw is a good example of a first-class lever when effort is applied to force one end up, the other end goes down, and vice versa. The shorter the distance between the fulcrum and the resistance, the easier it will be to move the resistance. As an example, consider whether it is easier to lift another person on a see-saw when they are sitting close to the middle or all the way at the end. A little practice will show you that it is much more difficult to lift a person the farther away he or she is on the see-saw.

First-Class Lever

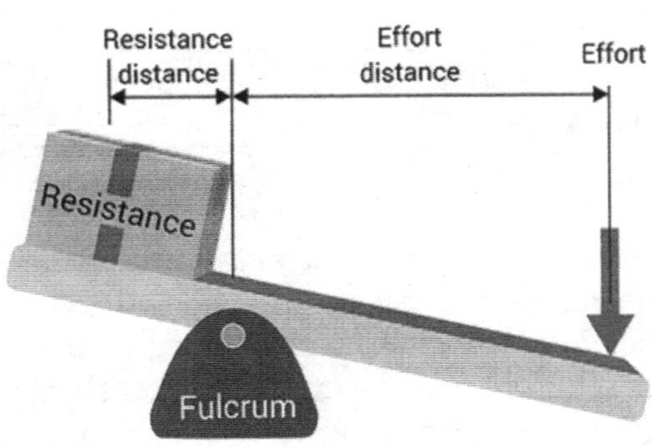

In a **second-class lever**, the resistance is in between the fulcrum and the effort. While a first-class lever is able to increase force and distance through mechanical advantage, a second-class lever is only able to increase force. A common example of a second-class lever is the wheelbarrow; the force exerted by your hand at one end of the wheelbarrow is magnified at the load. Basically, with a second-class lever, you are trading distance for force; by moving your end of the wheelbarrow a bit farther, you produce greater force at the load.

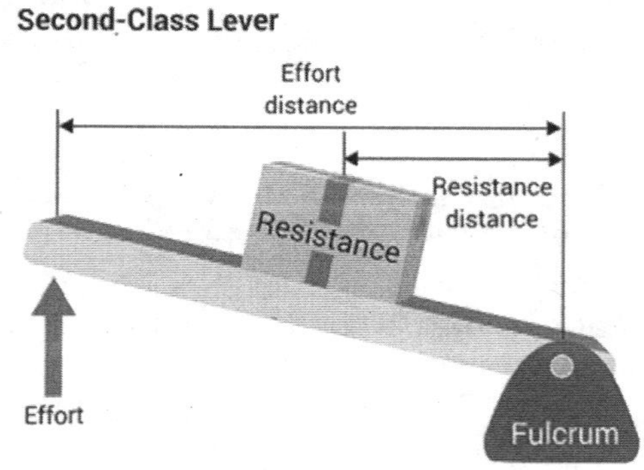

Third-class levers are used to produce greater distance. In a third-class lever, the force is applied in between the fulcrum and the resistance. A baseball bat is a classic example of a third-class lever; the bottom of the bat, below where you grip it, is considered the fulcrum. The end of the bat, where the ball is struck, is the resistance. By exerting effort at the base of the bat, close to the fulcrum, you are able to make the end of the bat fly quickly through the air. The closer your hands are to the base of the bat, the faster you will be able to make the other end of the bat travel.

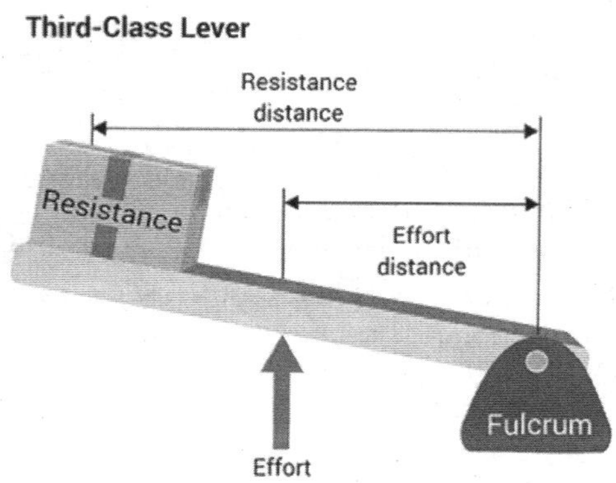

Review Video: Levers
Visit mometrix.com/academy and enter code: 103910

WHEEL AND AXLE

Another basic arrangement that makes use of simple machines is called the wheel and axle. When most people think of a wheel and axle, they immediately envision an automobile tire. The steering wheel of the car, however, operates on the same mechanical principle, namely that the force required to move the center of a circle is much greater than the force required to move the outer rim of a circle. When you turn the steering wheel, you are essentially using a second-class lever by increasing the output force by increasing the input distance. The force required to turn the wheel from the outer rim is much less than would be required to turn the wheel from its center.

The equation for the mechanical advantage of a wheel and axle is:

$$\textbf{Mechanical Advantage} = \frac{\textbf{radius}_{\textbf{wheel}}}{\textbf{radius}_{\textbf{axle}}}$$

For instance, a steering wheel with a radius of 12 inches has a greater mechanical advantage than a steering wheel with a radius of 10 inches; the same amount of force exerted on the rim of each wheel will produce greater force on the axle of the larger wheel.

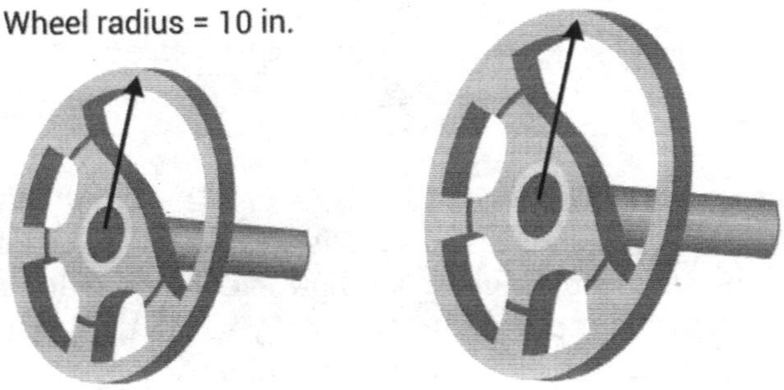

Thus, the mechanical advantage for each is:

$$\frac{10 \text{ inches}}{2 \text{ inches}} = 5 \qquad \frac{12 \text{ inches}}{2 \text{ inches}} = 6$$

Review Video: Wheel and Axle
Visit mometrix.com/academy and enter code: 574045

Pulleys

The pulley is a simple machine in which a rope is carried by the rotation of a wheel. Another name for a pulley is a block. Pulleys are typically used to allow the force to be directed from a convenient location. For instance, imagine you are given the task of lifting a heavy and tall bookcase. Rather than tying a rope to the bookcase and trying to lift it, it would make sense to tie a pulley system to a rafter above the bookcase and run the rope through it, so that you could pull down on the rope and lift the bookcase. Pulling down allows you to incorporate your weight (normal force) into the act of lifting, thereby making it easier.

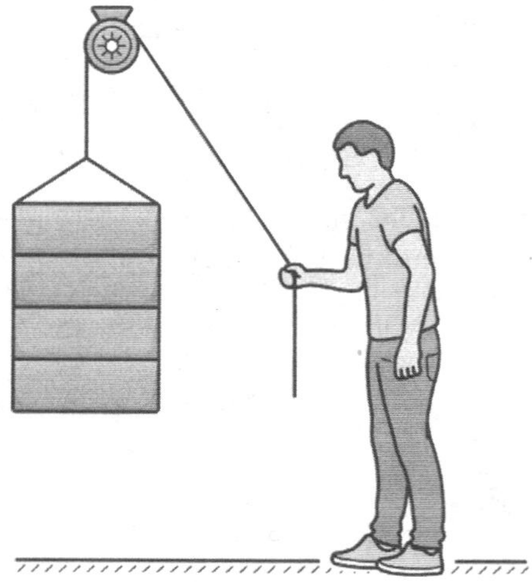

If there is just one pulley above the bookcase, you have created a first-class lever that will not diminish the amount of force that needs to be applied to lift the bookcase. There is another way to use a pulley, however, that can make the job of lifting a heavy object considerably easier. First, tie the rope directly to the rafter. Then, attach a pulley to the top of the bookcase and run the rope through it. If you can then stand so that you are above the bookcase, you will have a much easier time lifting this heavy object. This is because the weight of the bookcase is now being distributed: half of it is acting on the rafter, and half of it is acting on you. In other words, this arrangement allows you to lift an object with half the force. This simple pulley system, therefore, has a mechanical advantage of 2. Note that in this arrangement, the unfixed pulley is acting like a second-class lever. The price you pay for your mechanical advantage is that whatever distance you raise your end of the rope, the bookcase will only be lifted half as much.

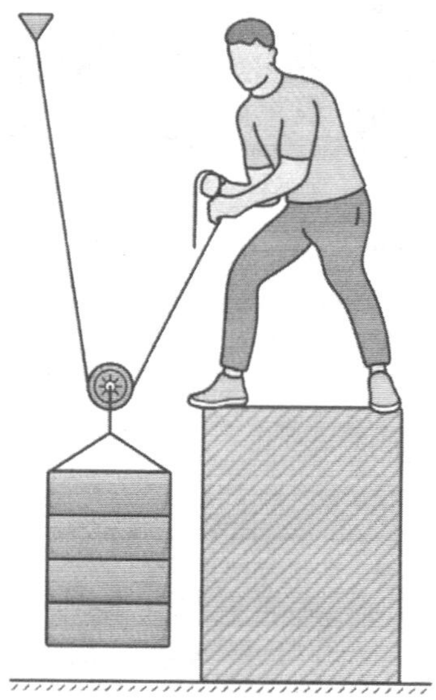

Of course, it might be difficult for you to find a place high enough to enact this system. If this is the case, you can always tie another pulley to the rafter and run the rope through it and back down to the floor. Since this second pulley is fixed, the mechanical advantage will remain the same.

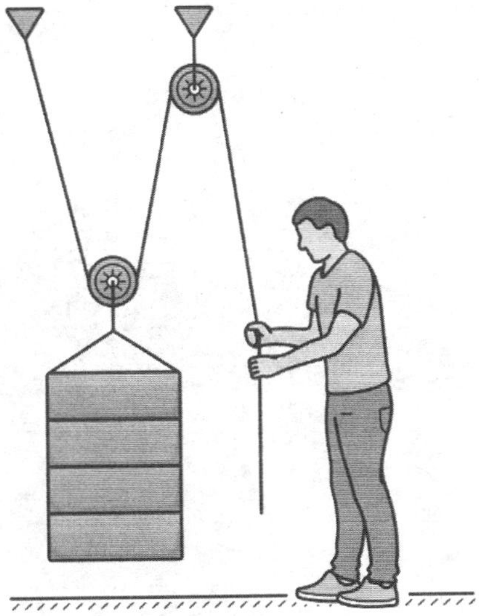

Inclined Plane

The inclined plane is perhaps the most common of the simple machines. It is simply a flat surface that elevates as you move from one end to the other. Consider how much easier it is for a person to walk up a long ramp than to climb a shorter but steeper flight of stairs; this is because the force required is diminished as the distance increases. Indeed, the longer the ramp, the easier it is to ascend.

Inclined planes often used to move heavy objects. For instance, moving a heavy box onto the back of a truck requires less force when pushing it up a ramp than when lifting it directly onto the truck bed. The longer the ramp, the greater the mechanical advantage, and the easier it will be to move the box. The mechanical advantage of an inclined plane is equal to the slant length divided by the rise of the plane.

$$\textbf{Mechanical Advantage} = \frac{\textbf{slant length}}{\textbf{rise}}$$

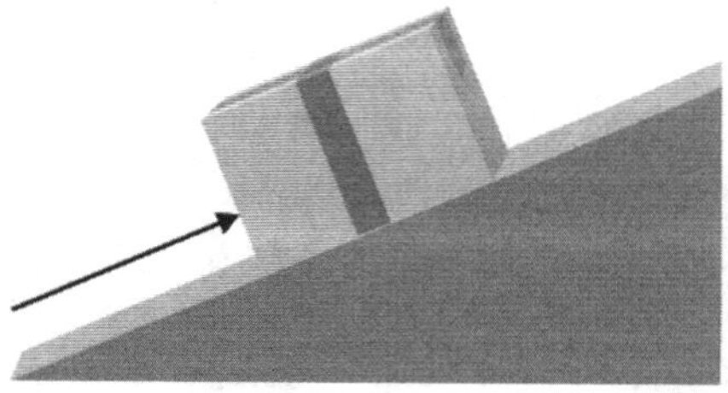

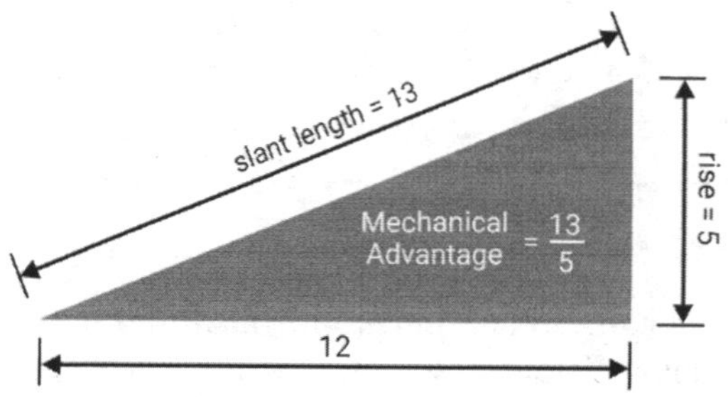

Screw

A screw is simply an inclined plane that has been wound around a cylinder so that it forms a sort of spiral.

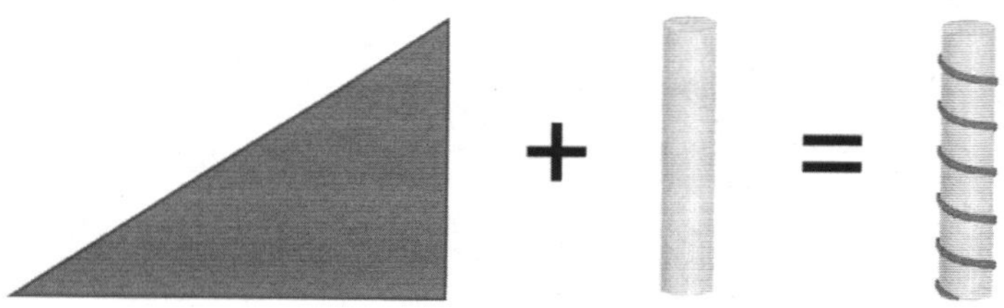

When it is placed into some medium, as for instance wood, the screw will move either forward or backward when it is rotated. The principle of the screw is used in a number of different objects, from jar lids to flashlights. The equation for the mechanical advantage is a modification of the inclined plane's equation.

Because the rise of the inclined plane is the length along a screw, length between rotations is the rise. The slant length is equal the circumference of one rotation ($2\pi r$).

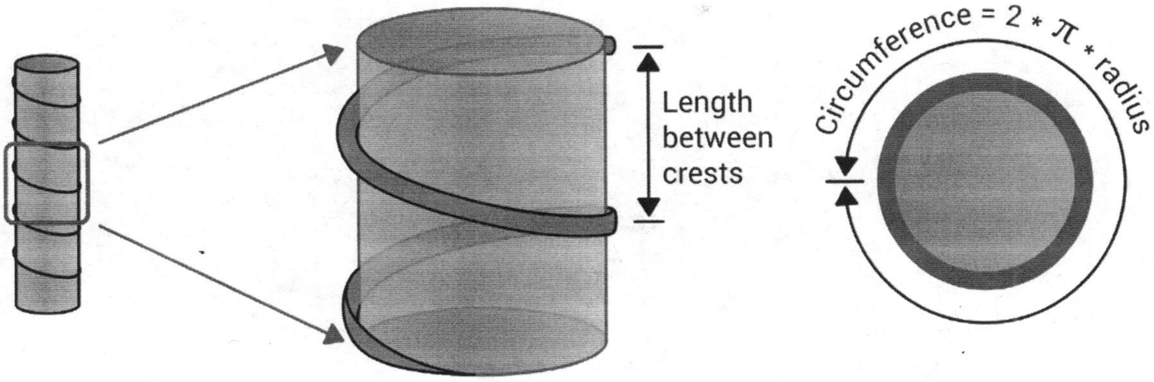

$$\textbf{Mechanical Advantage} = \frac{\textbf{2} \times \pi \times \textbf{radius}}{\textbf{length between crests}}$$

Wedge

A wedge is a variation on the inclined plane, in which the wedge moves between objects or parts and forces them apart. The unique characteristic of a wedge is that, unlike an inclined plane, it is designed to move. Perhaps the most familiar use of the wedge is in splitting wood. A wedge is driven into the wood by hitting the flat back end. The thin end of a wedge is easier to drive into the wood since it has less surface area and, therefore, transmits more force per area. As the wedge is driven in, the increased width helps to split the wood.

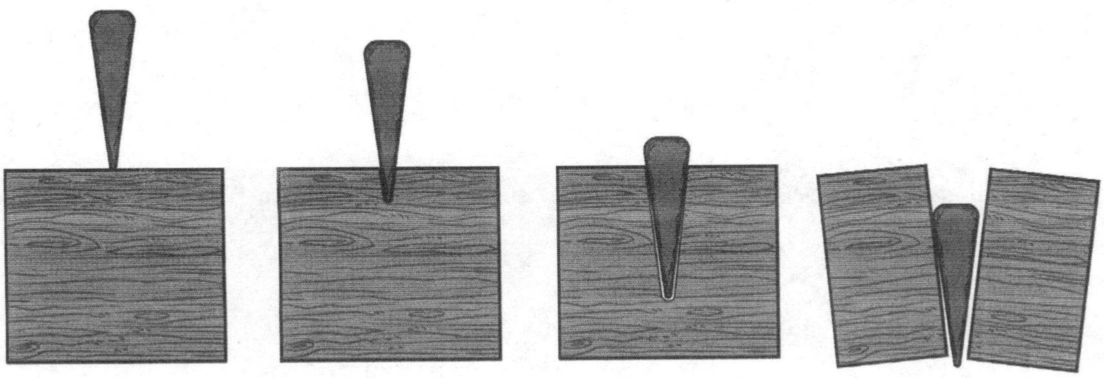

The longer and thinner the wedge, the greater the mechanical advantage. The equation for mechanical advantage of a wedge is:

$$\textbf{Mechanical Advantage} = \frac{\textbf{length}}{\textbf{width}}$$

Gears

Gears are a system of interlocking wheels that can create immense mechanical advantages. The amount of mechanical advantage, however, will depend on the gear ratio; that is, on the relation in size between the gears.

When a small gear is driving a big gear, the speed of the big gear is relatively slow; when a big gear is driving a small gear, the speed of the small gear is relatively fast.

The equation for the mechanical advantage is:

$$\textbf{Mechanical Advantage} = \frac{\textbf{torque}_{\textbf{output}}}{\textbf{torque}_{\textbf{input}}} = \frac{\textbf{r}_{\textbf{output}}}{\textbf{r}_{\textbf{input}}} = \frac{\textbf{\# of teeth}_{\textbf{output}}}{\textbf{\# of teeth}_{\textbf{input}}}$$

Note that mechanical advantage is greater than 1 when the output gear is larger. In these cases, the output velocity ($\boldsymbol{\omega}$) will be lower. The equation for the relative speed of a gear system is:

$$\frac{\omega_{input}}{\omega_{output}} = \frac{r_{output}}{r_{input}}$$

$$\textit{Mechanical Advantage} = \frac{\textit{teeth}_{\textit{output}}}{\textit{teeth}_{\textit{input}}} = \frac{20}{10} = 2$$

$$\textit{Mechanical Advantage} = \frac{\textit{teeth}_{\textit{output}}}{\textit{teeth}_{\textit{input}}} = \frac{16}{8} = 2$$

GEAR RATIOS

A gear ratio is a measure of how much the speed and torque are changing in a gear system. It is the ratio of output speed to input speed. Because the number of teeth is directly proportional to the speed in meshing gears, a gear ratio can also be calculated using the number of teeth on the gears. When the driving gear has 30 teeth and the driven gear has 10 teeth, the gear ratio is 3:1.

$$\text{Gear Ratio} = \frac{\#\text{ of teeth}_{\text{driving}}}{\#\text{ of teeth}_{\text{driven}}} = \frac{30}{10} = \frac{3}{1} = 3:1$$

This means that the smaller, driven gear rotates 3 times for every 1 rotation of the driving gear.

Uses of Gears

Gears are used to change the direction, location, and amount of output torque, as well as change the angular velocity of output.

Change output direction

Change torque location

Change torque amount

Change output velocity

Cams

In the study of motion, a final application often tested is the cam. A cam and follower system allows mechanical systems to have timed, specified, and repeating motion. Although cams come in varied forms, tests focus on rotary cams. In engines, a cam shaft coordinates the valves for intake and exhaust. Cams are often used to convert rotational motion into repeating linear motion.

Cams rotate around one point. The follower sits on the edge of the cam and moves along with the edge. To understand simple cams, count the number of bumps on the cam. Each bump will cause the follower to move outwards.

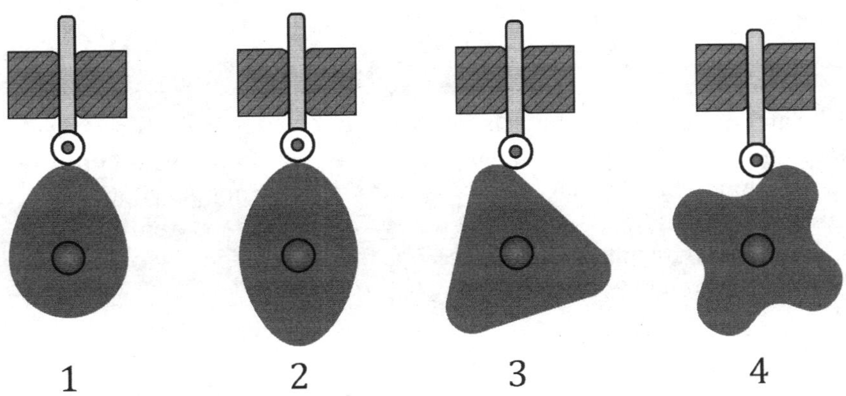

Another way to consider cams is to unravel the cam profile into a straight object. The follower will then follow the top of the profile.

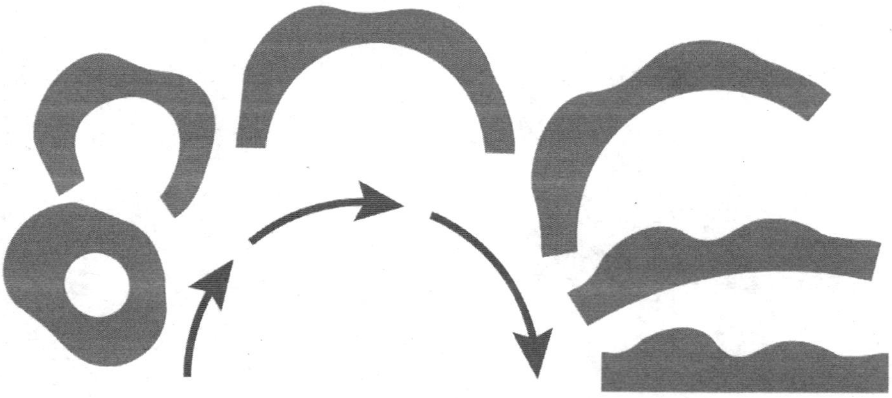

ENERGY

Energy is a word that has developed several different meanings in the English language, but in physics, it refers to the measure of a body's ability to do work. In physics, energy may not have a million meanings, but it does have many forms. Each of these forms, such as chemical, electric, and nuclear, is the capability of an object to perform work. However, the most commonly used concepts are mechanical energy and mechanical work. **Mechanical energy** is the sum of an object's kinetic and potential energies. While kinetic energy is linked to an object's motion, potential energy can be in a few different forms. The common forms of potential energy are gravitational and elastic.

KINETIC ENERGY

The **kinetic energy of an object** is that quality of its motion that can be related in a qualitative way to the amount of work performed on the object. Kinetic energy can be defined as $KE = \frac{mv^2}{2}$, in which m is the mass of an object and v is the magnitude of its velocity. Kinetic energy cannot be negative, since it depends on the square of velocity. Units for kinetic energy are the same as those for work: joules. Kinetic energy is a scalar quantity.

Changes in kinetic energy occur when a force does work on an object, such that the speed of the object is altered. This change in kinetic energy is equal to the amount of work that is done, and can be expressed as $W = KE_f - KE_i = \Delta KE$. This equation is commonly referred to as the work-kinetic energy theorem. If there are several different forces acting on the object, then W in this equation is the total work done by all the forces, or by the net force. This equation can be very helpful in solving some problems that would otherwise rely solely on Newton's laws of motion.

POTENTIAL ENERGY

Potential energy is the amount of energy that can be ascribed to a body or bodies based on configuration. There are a couple of different kinds of potential energy. **Gravitational potential energy** is the energy associated with the separation of bodies that are attracted to one another gravitationally. Any time you lift an object, you are increasing its gravitational potential energy. Gravitational potential energy can be found by the equation $PE = mgh$, where m is the mass of an object, $\boldsymbol{g}$ is the gravitational acceleration, and h is its height above a reference point, most often the ground.

Another kind of potential energy is **elastic potential energy**; elastic potential energy is associated with the compression or expansion of an elastic, or spring-like, object. Physicists will often refer to potential energy as being stored within a body, the implication being that it could emerge in the future.

Review Video: Potential and Kinetic Energy
Visit mometrix.com/academy and enter code: 491502

Elastic Potential Energy

Elastic potential energy is the potential for a certain amount of work to be done by one object on another using elastic compression or tension. The most common example is the spring. A spring will resist any compression or tension away from its equilibrium position (natural position). A small buggy is pressed into a large spring. The spring contains a large amount of elastic potential energy. If the buggy and spring are released, the spring will exert a force on the buggy, pushing it for a distance. This work will put kinetic energy into the buggy. The energy can be imagined as a liquid poured from one container into another. The spring pours its elastic energy into the buggy, which receives the energy as kinetic energy.

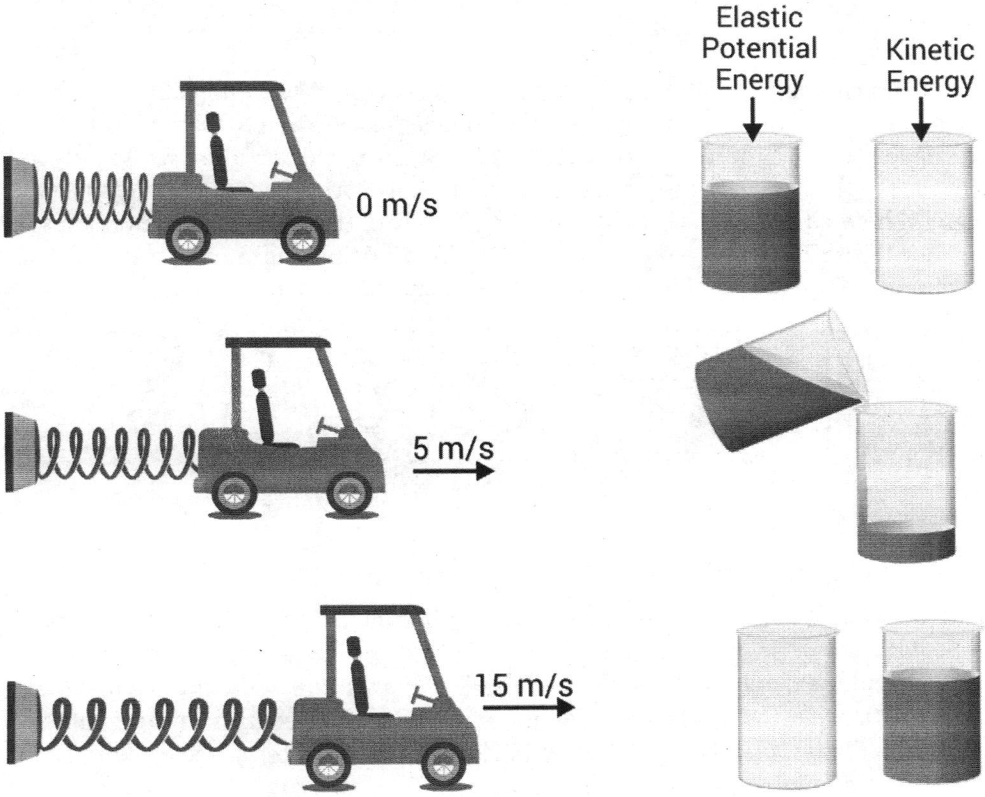

Conservative and Non-Conservative Forces

Forces that change the state of a system by changing kinetic energy into potential energy, or vice versa, are called **conservative forces**. This name arises because these forces conserve the total amount of kinetic and potential energy. Every other kind of force is considered non-conservative. One example of a conservative force is gravity. Consider the path of a ball thrown straight up into the air. Since the ball has the same amount of kinetic energy when it is thrown as it does when it returns to its original location (known as completing a closed path), gravity can be said to be a conservative force. More generally, a force can be said to be conservative if the work it does on an object through a closed path is zero. Frictional force would not meet this standard, of course, because it is only capable of performing negative work.

For example, imagine a ball moving perpendicular to the surface of the Earth, in other words straight up and down, with its weight being the only force acting on it. As the ball rises, the weight will be doing work on the ball, decreasing its speed and its kinetic energy and slowing it down until it momentarily stops. During this ascent, the potential energy of the ball will be rising. Once the ball begins to fall back down, it will lose potential energy as it gains kinetic energy. Mechanical energy is conserved throughout; the potential energy of the ball at its highest point is equal to the kinetic energy of the ball at its lowest point, just before to impact.

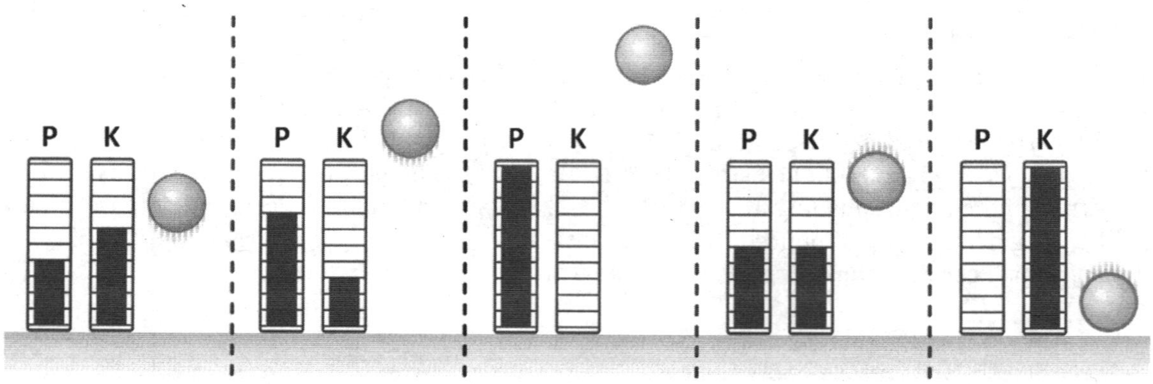

In systems where friction and air resistance are not negligible, we observe a different sort of result. For example, imagine a block sliding across the floor until it comes to a stop due to friction. Unlike a compressed spring or a ball flung into the air, there is no way for this block to regain its energy with a return trip. Therefore, we cannot say that the lost kinetic energy is being stored as potential energy. Instead, it has been dissipated and cannot be recovered. The total mechanical energy of the block-floor system has been not conserved in this case but rather reduced. The total energy of the system has not decreased, since the kinetic energy has been converted into thermal energy, but that energy is no longer useful for work.

One-Dimensional Analysis of Work Done By a Variable Force

If the force on an object varies across the distance the object is moved, then a simple product will not yield the work. If we consider the work performed by a variable force in one dimension, then we are assuming that the directions of the force and the displacement are the same. The magnitude of the force will depend on the position of the particle. In order to calculate the amount of work performed by a variable force over a given distance, we should first divide the total displacement into a number of intervals, each with a width of Δx. We may then say that the amount of work performed during any one interval is $\Delta W = \boldsymbol{F}_{avg}\Delta x$, where $\boldsymbol{F}_{avg}$ is the average force over the interval Δx. We can then say that the total amount of work performed is the sum of all work performed during the various intervals. By reducing the interval to an infinitesimal length, we obtain the integral:

$$W = \int_{x_1}^{x_2} \boldsymbol{F}_x dx$$

This integral requires that the force be a known function of x.

Work Performed by a Spring

If we move a block attached to a spring from point x_i to point x_f, we are doing work on the block, and the spring is also doing work on the block. To determine the work done by the spring on the block, we can substitute ***F*** from Hooke's law into our equation for work performed by a variable force, and arrive at this measure: $W = \frac{k(x_i^2 - x_f^2)}{2}$. This work will be positive if $x_i^2 > x_f^2$, and negative if the opposite is true. If $x_i = 0$ and we decide to call the final position x, then we may change our equation: $W = \frac{-kx^2}{2}$. It is important to keep in mind that this is the work done by the spring. The work done by the force that moves the block to its final position will be a positive quantity.

Like all simple harmonic oscillators, springs operate by **storing and releasing potential energy**. The amount of energy being stored or released by a spring is equal to the magnitude of the work done by the spring during that same operation. The total potential energy stored in a spring can be calculated as $PE = \frac{kx^2}{2}$. Neglecting the effects of friction and drag, an object oscillating on a spring will continue to do so indefinitely, since total mechanical energy (kinetic and potential) is conserved. In such a situation, the period of oscillation can be calculated as $T = 2\pi \times \sqrt{\frac{m}{k}}$.

Vectors and Scalars in Force and Motion

Vectors

Vectors are mathematical quantities with both **magnitude and direction**. A vector is most commonly described by the magnitude of its components in the relevant coordinate system. Vectors may exist in any number of dimensions, but for applications in mechanics they will most often be in either two or three. A vector is generally denoted by a letter either in boldface type or with an arrow above it.

Adding or subtracting vectors is as simple as adding or subtracting their components. For instance, given the two vectors $\mathbf{a} = \langle 1,5,7 \rangle$ and $\mathbf{b} = \langle 5,-3,3 \rangle$, $\mathbf{a} + \mathbf{b} = \langle (1+5),(5-3),(7+3) \rangle = \langle 6,2,10 \rangle$. If vectors are given as a length and an angle, it may be necessary to use trigonometry to convert these to orthogonal components.

Visually, adding a vector is accomplished by drawing the second vector starting from the endpoint of the first vector. To visually subtract a vector, draw both vectors starting from the origin. The difference will be the vector from the endpoint of the second to the endpoint of the first.

Vector addition has many of the same relevant properties as scalar addition. It is commutative, in that $\mathbf{a} + \mathbf{b} = \mathbf{b} + \mathbf{a}$, and associative, in that $(\mathbf{a} + \mathbf{b}) + \mathbf{c} = \mathbf{a} + (\mathbf{b} + \mathbf{c})$.

There are a few different ways to multiply vectors, though none of them is exactly the same as algebraic multiplication. For instance, one way to multiply vectors is to multiply a vector by a scalar. If we are to multiply vector **a** by scalar **s**, we can only multiply the magnitude of **a** by the absolute value of **s**. The direction of the product will be the same as **a** so long as **s** is positive; if **s** is negative, the resulting vector will be in the opposite direction. Remember that dividing **a** by **s**, is equivalent to multiplying **a** by $\frac{1}{\mathbf{s}}$. One common example of this kind of operation in physics is in the equation for force. To find force, we multiply mass (scalar) by acceleration (vector). Of course, since mass will always be positive, the direction of the resulting vector (force) will always be in the direction of the acceleration.

Resultant Force Vectors

Force has both magnitude and direction. Furthermore, multiple forces acting on one object combine in vector addition. This can be demonstrated by considering an object placed at the origin of the coordinate plane. If it is pushed along the positive direction of the *x*-axis, it will move in this direction. If the force acting on it is in the positive direction of the *y*-axis, it will move in that direction.

However, if both forces are applied at the same time, then the object will move at an angle to both the x- and y-axes, an angle determined by the relative amount of force exerted in each direction. In this way, we may see that the resulting force is a vector sum; a net force that has both magnitude and direction.

Resultant vectors from applied forces:

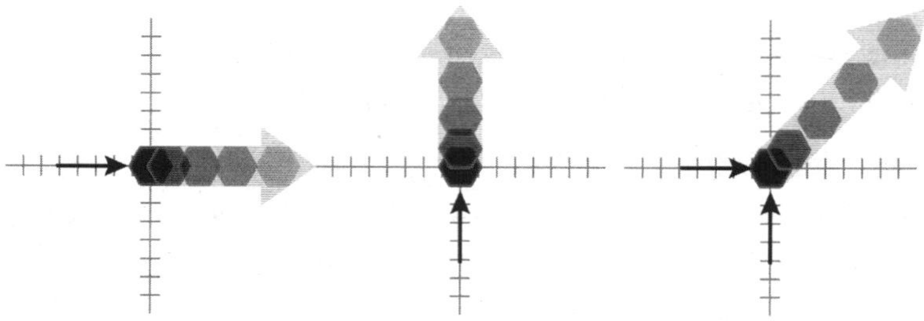

Review Video: Forces: Push-Pull
Visit mometrix.com/academy and enter code: 104731

Cross Products

When two vectors are being **multiplied for a vector product** ($\mathbf{a} \times \mathbf{b} = \mathbf{c}$), the equation will be written $\mathbf{c} = ab \sin \varphi$, where φ is the smaller of the two angles between **a** and **b**. Because in this form the multiplication of **a** and **b** is indicated with the $\times$, this resulting vector is often known as the cross product. Of course, if **a** and **b** are parallel, then $\mathbf{a} \times \mathbf{b} = 0$. The direction of **c** will be perpendicular to the plane that contains both **a** and **b** by the right-hand rule. It should be noted that the commutative law does not apply to this kind of multiplication. Instead, we may say that the cross product is an anticommutative function, meaning that $\mathbf{b} \times \mathbf{a} = -\mathbf{a} \times \mathbf{b}$. This kind of equation will be used in the formula for torque.

An alternative method for calculating the cross product is to take the determinant of a 3×3 matrix composed of the two vectors along with the unit vectors **i**, **j**, and **k**. So for vectors $\mathbf{a} = \langle 2,3,6 \rangle$ and $\mathbf{b} = \langle 1,1,4 \rangle$:

$$a \times b = \begin{vmatrix} \mathbf{i} & \mathbf{j} & \mathbf{k} \\ 2 & 3 & 6 \\ 1 & 1 & 4 \end{vmatrix} = \mathbf{i}(12-6) + \mathbf{j}(6-8) + \mathbf{k}(2-3)$$

So $\mathbf{a} \times \mathbf{b} = 6\mathbf{i} - 2\mathbf{j} - \mathbf{k}$. Conversely, $\mathbf{b} \times \mathbf{a} = -6\mathbf{i} + 2\mathbf{j} + \mathbf{k}$.

Dot Products

There are two different methods for multiplying two vectors: one way yields a **vector product**, and one way yields a **scalar product**. If we take the vectors **a** and **b** and decide to solve for a scalar product, we will set up this equation: $\mathbf{a} \cdot \mathbf{b} = ab \cos \varphi$. In this equation, a is the magnitude of the vector **a**, b is the magnitude of the vector **b**, and φ is the angle between **a** and **b**. Another way to arrive at the same scalar product is to multiply each component of one vector by the corresponding component in the other vector and sum the results: $\mathbf{a} \cdot \mathbf{b} = axbx + ayby + azbz$. Since there are only scalars on the right side of the equation, the resulting product will be a scalar. This product is often referred to as a dot product, since the left side of the equation is often written with the expression, "**a** · **b**" (a dot b). This kind of equation is exemplified by the formula for work, in which a scalar (work) is found by multiplying two vectors (force and displacement).

Displacement, Velocity, and Acceleration

Displacement

When something changes its location from one place to another, it is said to have undergone **displacement**. If we can determine the original and final position of the object, then we can determine the total displacement with the equation $\Delta \boldsymbol{x} = x_f - x_i$, where x_f is the final position and x_i is the initial position.

If the object has moved in the positive direction, then the final position will be greater than the original position, so we can say that the change was positive. If the final position is less than the original, however, displacement will be negative. Displacement along a straight line is an example of a vector quantity; it has both a magnitude and a direction. If an object travels from position $x = -5$ cm to $x = 5$ cm, it has undergone a displacement of 10 cm. If it traverses the same path in the opposite direction, its displacement is –10 cm. A vector that spans the object's displacement in the direction of travel is known as a displacement vector, with units of length.

Review Video: Displacement in Physics
Visit mometrix.com/academy and enter code: 236197

Determining Position

In order to determine anything about the motion of an object, we must first locate it. In other words, we must be able to describe its position relative to some reference point, often called an **origin**. If we consider the origin as the zero point of an axis, then positive values correspond to the location of an object one direction, and negative values are locations in the exact opposite direction. If a particle is located 5 cm from the origin in the positive direction of the x-axis, its location is said to be $x = 5$ cm. If another particle is 5 cm from the origin in the negative direction of the x-axis, its position is $x = -5$ cm. These two particles are 10 cm apart. A vector whose starting point is the origin and whose endpoint is the location of an object is that object's position vector, with units of length.

Velocity

Difference between Speed and Velocity

Often, people confuse the words *speed* and *velocity*. There is a significant difference. The average velocity is based on the amount of displacement, a vector. Alternately, the average speed is based on the distance covered or the path length. The equation for speed is:

$$\textbf{average speed} = \frac{\textbf{total distance traveled}}{\textbf{change in time}}$$

Notice that we used total distance and *not* change in position, because speed is path-dependent.

If the plane traveling between cities had needed to fly around a storm on its way, making the distance traveled 50 miles greater than the distance the car traveled, the plane would still have the same total displacement as the car.

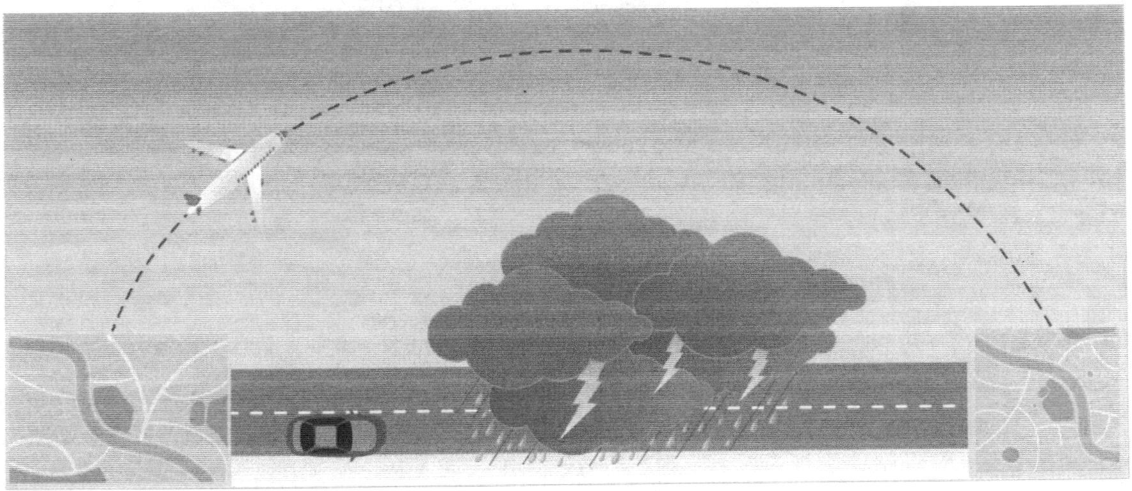

For this reason, the average speed can be calculated:

$$\text{plane average speed} = \frac{150 \text{ miles}}{1 \text{ hour}} = 150 \text{ miles per hour}$$

$$\text{car average speed} = \frac{100 \text{ miles}}{2 \text{ hours}} = 50 \text{ miles per hour}$$

Instantaneous Velocity

There are two types of velocity that are commonly considered in physics: average velocity and instantaneous velocity. In order to obtain the **instantaneous velocity** of an object, we must find its average velocity and then try to decrease Δt as close as possible to zero. As Δt decreases, it approaches what is known as a limiting value, bringing the average velocity very close to the instantaneous velocity. Instantaneous velocity is most easily discussed in the context of calculus-based physics.

Average Velocity

If we want to calculate the **average velocity** of an object, we must know two things. First, we must know its **displacement**, or the distance it has covered relative to a starting point. Second, we must know the **time it took to cover this distance**. Once we have this information, the formula for average velocity is: $\boldsymbol{v}_{avg} = \frac{(x_f - x_i)}{(t_f - t_i)}$, where the subscripts i and f denote the initial and final values of the position and time. In other words, the average velocity is equal to the change in position divided by the change in time. This calculation will indicate the average distance that was covered per unit of time. Average velocity is a vector and will always point in the same direction as the displacement vector (since time is a scalar and always positive).

Acceleration

Acceleration is the **change in the velocity** of an object. Like velocity, acceleration may be computed as an average or an instantaneous quantity. To calculate average acceleration, we may use the equation $\boldsymbol{a}_{avg} = \frac{v_f - v_i}{t_f - t_i}$, where the subscripts i and f denote the initial and final values of the velocity and time. The so-called instantaneous acceleration of an object can be found by reducing the time component to the limiting value until instantaneous velocity is approached. Acceleration will be expressed in units of distance divided by time squared; for instance, meters per second squared. Like position and velocity, acceleration is a vector quantity and will therefore have both magnitude and direction.

Review Video: Velocity and Acceleration
Visit mometrix.com/academy and enter code: 671849

Kinematics

Kinematic Equations

The phenomenon of constant acceleration allows physicists to construct a number of helpful equations. Perhaps the most fundamental equation of an object's motion is the **position equation**:

$$x_f = x_i + \boldsymbol{v}_i t + \frac{1}{2}\boldsymbol{a}t^2$$

If the object is starting from rest at the origin, this equation reduces to $x_f = \frac{at^2}{2}$. The position equation can be rearranged to give the **displacement equation**:

$$\Delta \boldsymbol{x} = \boldsymbol{v}_i t + \frac{1}{2}\boldsymbol{a}t^2$$

If the object's acceleration is unknown, the position or displacement may be found by the equation:

$$\Delta x = \frac{(v_f + v_i)t}{2}$$

If the position of an object is unknown, the velocity may be found by the equation:

$$v_f = v_i + at$$

Similarly, if the time is unknown, the velocity after a given displacement may be found by the equation:

$$v_f = \sqrt{(v_i^2 + 2a\Delta x)}$$

CONCEPT OF PROJECTILE MOTION

When we discuss **projectile motion**, we are referring to the movement of an object through two dimensions during a free fall. Two-dimensional motion may be described using the same equations as one-dimensional motion, but two equations must be considered simultaneously. For basic equations for projectile motion, it is often assumed that the rate of gravitational acceleration on the Earth is $g = 9.8 \text{ m/s}^2$, and that the effect of air resistance can be ignored (Note: take care with the sign on gravitational acceleration make sure that it always points toward the Earth). If a projectile is launched under such ideal conditions, we may say that its initial velocity is $\boldsymbol{v}_0 = v_0 \cos\theta\,\mathbf{i} + v_0 \sin\theta\,\mathbf{j}$. These two velocity components are sometimes written as $\boldsymbol{v}_{0x}$ and $\boldsymbol{v}_{0y}$, respectively.

PROJECTILE MOTION EXAMPLE

Simple projectile motion occurs when an object is in the air and experiencing only the force of gravity. We will disregard drag for this topic. Some common examples of projectile motion are thrown balls, flying bullets, and falling rocks. The characteristics of projectile motion are:

1. The horizontal component of velocity doesn't change
2. The vertical acceleration due to gravity affects the vertical component of velocity

Because gravity only acts downwards, objects in projectile motion only experience acceleration in the y-direction (vertical). The horizontal component of the object's velocity does not change in flight. This means that if a rock is thrown out off a cliff, the horizontal velocity (think of the shadow if the sun is directly overhead) will not change until the ball hits the ground.

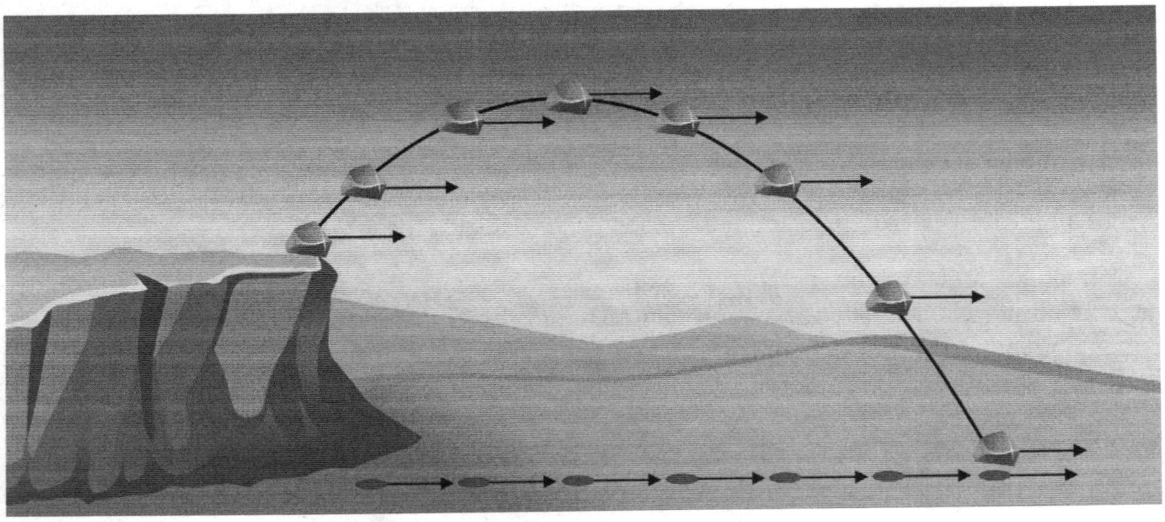

The velocity in the vertical direction is affected by gravity. Gravity imposes an acceleration of $g = 9.8\frac{\text{m}}{\text{s}^2}$ or $32\frac{\text{ft}}{\text{s}^2}$ downward on projectiles. The vertical component of velocity at any point is equal to:

$$\textbf{vertical velocity} = \textbf{original vertical velocity} - \textbf{g} \times \textbf{time}$$

When these characteristics are combined, there are three points of particular interest in a projectile's flight. At the beginning of a flight, the object has a horizontal component and a vertical component giving it a large speed. At the top of a projectile's flight, the vertical velocity equals zero, making the top the slowest part of travel. When the object passes the same height as the launch, the vertical velocity is opposite of the initial vertical velocity, making the speed equal to the initial speed.

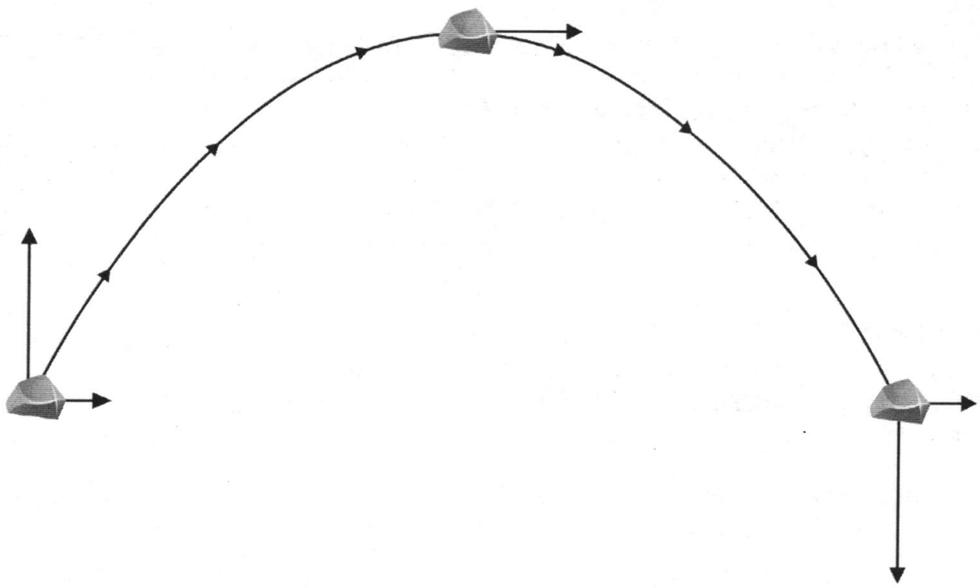

If the object continues falling below the initial height from which it was launched (e.g., it was launched from the edge of a cliff), it will have an even greater velocity than it did initially from that point until it hits the ground.

Review Video: Projectile Motion
Visit mometrix.com/academy and enter code: 719700

Example: If a cannon located at a height of 5 m above ground level fires a cannonball 250 m/s at an angle of $\frac{\pi}{6}$ from the horizontal, how far will the cannonball travel before hitting the ground?

When the cannonball hits the ground, it has been displaced by –5 m in the y-direction. Solving for the components of initial velocity yields $\boldsymbol{v}_{0x} = 216.5$ m/s and $\boldsymbol{v}_{0y} = 125$ m/s. Setting up the y-direction displacement equation results in the following: $-5 = 125t_f - 4.9{t_f}^2$. Solving for t_f yields an impact time of around 25.5 seconds. To find the horizontal distance covered, set up the displacement equation for the

x-direction: $\Delta \boldsymbol{x} = \boldsymbol{v}_{0x} t_f + \frac{1}{2} \boldsymbol{a}_x (t_f)^2$. Since we ignore the effects of air resistance, acceleration in the x-direction is zero, yielding a flight distance of 5,530 m.

Uniform Circular Motion

We may say that a particle is in **uniform circular motion** when it is traveling in a circle, or circular arc, and at a constant speed. Crucially, we must note that such a particle is accelerating, even though the magnitude of its velocity does not change. This is because velocity is a vector, and consequently, any change in its direction is an acceleration. So, if we take two points on an arc of radius, r, separated by an angle, θ, and want to determine the time it will take a particle to move between these two points at a constant speed, $|\boldsymbol{v}|$, we can use the equation: $\Delta t = \frac{r\theta}{|\boldsymbol{v}|}$. The quantity $\frac{|\boldsymbol{v}|}{r}$ is often written as $\boldsymbol{\omega}$, or angular velocity, having units of radians per second, so the time may also be computed as $\Delta t = \frac{\theta}{\omega}$. The speed, or absolute value of the velocity, of an object in uniform circular motion is also called the tangential speed, because the object is always moving in a direction tangent to the circle. Similarly, an increase in the magnitude of this velocity is called **tangential acceleration**.

A very important component of uniform motion is the centripetal acceleration. This is the acceleration that changes the direction of the velocity vector to follow the circular arc. It is directed toward the center of the circle or arc and is described by $\boldsymbol{a}_c = \frac{|\boldsymbol{v}|^2}{r} = r\boldsymbol{\omega}^2$.

Relative Motion and Inertial Reference Frames

When we describe motion as being **relative**, we mean that it can only be measured in relation to something else. If a moving object is considered as it relates to some stationary object or arbitrary location, it will have a different measured velocity than it would if it were compared to some other object that is itself in motion. In other words, the measure of an object's velocity depends entirely on the reference frame from which the measurement is taken. When performing measurements of this kind, we may use any reference point we like. However, once we have decided on a reference point, we must be consistent in using it as the basis for all of our measurements, or else we will go astray. Additionally, if we want to be able to apply Newton's laws of motion or Galilean principles of relativity, we must select an **inertial reference frame**: that is, a reference frame that is not accelerating or rotating. A car traveling at a constant speed in a straight line is an inertial reference frame. A car moving in uniform circular motion is not.

An object's velocity with respect to a frame fixed to the Earth can be computed by measuring its velocity from any inertial reference frame and combining that velocity by vector addition with the velocity of the inertial frame with respect to the Earth. For instance, if a man is traveling in the x-direction at 20 m/s, and he throws a rock out the window at a relative velocity of 15 m/s in the y-direction, the rock's velocity with respect to the Earth is found by adding the two vectors:

$$\boldsymbol{v}_r = 20\mathbf{i} + 15\mathbf{j} \text{ m/s}$$

LAWS OF MOTION

NEWTON'S LAWS

NEWTON'S FIRST LAW

Before Newton formulated his laws of mechanics, it was generally assumed that some force had to act on an object continuously in order to make the object move at a **constant velocity**. Newton, however, determined that unless some other force acted on the object (most notably friction or air resistance), it would continue in the direction it was pushed at the same velocity forever.

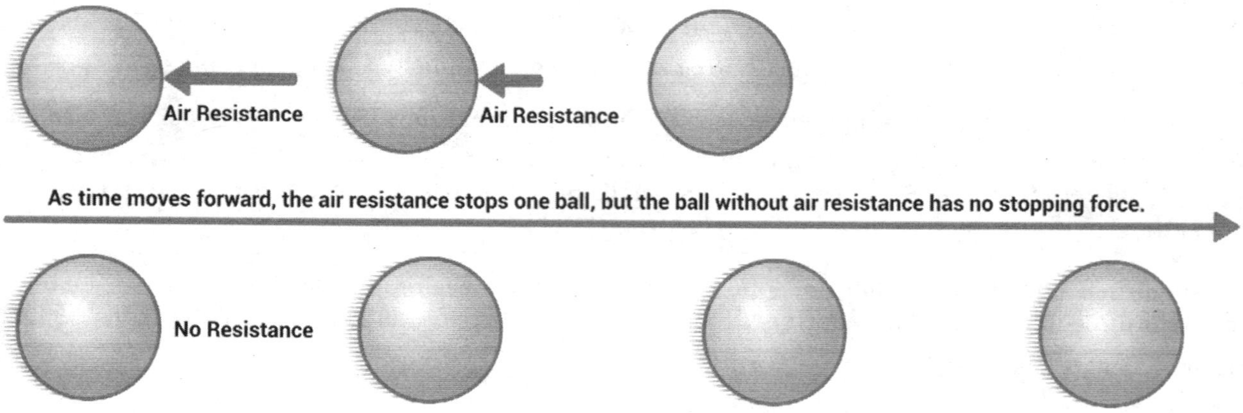

In this light, a body at rest and a body in motion are not all that different, and Newton's first law makes little distinction. It states that a body at rest will tend to remain at rest, while a body in motion will tend to remain in motion. This tendency of a body to remain in its present state of motion is referred to as **inertia**. In order for the body's state of motion to change, it must be acted on by a non-zero net force. **Net force** is the vector sum of all forces acting on a body. If this vector sum is zero, then there is no unbalanced force, and the body will remain in its present state of motion. It is important to remember that this law only holds in inertial reference frames.

Review Video: Newton's First Law of Motion
Visit mometrix.com/academy and enter code: 590367

NEWTON'S SECOND LAW

Newton's second law states that an **object's acceleration** is directly proportional to the net force acting on the object, and inversely proportional to the object's mass. It is generally written in equation form $\boldsymbol{F} = m\boldsymbol{a}$, where $\boldsymbol{F}$ is the net force acting on a body, m is the mass of the body, and $\boldsymbol{a}$ is its acceleration. It is important to note from this equation that since the mass is always a positive quantity, the acceleration vector is always pointed in the same direction as the net force vector. Of course, in order to apply this equation correctly, one must clearly identify the body to which it is being applied. Once this is done, we may say that $\boldsymbol{F}$ is the vector sum of all forces acting on that body, or the net force. This measure includes only those forces that are external to the body; any internal forces, in which one part of the body exerts force on another, are discounted.

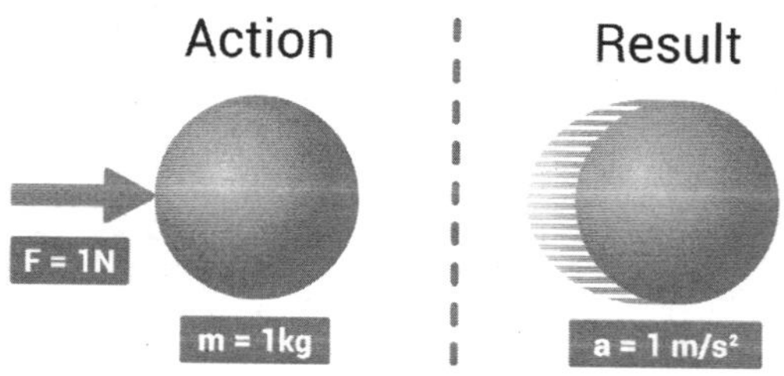

Newton's second law somewhat encapsulates his first, because it includes the principle that if no net force is acting on a body, the body will not accelerate. As was the case with his first law, Newton's second law may only be applied in inertial reference frames.

Review Video: Newton's Second Law of Motion
Visit mometrix.com/academy and enter code: 737975

NEWTON'S THIRD LAW

Newton's third law of motion can be stated as: **for every force, there is an equal and opposite force**. When a hammer strikes a nail, the nail hits the hammer just as hard. If we consider two objects, A and B, then we may express any contact between these two bodies with the equation $\boldsymbol{F}_{AB} = -\boldsymbol{F}_{BA}$. It is important to note in this kind of equation that the order of the subscripts denotes which body is exerting the force. Although the two forces are often referred to as the **action** and **reaction** forces, in physics there is really no such thing. There is no implication of cause and effect in the equation for Newton's third law. At first glance, this law might seem to forbid any movement at all. We must remember, however, that these equal, opposite forces are exerted on different bodies with different masses, so they will not cancel each other out.

As an example, consider two spring-based scales, both tipped on their sides, with the weighing surfaces facing each other. If scale #1 is pressing scale #2 into the wall, it exerts a force on scale #2, measurable by the reading on scale #2. However, because scale #1 is exerting a force on scale #2, scale #2 is exerting a force on scale #1 with an opposite direction, but the same magnitude.

Review Video: Newton's Third Law of Motion
Visit mometrix.com/academy and enter code: 838401

Equilibrium and Friction

Normal Force

The word *normal* is used in mathematics to mean perpendicular, and so the force known as normal force should be remembered as the perpendicular force exerted on an object that is resting on some other surface. For instance, if a box is resting on a horizontal surface, we may say that the normal force is directed upwards through the box (the opposite, downward force is the weight of the box). If the box is resting on a wedge, the normal force from the wedge is not vertical but is perpendicular to the surface.

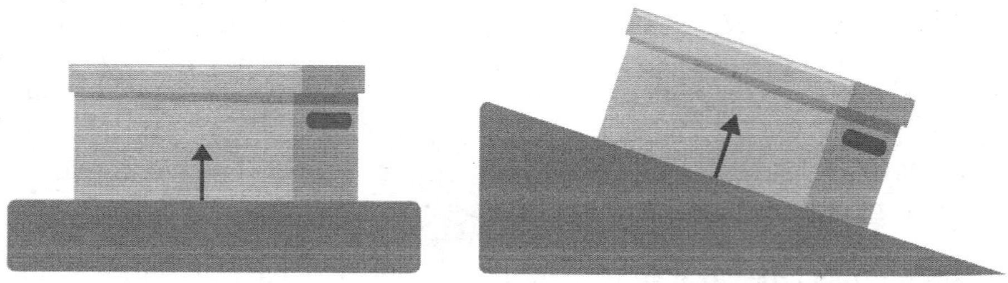

Static and Kinetic Frictional Forces

In order to illustrate the concept of friction, let us imagine a book resting on a table. As it sits there, the force of its weight ($\boldsymbol{W}$) is equal and opposite to the normal force ($\boldsymbol{N}$). If, however, we were to exert a force ($\boldsymbol{F}$) on the book, attempting to push it to one side, a frictional force ($\boldsymbol{f}$) would arise, equal and opposite to our force. This kind of frictional force is known as **static frictional force**.

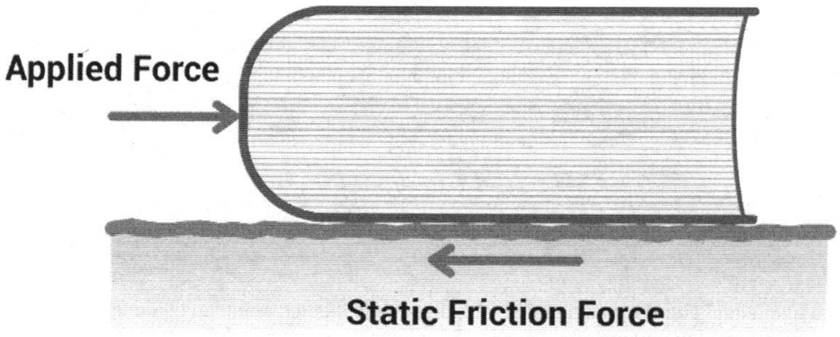

As we increase our force on the book, however, we will eventually cause it to accelerate in the direction of our force. At this point, the frictional force opposing us will be known as **kinetic frictional force**.

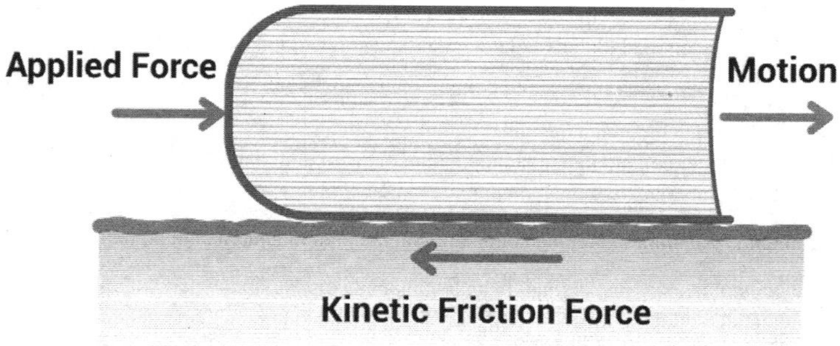

For the most part, kinetic frictional force is lower than static frictional force, and so the amount of force needed to maintain the movement of the book will be less than that needed to initiate movement. For wheels and spherical objects on a surface, static friction at the point of contact allows them to roll, but there is a frictional force that resists the rolling motion as well, due primarily to deformation effects in the rolling material. This is known as rolling friction, and tends to be much smaller than either static or kinetic friction.

COEFFICIENT OF FRICTION

If an object does not move when a horizontal force $\boldsymbol{F}$ is applied, then the **static frictional force** $(\boldsymbol{f}_s)$ is exactly equal and opposite to $\boldsymbol{F}$, i.e., $\boldsymbol{f}_s = -\boldsymbol{F}$. Static frictional force has a maximum value, however, which is expressed as $\boldsymbol{f}_{s,max} = \mu_s N$, in which μ_s is the coefficient of static friction, and N is the magnitude of the normal force. If the magnitude of horizontal force applied to an object exceeds the maximum value of static friction, the object will begin to move. Once the object has begun to slide, the frictional force will generally decrease. The value to which the frictional force will diminish is expressed as $\boldsymbol{f}_k = \mu_k N$, in which μ_k is the coefficient of kinetic friction. For objects inclined to roll, such as balls or wheels, there is a rolling frictional force that resists the continued rolling of such an object. This force is expressed by $\boldsymbol{f}_r = \mu_r N$, in which μ_r is the coefficient of rolling friction. All of these frictional coefficients are dimensionless. Since the value of the frictional force depends on the interaction of the body and the surface, it is usually described as friction between the two.

Review Video: Friction
Visit mometrix.com/academy and enter code: 716782

EQUILIBRIUM

We may say that an object is in a **state of equilibrium** when it has a **constant linear momentum** $(\boldsymbol{p})$ at its center of mass, or when **angular momentum** $(\boldsymbol{L})$ **is also constant about the center of mass**. In other words, a wheel may be in equilibrium when it is spinning at a constant speed, and a hockey puck may be in equilibrium as it slides across ice. These are both examples of **dynamic equilibrium**. The phrase **static equilibrium**, however, is reserved for objects in which both linear and angular momentum are at zero. An object sitting on a table could be considered as being in static equilibrium.

BALANCED FORCES

An object is in equilibrium when the sum of all forces acting on the object is zero. When the forces on an object sum to zero, the object does not accelerate. Equilibrium can be obtained when forces in the y-direction sum to zero, forces in the x-direction sum to zero, or forces in both directions sum to zero.

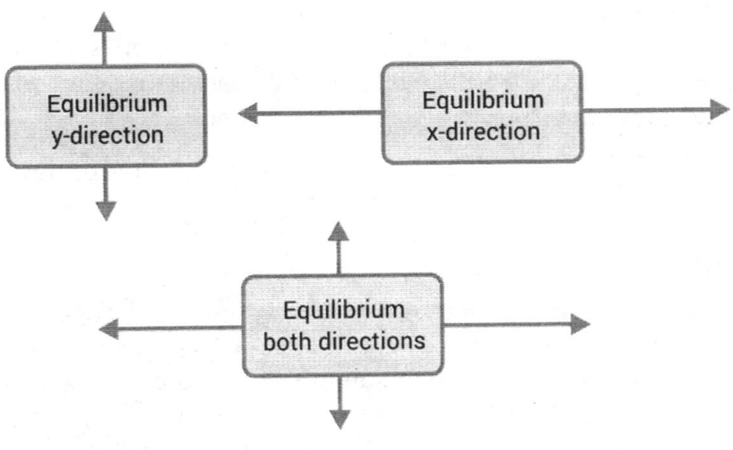

In most cases, a problem will provide one or more forces acting on an object and ask for a force to balance the system. The force will be the opposite of the current force or sum of current forces.

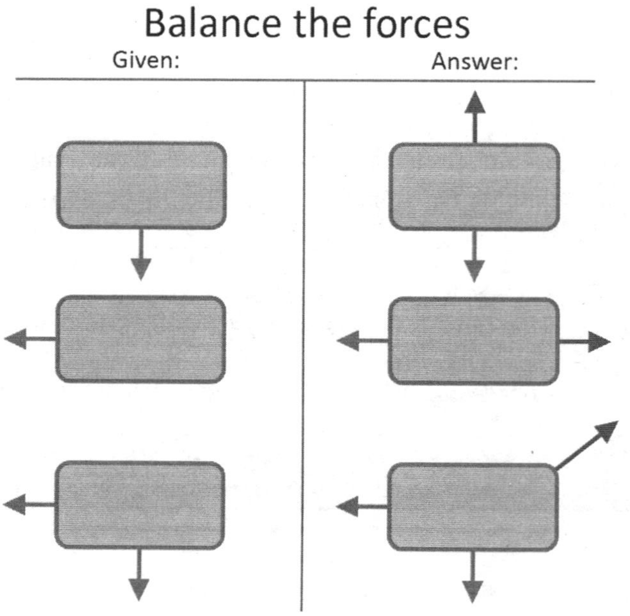

Using Equilibrium Conditions

For a **body in equilibrium**, the net force vector and the net torque vector will both be equal to zero. For the most common cases, two-dimensional systems, these conditions can be fully expressed by one or two force summation equations and one torque summation equation. Torque summations may be taken about any point on the body, though strategic placement can make calculations simpler. To determine the **torque exerted by a force**, multiply the magnitude of the force by the perpendicular distance to the point of interest. It will be necessary to decide in advance which direction of torque (clockwise or counterclockwise) will be considered positive.

For example, if we have a bar of known mass, m, that is suspended by cables at each end and whose center of mass is two thirds of the way along its length, L, we can use the equilibrium conditions to determine the tension in each cable. Gravity exerts a force of $-\boldsymbol{mg}$ on the bar's center of mass. Translational equilibrium conditions tell us that $\boldsymbol{T}_1 + \boldsymbol{T}_2 - \boldsymbol{mg} = 0$. Setting the total torque about the center of mass equal to zero, considering counterclockwise torque to be positive, yields the equation $\boldsymbol{T}_2\left(\frac{L}{3}\right) - \boldsymbol{T}_1\left(\frac{2L}{3}\right) = 0$. Solving these equations results in $\boldsymbol{T}_1 = \frac{mg}{3}$ and $\boldsymbol{T}_2 = \frac{2mg}{3}$. This result makes sense since the center of mass is closer to the second cable.

Translational and Rotational Equilibrium

If a body is in **translational equilibrium**, then its linear momentum will be constant, and there will be a net force of zero. Likewise, a body in rotational equilibrium will have a constant angular momentum, and again there will be a net torque of zero. Both of these equations are vector equations, and as such are both equivalent to three scalar equations for the three dimensions of motion, though in most instances, only one or two dimensions will be considered at a time. We may say that the two requirements for a body to be in equilibrium are that the vector sum of all the external forces acting on the body must be zero, and the vector sum of all the external torques acting on the body must also be zero. Conversely, if we are told that a body is in equilibrium, we may assume that both of these conditions will hold, and that we can use them to find unknown forces or torques.

Harmonic and Circular Motion

Polar Coordinate System

Polar coordinates were designed to be useful in situations in which circular arcs are more common than straight lines and right angles. Instead of having x- and y-coordinates, an object's location is described by its **distance from the origin**, r, and the angle between its position vector and the positive x-axis, commonly denoted as θ.

The two coordinate systems are related by the following equations:

$$x = r\cos\theta,\ y = r\sin\theta$$

$$r = \sqrt{(x^2 + y^2)},\ \theta = \tan^{-1}\left(\frac{y}{x}\right)$$

The direction and nature of the conversion will dictate which set of equations to use.

The polar coordinate system simplifies many calculations of **circular motion**. Instead of a velocity in the x- or y-direction, velocity may be described by motion toward or away from the origin and an increase or decrease in the angle θ. For **uniform circular motion**, the change in r is zero, and the rate of change of angle θ is constant. The only acceleration on the body is the centripetal acceleration, given by $\boldsymbol{a}_c = \frac{|\boldsymbol{v}|^2}{r} = r\boldsymbol{\omega}^2$, where $\boldsymbol{\omega}$ is the rate of change in angle θ, known as the rotational velocity, keeping the body in its circular arc. This acceleration is caused by a centripetal force that pulls the object toward the center of the circle. By Newton's second law, this force has a magnitude given by $\boldsymbol{F} = m\boldsymbol{a}_c = \frac{m|\boldsymbol{v}|^2}{r} = mr\boldsymbol{\omega}^2$.

Simple Harmonic Motion

Simple harmonic motion in a single dimension, x, is described by the equation $x = A\cos(\omega t + \varphi)$, where A is the amplitude of oscillation, ω is the angular frequency of oscillation, and φ is the phase. The particular trigonometric operator used in the equation is not of great importance as sine may be substituted for cosine given a proper modification of the phase. Graphically, the motion of a harmonic oscillator starting from rest at maximum displacement is shown by the graph below. This graph assumes no energy lost to friction or drag.

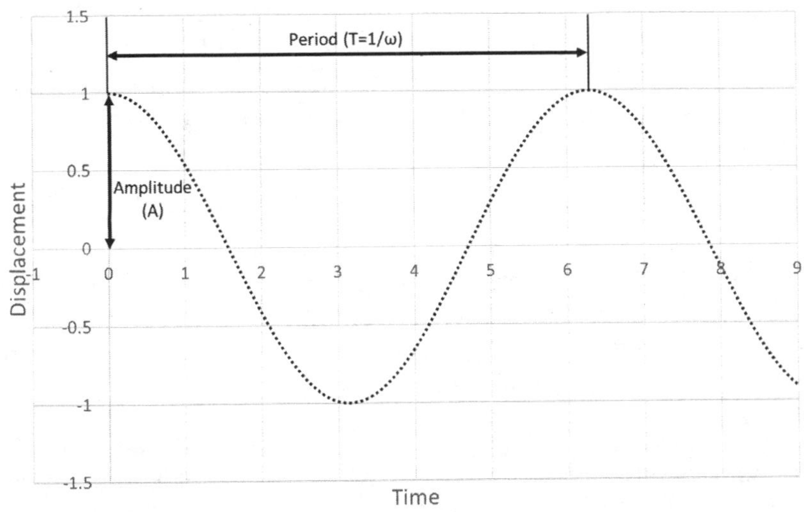

Hooke's Law

The work performed by a spring is one of the classic examples of **work performed by variable force**. When a spring is neither compressed nor extended, we may say that it is in a relaxed state. Any time the spring is taken out of this state, whether by being stretched or compressed, it will exert what is called a restoring force, as it attempts to return to its relaxed state. In most cases, we can say that the force, $\boldsymbol{F}$, exerted by the spring is proportional to the displacement of the free end from its position during the relaxed state. This is known as Hooke's law, and is expressed $\boldsymbol{F} = -k\boldsymbol{x}$, where k is the spring constant or stiffness. The x-coordinate in this equation corresponds to an axis where $\boldsymbol{x} = 0$ is the coordinate of the relaxed position. The negative sign in this equation indicates that the force is always opposite to the displacement.

Simple Pendulum

A **pendulum** is a **harmonic oscillator** that depends on the force of gravity for its motion. If we consider a simple pendulum composed of a mass hanging from an inelastic, massless string, then we may describe its restoring force as $\boldsymbol{F} = -m\boldsymbol{g}\sin\theta$, in which θ is the angle by which the mass is removed from its resting position. If the angle is very small, less than 15° or $\frac{\pi}{12}$, then $\theta \approx \sin\theta$, and the motion of the pendulum is like that of a simple harmonic oscillator. If this is the case, then the period of our simple pendulum can be found as $T = 2\pi\sqrt{\left(\frac{L}{g}\right)}$, where L is the length of the string. Again, this only holds if the angular amplitude θ_{max} is very small.

Like springs, pendulums operate by **converting energy** between kinetic and potential. Unlike springs, the potential energy stored in pendulums is gravitational potential energy. As the mass is displaced from its resting state, its height above ground increases. The potential energy stored in a simple pendulum can be calculated as $PE = mgL(1 - \cos\theta)$.

Linear Momentum and Impulse

In physics, **linear momentum** can be found by **multiplying the mass and velocity** of a particle ($\boldsymbol{p} = m\boldsymbol{v}$). Momentum is measured in kg·m/s. Like velocity, momentum is a vector quantity and will always have the same direction as the velocity. Newton's second law describes **momentum**, stating that the rate of change of momentum is proportional to the force exerted and is in the direction of the force. Impulse is the application of force over a period of time, Δt. If a constant net force of 10 N is exerted on an object for 5 seconds, it gives the object an impulse of 50 N-s. An impulse of 50 N-s corresponds to a change in momentum of 50 kg·m/s in the direction of the force. In equation form, $\boldsymbol{F}\Delta t = m\Delta\boldsymbol{v}$, where $\boldsymbol{F}$ is a constant net force. If the force is varying, it will be necessary to integrate the force over time.

For example, suppose a 2-kg block is initially at rest on a frictionless surface and a constant net force of 8 N is exerted on the block for 5 seconds. In order to determine how fast the block is moving, we need to calculate the impulse that was given to it ($\boldsymbol{F}\Delta t$ = 40 N-s). This means that the change in momentum of the block was 40 kg·m/s. Since the block has a mass of 2 kg, this translates to an increase in velocity of 20 m/s. Thus, the block will be traveling at 20 m/s after 5 seconds.

Linear Momentum and Collisions

In a closed and isolated system (i.e., one in which no particles leave or enter and on which the sum of external forces is zero), we can assume that the momentum of the system will neither increase nor decrease. If we write the equation for the linear momentum of the system such that the net external force is equal to zero, we will find that linear momentum, $\boldsymbol{p}$, is a constant. The equation for linear momentum is a vector equation, and, as such, it can be divided into component equations for each dimension.

Some of the most popular examples used to demonstrate conservation of linear momentum involve two objects colliding on a frictionless surface. These collisions are generally categorized as either elastic or inelastic. In a perfectly **elastic** collision, both total momentum and total kinetic energy of the system are conserved. In a perfectly **inelastic** collision, only the total momentum of the system is conserved, as the two bodies combine to form a single body; however, in reality, most actual collisions fall somewhere between these two extremes. Unless a collision is specified as being perfectly elastic, it should be assumed that only momentum is conserved.

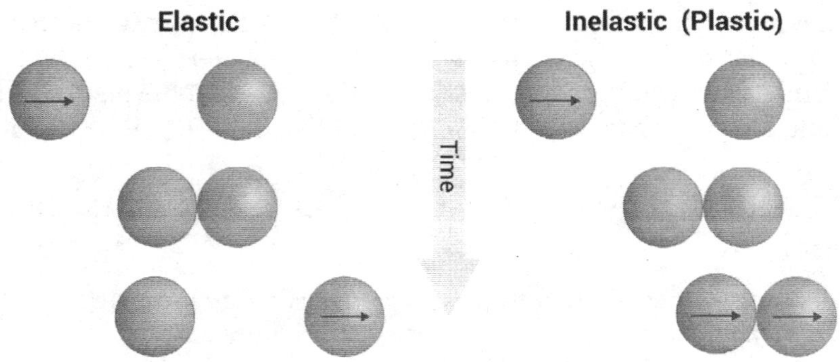

Examples of One-Dimensional Collisions

All examples assume a frictionless surface.

A 0.01-kg bullet traveling at 400 m/s strikes a stationary block of wood that weighs 10 kg and buries itself in the wood. What is the final velocity of the block and the bullet?

The bullet initially has 4 kg·m/s of momentum. The block of wood, beginning at rest, has no momentum. Thus, the final momentum is 4 kg·m/s. Given the new combined mass of 10.01 kg, the final velocity is approximately 0.4 m/s.

Two blocks, with masses of 10 kg and 40 kg, are traveling toward one another at -20 m/s and 10 m/s, respectively. Assuming the collision was perfectly elastic, find the final velocities of each body. Assuming it was perfectly inelastic, find the final velocity of the resulting single body.

For elastic collisions, two conditions hold: $KE_i = KE_f$ and $\boldsymbol{p}_i = \boldsymbol{p}_f$. Calculating initial conditions yields $KE_i =$ 4,000 J and $\boldsymbol{p}_i = 200\ \text{kg} \cdot \text{m/s}$ for both blocks. Equating these to the final values of each yields $5\boldsymbol{v}_{1f}{}^2 + 20\boldsymbol{v}_{2f}{}^2 = 4{,}000$ and $10\boldsymbol{v}_{1f} + 40\boldsymbol{v}_{2f} = 200$. Solving both equations simultaneously gives $\boldsymbol{v}_{1f} = 28$ m/s and $\boldsymbol{v}_{2f} = -2$ m/s.

The inelastic case is much simpler. Since the two blocks merge to form one, the final momentum, $200\ \text{kg} \cdot \text{m/s}$, is divided by the combined mass to give the final velocity of 4 m/s.

Conservation of Energy and Momentum

Applying Conservation of Rotational Energy and Angular Momentum

A metal hoop of mass m and radius r is released from rest at the top of a hill of height h. Assuming that it rolls without sliding and does not lose energy to friction or drag, what will be the hoop's angular and linear velocities upon reaching the bottom of the hill?

The hoop's initial energy is all potential energy, $PE = mgh$. As the hoop rolls down, all of its energy is converted to **translational** and **rotational kinetic energy**. Thus, $mgh = \frac{1}{2}m\boldsymbol{v}^2 + \frac{1}{2}I\boldsymbol{\omega}^2$. Since the moment for a hoop is $I = mr^2$, and $\boldsymbol{\omega} = \frac{v}{r}$, the equation becomes $mgh = \frac{1}{2}m\boldsymbol{v}^2 + \frac{1}{2}mr^2\left(\frac{v^2}{r^2}\right)$, which further simplifies to $gh = \boldsymbol{v}^2$. Thus, the resulting velocity of the hoop is $\boldsymbol{v}_f = \sqrt{gh}$, with an angular velocity of $\boldsymbol{\omega}_f = \frac{v_f}{r}$. Note that if you were to forget about the energy converted to rotational motion, you would calculate a final velocity of $\boldsymbol{v}_f = \sqrt{2gh}$, which is the **impact velocity** of an object dropped from height h.

Angular momentum, $\boldsymbol{L}$, of an object is defined as its moment of inertia multiplied by its angular velocity, or $\boldsymbol{L} = I\boldsymbol{\omega}$. Consider a planet orbiting the sun with an elliptical orbit where the small radius is r_S and large radius is r_L. Find the angular velocity of the planet when it is at distance r_S from the sun if its velocity at r_L is $\boldsymbol{\omega}_L$.

Since the size of a planet is almost insignificant compared to the interplanetary distances, the planet may be treated as a single particle of mass m, giving it a moment about the sun of $I = mr^2$. Since the gravitational force is incapable of exerting a net torque on an object, we can assume that the planet's angular momentum about the sun is a constant, $\boldsymbol{L}_L = \boldsymbol{L}_S$. Thus, $m{r_L}^2\boldsymbol{\omega}_L = m{r_S}^2\boldsymbol{\omega}_S$. Solving this equation for $\boldsymbol{\omega}_S$ yields $\boldsymbol{\omega}_S = \boldsymbol{\omega}_L\left(\frac{r_L}{r_S}\right)^2$.

Mass-Energy Relationship

Because mass consists of atoms, which are themselves formed of subatomic particles, there is an energy inherent in the composition of all mass. In other words, it would require a significant input of energy to form all the atoms in a given mass from their most basic particles. This rest energy is the energy that Einstein refers to in his famous mass-energy relation $E = mc^2$, where c is the speed of light in a vacuum. In theory, if all the particles in a given mass were converted directly to energy (e.g., by matter-antimatter annihilation), it would give off energy $E = mc^2$. For example, if this were to happen to a single gram of mass, the resulting outburst of energy would be $E = 9 \times 10^{13}$ J, enough energy to provide power for over 2,000 average households for a whole year.

In some nuclear reactions, small amounts of mass are converted to energy. The amount of energy released can be calculated through the same relation, $E = mc^2$. Most such reactions involve mass losses on the order of 10^{-30} kg.

Fluid Mechanics

Basics of Fluids

While it may sound obvious, fluids can best be defined as **substances that flow**. A fluid will conform, slowly or quickly, to any container in which it is placed. This is because a fluid is unable to maintain a force tangential to its surface. In other words, **fluids cannot withstand shearing stress**. They can, on the other hand, exert a force perpendicular to their surface. Both liquids and gases are considered to be fluids. Fluids, essentially, are those substances in which the atoms are not arranged in any permanent, rigid way. In ice, for instance, molecules are all lined up in a crystalline lattice, while in water and steam, the only intermolecular arrangements are haphazard connections between neighboring molecules.

Fluid Density and Pressure

The **density of a fluid** is generally expressed with the symbol ρ. The density may be found with the simple equation $\rho = \frac{m}{V}$, mass per unit volume. Density is a scalar property, meaning that it has no direction component. It is typically measured in SI units of kilograms per cubic meter. While the density of a gas will tend to fluctuate considerably depending on the level of pressure, the density of a liquid is comparatively stable. The density of water is most often taken to be 1,000 kg/m^3.

The **pressure of a fluid** is calculated as $P = \frac{F}{A}$, force per unit area. To find the pressure at a given depth in a fluid, or the hydrostatic pressure, the pressure can be calculated as $P = \rho g h$, where h is the fluid depth. For instance, the pressure of water is greater the deeper you are below the surface.

Pressure, like fluid density, is a scalar, and does not have a direction. The equation for pressure is concerned only with the magnitude of the force, not with the direction in which it is pointing. The SI unit of pressure is the Newton per square meter, or pascal.

Archimedes' Principle

If an object is submerged in water, it will have a **buoyant force** exerted on it in the upward direction. This force is caused by the water pressure acting on the bottom surface of the object. The deeper the object is submerged, the greater the pressure at the bottom surface. Often, of course, this buoyant force is much too small to keep an object from sinking to the bottom. This idea of buoyancy is summarized in **Archimedes' principle**: a body wholly or partially submerged in a fluid will be buoyed up by a force equal to the weight of the fluid displaced by the body.

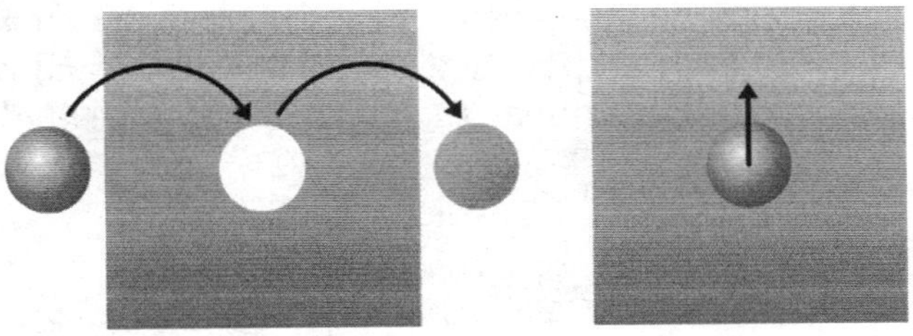

Thus, an object's ability to remain afloat in a fluid depends on its density relative to that of the fluid. If the fluid has a higher density than the object then the object will float. Otherwise, the object will sink. This principle can also be used to find the weight of a floating object by calculating the volume of fluid that it has displaced. For instance if a cube with a volume of 1 m^3 is floating in water to a depth of 0.25 m, the cube is displacing 0.25 m^3 of water. This is the equivalent of 250 kg of water, creating a buoyancy force of 2,450 N. Thus, the block weighs 2,450 N, has a mass of 250 kg, and has a density of 250 kg/m^3.

Pascal's Principle

Pascal's principle states that a change in the pressure applied to an enclosed fluid is **transmitted** undiminished to **every portion** of the fluid, as well as to the walls of the containing vessel. Imagine, for instance, a container filled with liquid, on top of which rests a piston loaded down with a lead weight. The atmosphere, lead weight, and piston will combine to exert pressure P_{ext} on the liquid, so the total pressure will be $P = P_{ext} + \rho g h$, for every point at height h within the fluid. Imagine again, an enclosed fluid in a container with two pistons on top, one with area $A_1 = 2 \text{ m}^2$ and the other with area $A_2 = 4 \text{ m}^2$. Since the pressure will be the same at both pistons, the upward force on the larger piston will be twice that of the smaller, since it has a larger area and the force is equal to the pressure times the area over which it is applied.

Drag Force

Friction can also be generated when an object is moving through air or liquid. A drag force occurs when a body moves through some fluid (either liquid or gas) and experiences a force that opposes the motion of the body. The drag force is greater if the air or fluid is thicker or is moving in the direction opposite to the object. Obviously, the higher the drag force, the greater amount of positive force required to keep the object moving forward. This is one reason ideal fluid questions assume that the fluids are non-viscous.

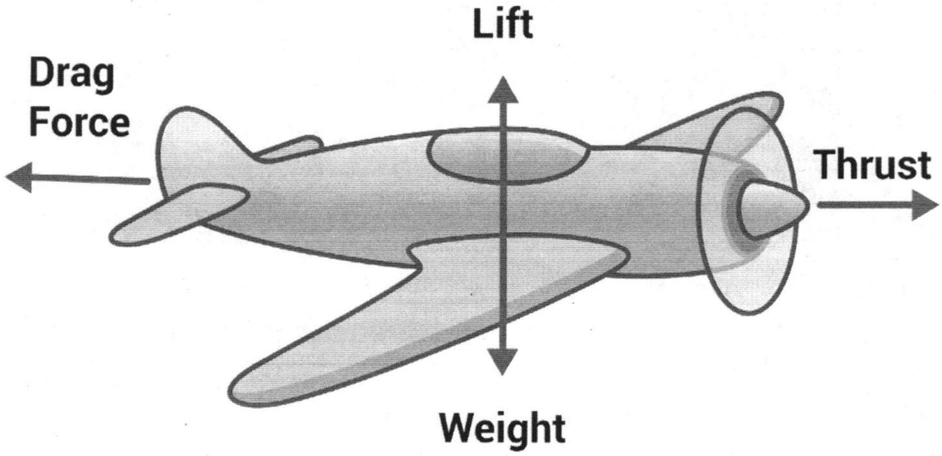

Ideal Fluids in Motion

Since the motion of actual fluids is extremely complex, physicists usually refer to **ideal fluids** when they make their calculations. Using ideal fluids in equations is a bit like discounting friction in other calculations; it tends to make the process more mathematically manageable. So, when we deal with ideal fluids, we are making four assumptions. First, we are assuming that the **flow is steady**; in other words, the velocity of every part of the fluid is the same. Second, we assume that fluids are **incompressible**, and therefore have a consistent density. Third, we assume that fluids are **non-viscous**, meaning that they flow easily and without resistance. Finally, we assume that the flow of ideal fluids is **irrotational**: that is, particles in the fluid will not rotate around a center of mass.

Flow Rates

When liquids flow in and out of containers at certain rates, the change in volume is the volumetric flow in minus the volumetric flow out. Volumetric flow is essentially the amount of volume moved past some point divided by the time it took for the volume to pass.

$$\textbf{Volumetric flow rate} = \frac{\textbf{volume moved}}{\textbf{time for the movement}}$$

If the flow into a container is greater than the flow out, the container will fill with the fluid. However, if the flow out of a container is greater than the flow into a container, the container will drain of the fluid.

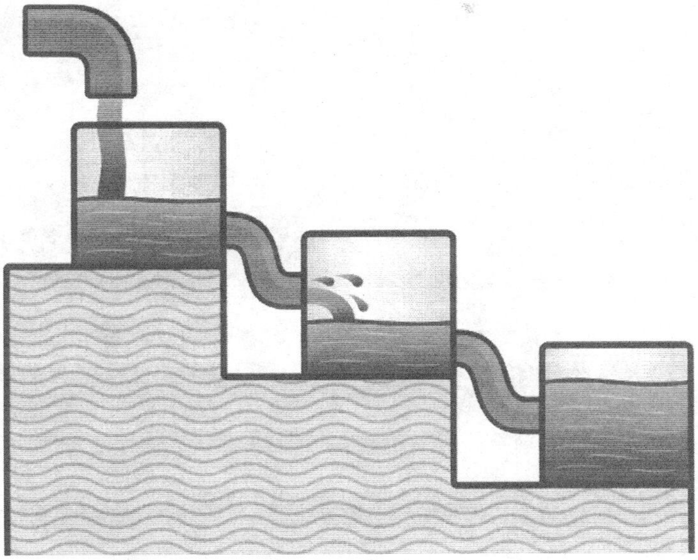

Streamlines, Tube of Flow, Volume Flow Rate, and the Equation of Continuity

A **streamline** is the path traced out by a very small unit of fluid, which we will refer to as a particle. Although the velocity of a particle may change in both magnitude and direction, streamlines will never cross one another. In many instances of flow, several streamlines will group together to form what is called a tube of flow. If we were to make two cross-sections of a tube of flow, with areas A_1 and A_2, we would find that since fluid is incompressible, the same amount of fluid passes through the two cross-sections over the same interval of time. This is expressed by the equation $Q = Av$, in which Q is known as the volumetric flow rate and is constant for a given tube of flow. This equation is known as the **equation of continuity**; it suggests that flow will be faster in areas of the tube that are narrower. One very important equation derived from this principle is $A_1v_1 = A_2v_2$. Given that a pipe narrows its cross-section from A_1 to A_2, and the fluid velocity in A_1 is v_1, the velocity in A_2 must be $v_2 = \frac{A_1v_1}{A_2}$. Also important to note is that the mass flow rate is directly related to the volumetric flow rate by the equation $m_{flow} = \rho vA = \rho Q$.

Bernoulli's Equation

Let us imagine an ideal fluid in a tube of flow. By applying the **law of conservation of energy** with ideal fluid assumptions, we can arrive at **Bernoulli's equation**: $P + \rho gh + \frac{\rho v^2}{2} = C$, where C is a constant for a given tube of flow. Basically, this equation states that in the absence of an external input of energy or a significant elevation change, any increase in velocity will require a decrease in fluid pressure. And under similar circumstances, an increase in pressure will necessarily cause a decrease in velocity. It is essentially just a reformulation of the law of conservation of mechanical energy for fluid mechanics. Bernoulli's principle is used to explain a number of physical phenomena, including the lift force on the wings of an aircraft.

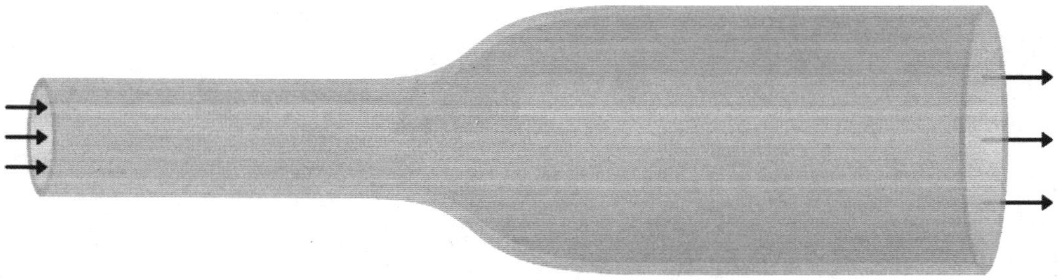

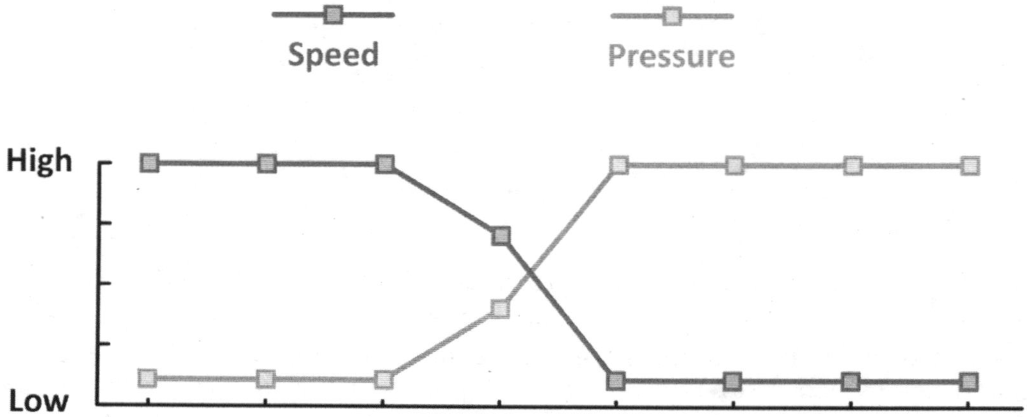

Rotational Motion

Angular Motion and the Axis of Rotation

When a body is moving in a straight line, it is said to be moving in **translation**. When, on the other hand, it is moving around some fixed axis, it is said to be in **rotation**. For a rotating object, the fixed axis is called the axis of rotation. Every point on the body will move in a circle that has this axis as its center, and every point will move through the same angle over the same interval of time. Angles may be measured in one of three units: degrees, radians, or revolutions. A full rotation is equal to 360 degrees, 2π radians, or 1 revolution. On a circle, one radian is the angle that measures an arc length equal to the radius of the circle. Since a circle's circumference is 2π times the radius, one full rotation is equal to 2π radians.

Angular motion has many correlations to linear motion. For an angle of rotation, θ, the linear distance traveled is $\boldsymbol{x} = r\theta$. For angular velocity, $\boldsymbol{\omega}$, the linear velocity is $\boldsymbol{v} = r\boldsymbol{\omega}$. For angular acceleration, $\boldsymbol{\alpha}$, the linear acceleration is $\boldsymbol{a} = r\boldsymbol{\alpha}$. When discussing angular motion in this way, the angular unit is always radians.

Rotational Kinematics

Concept: Increasing the radius increases the linear speed

Calculation: Linear speed $=$ radius $\times$ rotational speed

In practice, simple rotation is when an object rotates around a point at a constant speed. Most questions covering rotational kinematics will provide the distance from a rotating object to the center of rotation (radius) and ask about the linear speed of the object. A point will have a greater linear speed when it is farther from the center of rotation.

If a potter is spinning his wheel at a constant speed of one revolution per second, the clay six inches away from the center will be going faster than the clay three inches from the center. The clay directly in the center of the wheel will not have any linear velocity.

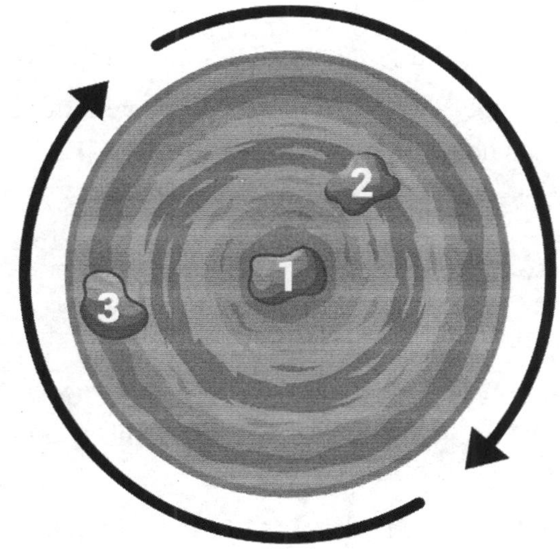

To find the linear speed of rotating objects using radians, we use the equation:

$$\textbf{linear speed} = (\textbf{rotational speed [in radians]}) \times (\textbf{radius})$$

Using degrees, the equation is:

$$\textbf{linear speed} = (\textbf{rotational speed [in degrees]}) \times \frac{\boldsymbol{\pi}\ \textbf{radians}}{\textbf{180 degrees}} \times (\textbf{radius})$$

To find the speed of the pieces of clay, we use the known values (rotational speed of 1 revolution per second, radii of 0 inches, 3 inches, and 6 inches) and the knowledge that one revolution = 2π.

$$\text{clay \#1 speed} = \left(2\pi \frac{\text{rad}}{\text{s}}\right) \times (0 \text{ inches}) = 0 \frac{\text{inches}}{\text{second}}$$

$$\text{clay \#2 speed} = \left(2\pi \frac{\text{rad}}{\text{s}}\right) \times (3 \text{ inches}) = 18.8 \frac{\text{inches}}{\text{second}}$$

$$\text{clay \#3 speed} = \left(2\pi \frac{\text{rad}}{\text{s}}\right) \times (6 \text{ inches}) = 37.7 \frac{\text{inches}}{\text{second}}$$

Review Video: Linear Speed
Visit mometrix.com/academy and enter code: 327101

Rotational Motion

Newton's second law, commonly stated as $\boldsymbol{F} = m\boldsymbol{a}$, is applied to rotational motion by the equation $\boldsymbol{\tau} = I\boldsymbol{\alpha}$. That is, the torque is equal to the moment of inertia times the angular acceleration. **Torque** is calculated as the magnitude of an applied force times its perpendicular distance from the body's center of mass. A body's moment of inertia depends on both its mass and its configuration. Each particle in a body contributes a moment of $I = mr^2$, where m is the particle's mass and r is its distance from the center of mass. Thus, for a thin ring or a thin, hollow sphere, the moment for the body is $I = mr^2$. Some other commonly encountered shapes are spheres $\left(I = \left(\frac{2}{5}\right)mr^2\right)$ and disks $\left(I = \left(\frac{1}{2}\right)mr^2\right)$. A closely related property of these shapes is the radius of gyration, k. This quantity is the average distance of mass from the center. It can be found by the equation $k = \sqrt{\left(\frac{I}{M}\right)}$. Similarly, the moment of inertia may be found as $I = mk^2$.

Another important corollary with linear motion is momentum. An object's angular momentum may be calculated as $\boldsymbol{L} = I\boldsymbol{\omega}$. All the same conservation rules for linear momentum apply to angular momentum as well. Additionally, there is a kinetic energy associated with rotational motion. It is calculated as $KE_r = \frac{I\omega^2}{2}$. When calculating kinetic energy for an object that is in both linear and angular motion, the total kinetic energy is the sum of the translational and rotational kinetic energy, $KE = \frac{mv^2}{2} + \frac{I\omega^2}{2}$.

Concept: Torque is a twisting force on an object

Calculation: Torque = radius × force

Torque, like force, is a vector and has magnitude and direction. As with force, the sum of torques on an object will affect the angular acceleration of that object. The key to solving problems with torque is understanding the lever arm. A better description of the torque equation is:

Torque = force × the distance perpedicular to the force from the center of rotation

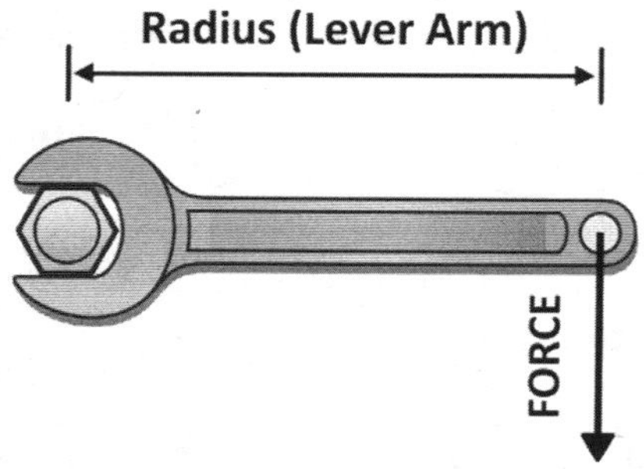

Because torque is directly proportional to the radius, or lever arm, a greater lever arm will result in a greater torque with the same amount of force. The wrench on the right has twice the radius and, as a result, twice the torque.

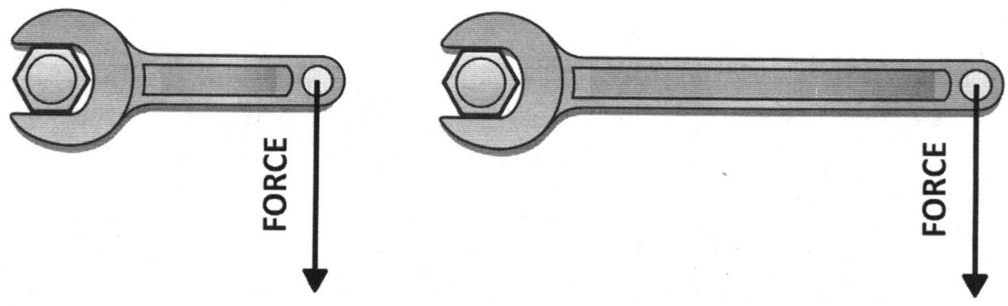

Alternatively, a greater force also increases torque. The wrench on the right has twice the force and twice the torque.

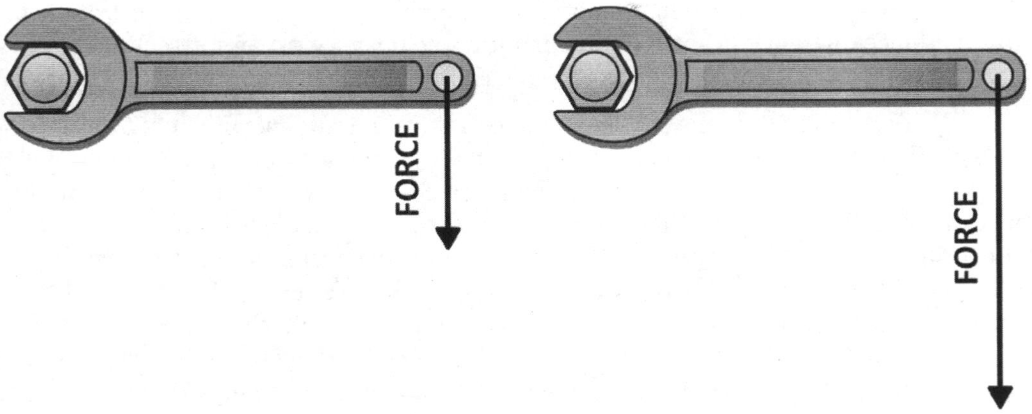

Two-Dimensional Collisions

All examples assume a frictionless surface.

Two blocks weighing 5 kg and 10 kg with velocities of $v_1 = 9\mathbf{i}$ m/s and $v_2 = 3\mathbf{j}$ m/s, respectively, are on a collision course. Assuming the collision is perfectly inelastic, find the velocity of the combined block after collision.

Since each block initially has velocity in only one dimension, it is a simple calculation to find the initial momentum values: $\boldsymbol{p}_x = 45 \text{ kg} \cdot \text{m/s}$ and $\boldsymbol{p}_y = 30 \text{ kg} \cdot \text{m/s}$. With the new combined mass of 15 kg, the final velocity vector will be $\boldsymbol{v}_f = 3\mathbf{i} + 2\mathbf{j}$ m/s.

Two hockey pucks both weighing 0.15 kg with velocity vectors $v_1 = 20\mathbf{i} + 30\mathbf{j}$ m/s and $v_2 = -50\mathbf{i} - 10\mathbf{j}$ m/s are headed toward a collision. Suppose that the final velocity of one puck is $v_{2f} = -10\mathbf{i} + 15\mathbf{j}$ m/s. Find the final velocity vector of the other puck.

We must ensure that momentum is conserved in both dimensions. The initial momentum in the x- and y-directions is calculated to be $\boldsymbol{p}_{xi} = -4.5 \text{ kg} \cdot \text{m/s}$ and $\boldsymbol{p}_{yi} = 3 \text{ kg} \cdot \text{m/s}$. Since we know the final velocity of one of the pucks, we can find the other's final velocity to be $\boldsymbol{v}_{1f} = -20\mathbf{i} + 5\mathbf{j}$ m/s.

UNIVERSAL GRAVITATION AND ORBITAL MOTION

NEWTON'S LAW OF GRAVITATION

One of Newton's major insights into the behavior of physical objects was that every object in the universe exerts an **attractive force on every other body**. In quantitative terms, we may say that the gravitational force with which particles attract one another is given by $\boldsymbol{F} = \frac{Gm_1m_2}{r^2}$, in which r is the distance between the particles, m_1 and m_2 are the masses of the particles, and G is the gravitational constant, $G = 6.674 \times 10^{-11}$ N-m^2/kg^2. Newton expressed this relation by saying that a uniform spherical shell of matter attracts a particle outside the shell as if all the shell's matter were concentrated at its center. In the case of gravitation on Earth, objects behave as if there was a single particle located at the center of the Earth with the mass of the entire Earth (M_E). Thus, regardless of an object's distance from the surface of the Earth, it can be approximated as a particle due to the effective distance from the Earth's center of mass. The difference in the gravitational pull on an object at sea level and at the highest point on the Earth's surface is about 0.25%. Thus, the gravitational acceleration anywhere on the Earth's surface is considered to be a constant 9.81 m/s^2. For an object orbiting the Earth, such as a satellite, its period of orbit can be found by equating the gravitational force to the centripetal force, giving the equation $\frac{GM_Em}{r^2} = mr\omega^2 = mr\left(\frac{2\pi}{T}\right)^2$. Solving for the period yields $T = \sqrt{\frac{4\pi^2r^3}{GM_E}}$.

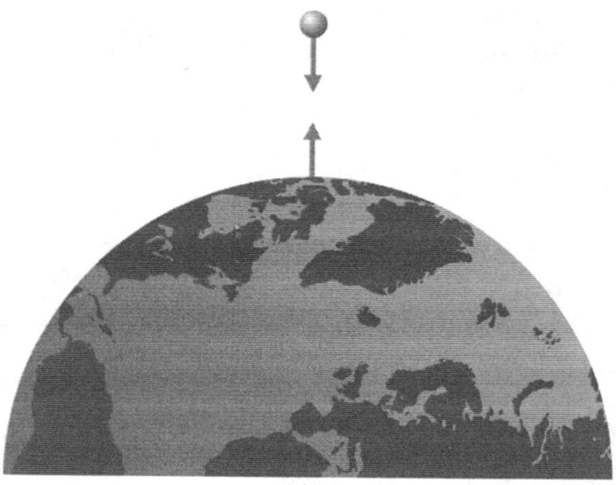

Review Video: Newton's Law of Gravitation
Visit mometrix.com/academy and enter code: 709086

KEPLER'S LAWS

KEPLER'S FIRST LAW

Kepler's first law describing the movement of planets states that **all planets move in elliptical orbits**, with the sun at one focus. If we are to consider the motion of one planet around the sun, we will assume that its mass is much smaller than that of the sun, such that the center of mass of the system is almost in the middle of the sun. The orbit of the planet will then be defined by the semimajor axis, a (that is, half the length of the ellipse), the semiminor axis, b (half the width of the ellipse), and the eccentricity, e (the degree to which the orbit is not circular, $e = \sqrt{1 - \frac{b^2}{a^2}}$). The orbits of the planets are only slightly elliptical, though they are often exaggerated on diagrams. In a planetary orbit, the distance from the center of the ellipse to either focus is $d = ae$. The maximum and minimum distances of a planet from the sun are given by $r_{max} = \frac{b^2}{(a-d)}$ and $r_{min} = \frac{b^2}{(a+d)}$.

KEPLER'S SECOND LAW

Kepler's second law for planets and satellites states that any line connecting a planet to the sun will sweep out **equal areas in equal times**, regardless of where the planet is in its orbit. In other words, the planet will move most slowly when it is far away from the sun, and fastest when it is closest. This law is directly connected to the law of conservation of angular momentum.

KEPLER'S THIRD LAW

Kepler's third law for planets states that the square of the period of any planet is proportional to the cube of the semimajor axis of its orbit. This relation can be expressed $T^2 = \left(\frac{4\pi^2}{Gm}\right) r^3$. The quantity in parentheses in this equation is a constant, its only variable being the mass of the central body. This equation holds up for elliptical orbits as well.

WEIGHT AND MASS

WEIGHT

Not to be confused with mass (quantity of matter), weight the term for the force due to the gravitational attraction between the masses of the two bodies. This force is described by the expression $\frac{Gm_1m_2}{r^2}$, where G is the gravitational constant, m_1 and m_2 are the masses of the two objects, and r is the distance between the centers of mass. Since the majority of humans are concerned with events close to the surface of the Earth, one of the masses (M_E) and the distance (R_E) are essentially constant and are combined into $\boldsymbol{g}$, which is the acceleration due to gravity near the surface of the Earth $\left(\boldsymbol{g} = \frac{GM_E}{(R_E)^2}\right)$. Thus, we can express weight as $\boldsymbol{W} = m\boldsymbol{g}$. Since it is a force, the SI unit for weight is the Newton. As a vector, $\boldsymbol{W}$ can be expressed as either $-mg\mathbf{j}$ or $-W\mathbf{j}$, in which $\mathbf{j}$ is the direction on the axis pointing away from the Earth.

Review Video: Mass, Weight, Volume, Density, and Specific Gravity
Visit mometrix.com/academy and enter code: 920570

Waves and Optics

TYPES OF WAVES AND THEIR CHARACTERISTICS

TRANSVERSE AND LONGITUDINAL WAVES

Transverse waves have oscillations that are **perpendicular** to the direction of motion. A light wave is an example of a transverse wave. A group of light waves traveling in the same direction will be oscillating in several different planes. Light waves are said to be polarized when they are filtered such that only waves oscillating in a particular plane are allowed to pass, with the remainder being absorbed by the filter. If two such polarizing filters are employed successively and aligned to allow different planes of oscillation, they will block all light waves.

Longitudinal waves are waves that oscillate in the **same direction** as their primary motion. Their motion is restricted to a single axis, so they may not be polarized. A sound wave is an example of a longitudinal wave.

VELOCITY, AMPLITUDE, WAVELENGTH, AND FREQUENCY

- The **velocity of a wave**, v, is the rate at which it travels in a given medium. It is defined in the same way that velocity of physical objects is defined, a change in position divided by a change in time. A single wave may have a different velocity for every medium in which it travels. Some types of waves, such as light waves, do not require a medium.
- **Amplitude**, A, is one measure of a wave's strength. It is half the verticle distance between the highest and lowest points on the wave, the crest and trough, respectively. The vertical midpoint, halfway between the crest and trough, is sometimes called an equilibrium point, or a node.

- The **wavelength**, λ, is the horizontal distance between successive crests or troughs, or the distance between the first and third of three successive nodes.
- **Frequency**, f, is the number of crests or troughs that pass a particular point in a given period of time. It is the inverse of the period, the time required for the wave to cycle from one crest or trough to the next. Frequency is generally measured in hertz, or cycles per second.

Velocity, wavelength, and frequency are not independent quantities. They are related by the expression $v = \lambda f$. Note that amplitude, however, is independent from these quantities.

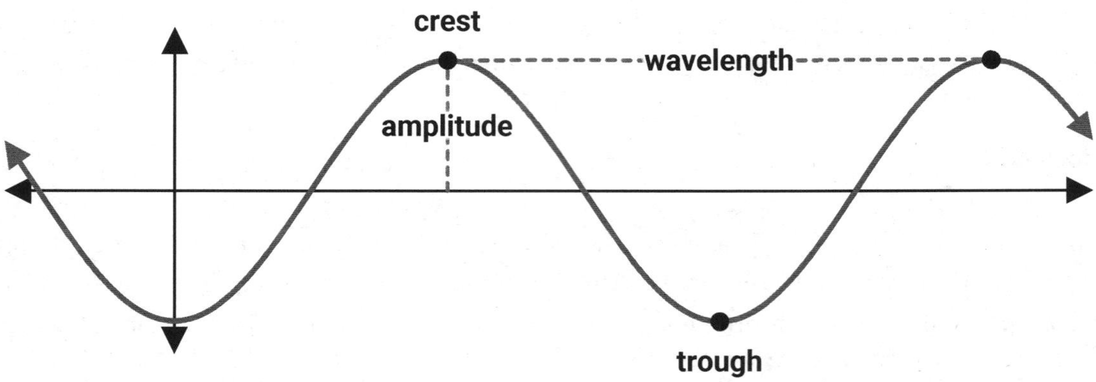

INTENSITY

The **intensity** I of a wave is equivalent to the flux through a given area over a period of time. It may also be defined as the energy density of a wave times its velocity. Intensity has units of watts per square meter. This can be seen in light waves as well. The intensity of light decreases as the distance from the light source increases. The inverse square law states that the intensity is inversely proportional to the square of the distance from the source. It is also directly proportional to the power P of the light source. This is shown mathematically by the expression $I = \frac{CP}{r^2}$, where C is the proportionality constant. This may be better understood by imagining the light waves emanating from a source as an expanding sphere. As their distance r from the source increases, the area over which they must divide themselves increases at a rate of $4\pi r^2$.

STANDING WAVES

A **standing wave** is the result of **interference** between two waves of the same frequency moving in opposite directions. These waves, although in constant motion, have certain points on the path where the amplitude is zero referred to as **nodes**. One example of a standing wave is a plucked guitar string. Since the string is attached at both ends, the fixed ends will be nodes. The primary tone will be that of the fundamental, or first harmonic, shown in the first figure below. It has a wavelength of twice the length of the string, L. The other three pictures below are those of the second through fourth harmonics. The nth harmonic has wavelength and frequency of $\lambda_n = \frac{2L}{n}$ and $f_n = \frac{nv}{2L}$, where v is wave velocity.

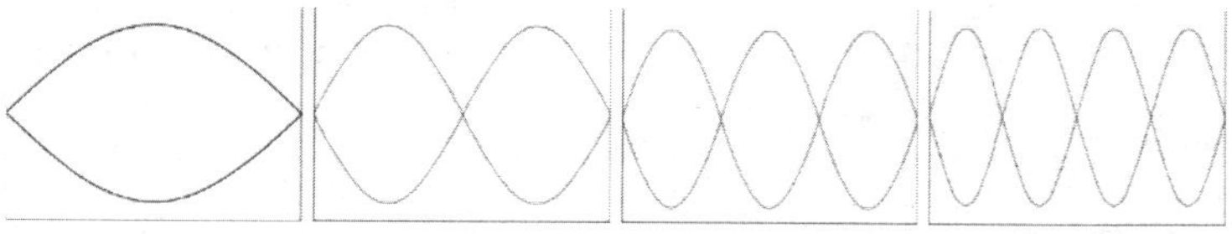

This same phenomenon occurs inside the tubes of wind instruments, though it is much more difficult to visualize. With a tube, however, there will be one or two open ends. Rather than a node, each open end will coincide with an **antinode**: that is, a crest or trough. For waves in a tube with two open ends, the wavelength and frequency calculations are the same as those for the plucked string. For the case with one open end, only the odd harmonics will be seen. The frequency of the nth harmonic becomes $f_n = \frac{nv}{4L}$, where n is odd.

Reflection, Refraction, Interference, and Diffraction of Waves

Reflection, Transmission, and Absorption

When light waves make contact with matter, they are either reflected, transmitted, or absorbed. If the light is **reflected** from the surface of the matter, the **angle** at which it hits the surface will be the same as the angle at which it leaves. If the ray of light is perpendicular to the surface, it will be reflected back in the direction from which it came.

When light is **transmitted** from one medium to another, its direction may be **altered** upon entering the new medium. This is known as **refraction**. The degree to which the light is refracted depends on the index of refraction, n, for each medium.

Light that is neither reflected nor transmitted will be **absorbed** by the surface and **stored as heat** energy. Because there are no ideal surfaces, most light and matter interaction will be a combination of two or even all three of these. Another result of imperfect surfaces is **scattering**, which occurs when waves are reflected in multiple directions. Rayleigh scattering is the specific case of a light wave being scattered by tiny particles that single out particular wavelengths. Dust particles in the atmosphere scatter primarily the blue wavelength of sunlight to give our sky a predominantly blue hue.

Review Video: Reflection, Transmission, and Absorption of Light
Visit mometrix.com/academy and enter code: 109410

Snell's Law

When light is transmitted from one medium to another, its direction may be altered upon entering the new medium. This is known as **refraction**. The degree to which the light is refracted depends on the index of refraction, n, for each medium. The **index of refraction** is a ratio of the speed of light in a vacuum to the speed of light in the medium in question, $n = \frac{c}{v_m}$. Since light can never travel faster than it does in a vacuum, the index of refraction is always greater than one. Snell's law gives the equation for determining the angle of refraction: $n_1 \sin(\theta_1) = n_2 \sin(\theta_2)$, where n is the index of refraction for each medium, and θ is the angle the light makes with the normal vector on each side of the interface between the two media.

We will examine a special case by trying to determine the angle of refraction for light traveling from a medium with $n_1 = 3$ to another medium with $n_2 = 1.5$. The light makes an angle $\theta_1 = 35°$ with the normal. Using Snell's law, we find that $\sin(\theta_2) = 1.15$. Since this is not mathematically possible, we conclude that the light cannot be refracted. This case is known as total internal reflection. When light travels from a more dense medium to a less dense medium, there is a minimum angle of incidence, beyond which all light will be reflected. This critical angle is $\theta_1 = \sin^{-1}\left(\frac{n_2}{n_1}\right)$. Fiber-optic cables make use of this phenomenon to ensure that the signal is fully reflected internally when it veers into the outer walls of the fiber.

Resonance and Natural Frequency

Every physical object has one or more **natural frequencies**, or frequencies at which it will naturally vibrate. The natural frequency is based on the object's dimensions, density, orientation, and other factors. If the object is acted on by a periodic force, it will vibrate at its natural frequency, regardless of the forcing frequency. If the excitation force is operating at the object's natural frequency, the object will experience **resonance**, in which the object receives all of the energy exerted by the excitation force. The amplitude of the vibration will increase rapidly and without bound until either the excitation force changes frequency or the natural frequency of the object is altered.

Diffraction and Dispersion

Diffraction occurs when a wave encounters a physical object. It includes phenomena such as bending, diverging, and other aperture effects. When light emerges from a single small slit, a rippling effect may be observed. The results of Young's double-slit experiment are due to diffraction as the light waves from these slits diverge. Similarly, light emerging from a circular aperture will project concentric light and dark rings due to diffraction. Diffraction grating is an arrangement of material whose reflective properties are intentionally varied at equally spaced intervals. Due to the arrangement, incident light is reflected in specific directions, known as diffraction orders, based on its wavelength.

Dispersion occurs when light consisting of multiple wavelengths enters a medium whose propagation behavior depends on the wavelength of transmitted light. This is what is observed when light passes through a prism, splitting it into its component colors.

Review Video: Diffraction of Light Waves
Visit mometrix.com/academy and enter code: 785494

YOUNG'S DOUBLE-SLIT EXPERIMENT

Thomas Young's **double-slit experiment** visually demonstrated the interference between two sets of light waves. It consisted of shining light through two thin, closely spaced parallel slits and onto a screen. The interference between light waves from the two slits caused a pattern of alternately light and dark bands to appear on the screen, due to constructive and destructive interference, respectively. The dimensions of the experimental setup can be used to determine the wavelength of the light being projected onto the screen. This is given by the equation $\lambda = y\frac{d}{x}$, where y is the distance between the centers of two light bands, d is the distance between the slits, and x is the distance from the slits to the screen. Thin-film interference is caused when incident light is reflected both by a partially reflective thin layer on a surface and by the surface itself. This interference may be constructive or destructive.

WAVE SUPERPOSITION AND INTERFERENCE

The principle of **linear superposition** states that two or more waves occupying the same space create an effect equal to the sum of their individual amplitudes at that location. This is known as interference. If the resultant amplitude is larger than either individual amplitude, it is constructive interference. Similarly, if the interference reduces the effect, it is considered destructive.

Some special cases of interference are standing waves and beats, in which two waves having the same and nearly the same frequency, respectively, interfere with one another. Another concept related to interference is phase. If two waves with the same frequency are in phase, then they have perfectly constructive interference. The nodes in each wave will line up, as will the respective crests and troughs. If those same two waves are 180 degrees out of phase, they will experience perfectly destructive interference. The nodes will still line up, but each crest will be aligned with a trough, and vice versa. From this it can be seen that constructive interference results in a larger wave amplitude than destructive interference. If two identical waves are 180 degrees out of phase, the resultant wave will have zero amplitude. This effect is the design impetus for some noise-cancellation technology.

DOPPLER EFFECT

One common phenomenon of wave motion is the **Doppler effect.** It occurs when there is a **disparity** between the emitted frequency and the observed frequency of a wave. It is the caused by **relative motion** between the **wave source** and the **observer**. If the source and observer are both moving toward one another, the observed frequency is determined by the following equation: $f_o = f_e\frac{(v_w+v_o)}{(v_w-v_s)}$, where v_w is the speed of the wave. If the source or the observer is moving in the opposite direction, its sign must be reversed. The Doppler effect can occur with any wave (light, water, pressure, etc.), but it is most commonly observed when sound waves change pitch due to an observer's change in position relative to a loud train horn or emergency vehicle siren. The effect is also employed in the operation of speed-detecting radar guns. Microwaves are emitted at a known frequency and, after being reflected by the target, return at a different frequency, giving the object's speed.

SOUND WAVES

The **pitch of a sound** as it reaches one's ear is based on the frequency of the sound waves. A high-pitched sound has a higher frequency than a low-pitched sound. Like all waves, sound waves transmit energy. The rate at which this energy is transmitted is the sonic power. Loudness, or intensity of sound, is the sonic power received per unit area.

When a pair of sound waves with slightly different frequencies interfere with one another causing a periodic variation in sound intensity or a **beat**. The frequency of the variation, called the **beat frequency**, is equal to the difference between frequencies of the two sound waves. The phenomenon is used when tuning two instruments to one another. As the two pitches get closer, the beat frequency will become smaller and smaller until it disappears entirely, indicating that the instruments are in tune.

Review Video: Sound
Visit mometrix.com/academy and enter code: 562378

ELECTROMAGNETIC WAVES AND ELECTROMAGNETIC SPECTRUM

ELECTROMAGNETIC SPECTRUM

The **electromagnetic spectrum** is the range of all wavelengths and frequencies of known electromagnetic waves. Visible light occupies only a small portion of the electromagnetic spectrum. Some of the common classifications of electromagnetic waves are listed in the table below with their approximate frequency ranges.

Classification	Freq. (Hz)
Gamma Rays	$\sim 10^{19}$
X-Rays	$\sim 10^{17} - 10^{18}$
Ultraviolet	$\sim 10^{15} - 10^{16}$
Visible Light	$\sim 10^{14}$
Infra-red	$\sim 10^{11} - 10^{14}$
Microwaves	$\sim 10^{10} - 10^{11}$
Radio/TV	$\sim 10^{6} - 10^{9}$

Electromagnetic waves travel at the speed of light, $c = 3 \times 10^8$ m/s. To find the wavelength of any electromagnetic wave, simply divide c by the frequency. Visible light occupies a range of wavelengths from approximately 380 nm (violet) to 740 nm (red). The full spectrum of color can be found between these two wavelengths.

Review Video: Electromagnetic Spectrum
Visit mometrix.com/academy and enter code: 771761

Review Video: Light
Visit mometrix.com/academy and enter code: 900556

Geometric Optics

Thin Lenses

A **lens** is an optical device that **redirects light** to either converge or diverge in specific geometric patterns. Whether the lens converges or diverges is dependent on the lens being **convex** or **concave**, respectively. The particular angle of redirection is dictated by the lens's focal length. For a **converging lens**, this is the distance from the lens that parallel rays entering from the opposite side would intersect. For a **diverging lens**, it is the distance from the lens that parallel rays entering the lens would intersect if they were reverse extrapolated. However, the focal length of a diverging lens is always considered to be negative. A thin lens is a lens whose focal length is much greater than its thickness. By making this assumption, we can derive many helpful relations.

Convex Lens

View through a convex lens

Concave Lens

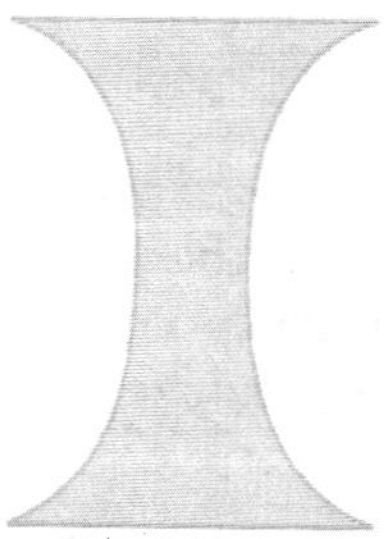

View through a concave lens

Real and Virtual Images

In optics, an **object's image** is what is seen when the object is viewed through a lens. The location of an object's image is related to the lens's **focal length** by the equation $\frac{1}{d_o}+\frac{1}{d_i}=\frac{1}{f}$, where f is the focal length, and d_o and d_i are the distance of the object and its image from the lens, respectively. A positive d_i indicates that the image is on the opposite side of the lens from the object. If the lens is a magnifying lens, the height of the object may be different from that of its image, and may even be inverted. The object's magnification, m, can be found as $m=\frac{-d_i}{d_o}$. The value for the magnification can then be used to relate the object's height to that of its image: $m=\frac{y_i}{y_o}$. Note that if the magnification is negative, then the image has been inverted.

Images may be either **real** or **virtual**. Real images are formed by light rays passing through the image location, while virtual images are only perceived by reverse extrapolating refracted light rays. Diverging lenses cannot create real images, only virtual ones. Real images are always on the opposite side of a converging lens from the object and are always inverted.

Concave Mirrors

Concave mirrors will create an image of an object in varying ways depending on the location of the object. The table below details the location, orientation, magnification, and nature of the image. The five object locations to be examined are between the mirror and the focal point (1), at the focal point (2), between the focal point and the center of curvature, or twice the focal point (3), at the center of curvature (4), and beyond the center of curvature (5).

Object	Image Location	Orientation	Magnification	Type
1	$d_i < 0$	upright	$m > 1$	virtual
2	none	none	none	none
3	$d_i > 2f$	inverted	$m < -1$	real
4	$d_i = 2f$	inverted	$m = -1$	real
5	$f < d_i < 2f$	inverted	$0 > m > -1$	real

Note in case 5 that the image may effectively be located at the focal point. This is the case for objects at extremely great, or near infinite, distances from the mirror. The magnification at these distances will be very small and a true infinite distance would result in a magnification of zero.

Plane Mirrors and Spherical Mirrors

Plane mirrors have very simple properties. They reflect only **virtual images**, they have no magnification, and the object's distance from the mirror is always equal to that of its image. Plane mirrors will also appear to reverse the directions left and right.

Spherical mirrors follow the same governing equations for finding image height, location, orientation, and magnification as do thin lenses; however, the sign convention for image location is reversed. A positive image location denotes that it is on the same side as the object. Spherical mirrors may be either **concave** or **convex.** Convex mirrors are by far the simpler of the two. They will always reflect virtual, upright images with magnification between zero and one. Concave mirrors have varying behavior based on the object location.

Simple Magnifier, the Microscope, and the Telescope

A simple magnifier, or commonly a **magnifying glass**, is a converging lens that creates an enlarged virtual image near the observer's eye. The object must be within a certain distance, about 25 cm or 10 inches, from the magnifier for it to operate properly. Otherwise, the image will be blurry.

A **microscope** is a magnifying device that is used to examine very small objects. It uses a series of lenses to capture light coming from the far side of the sample under examination. Often microscopes will have interchangeable magnification lenses mounted on a wheel, allowing the user to adjust the level of magnification by rotating in a different lens. Optical microscopes will generally be limited to a magnification of 1,500.

Telescopes are used to view very distant objects, most often celestial bodies. Telescopes use both lenses and mirrors to capture light from a distant source, focus it, and then magnify it. This creates a virtual image that is very much smaller than the object itself, and yet much larger than the object appears to the naked eye.

Prisms

Prisms are optical devices that alter the path or nature of light waves. Glass and plastic are the two most prevalent materials used to make prisms. There are three different types of prisms in common use. The most familiar of these is the dispersive prism, which splits a beam of light into its constituent wavelengths. For sunlight, this results in the full spectrum of color being displayed. These prisms are generally in the familiar triangular prism shape.

Polarizing prisms, as their name suggests, polarize light, but without significantly reducing the intensity, as a simple filter would. Waves that are oscillating in planes other than the desired plane are caused to rotate, so that they are oscillating in the desired plane. This type of prism is commonly used in cameras.

Reflective prisms are much less common than either of the others. They reflect light, often through the use of the total internal reflection phenomenon. Their primary use is in binoculars.

Electricity and Magnetism

Electrostatics

Electric Field Equation

In order to define a particular **electric field**, we may place an object with positive charge, q_0, called a test charge, somewhere near the charged particle, and then measure the **force exerted** on the object. We may then say that electric field $\boldsymbol{E}$ at that point is $\boldsymbol{E} = \frac{\boldsymbol{F}}{q_0}$. Electric field is a vector, and the direction of $\boldsymbol{E}$ will be the direction of the force acting on the test charge. If we want to fully define some region of an electric field, we must find measures for the field at every point within that region. The SI units for electric field are Newtons per coulomb (N/C). When performing this operation, we will assume that the presence of the test charge does not affect in any way the charge distribution of the electric field.

Coulomb's Law

If two particles have charge magnitudes q_1 and q_2, and are separated by distance r, then the electrostatic force of attraction or repulsion between them can be calculated as $\boldsymbol{F} = \frac{kq_1q_2}{r^2}$, in which the constant k is approximately $9 \times 10^9\ \frac{\text{N}\cdot\text{m}^2}{\text{C}^2}$. This is known as **Coulomb's law**. We should note the similarity to Newton's equation for the gravitational force between two particles, $\boldsymbol{F} = \frac{Gm_1m_2}{r^2}$. The main difference between these two equations is that while electrical force may be attractive or repulsive, **gravitational force is always attractive**. No experiment has ever contradicted Coulomb's law, even those conducted at the subatomic level. The constant k in the equation is called Coulomb's constant or the electrostatic constant. An important principle when calculating electrostatic force, if more than two particles are involved, is the law of superposition. If we are looking for the force exerted on a particle by two or more other particles, we must determine the individual force from each of the other particles, and take the vector sum of those forces to determine the total effect.

Review Video: Static Electricity
Visit mometrix.com/academy and enter code: 113722

Gauss's Law for Electric Flux

Flux is a concept that is applicable in many areas of science. It is a measure of flow through a given area. Electric flux, Φ, is a measure of the electric field flowing perpendicularly through a particular area. It can be calculated by the equation $\Phi = \boldsymbol{E} \cdot \boldsymbol{A} = \boldsymbol{EA}\cos\theta$, where θ is the angle between the direction of $\boldsymbol{E}$ and $\boldsymbol{A}$ (the normal vector of the area).

Gauss's law states that the electric flux through an enclosing surface is directly related to charge enclosed by the surface. This relation is given by the equation $\Phi = \frac{Q}{\varepsilon_0}$, where Q is the total enclosed carge and ε_0 is a constant known as the permittivity of free space. The shape of the enclosing surface should be chosen to accommodate the finding of $\boldsymbol{E} \cdot \boldsymbol{A}$. Most often, this will be a sphere or cylinder, since these surfaces are perpendicular to field lines emanating from a point or line charge, respectively. Combining the the flux equation with Gauss's law yields the relation, $\frac{Q}{\varepsilon_0} = \boldsymbol{E} \cdot \boldsymbol{A}$. Units for electric flux are $\frac{\text{N}\cdot\text{m}^2}{\text{C}}$.

ELECTRICAL PROPERTIES OF MATERIALS

COMMON MEANS OF TRANSFERRING ELECTRICAL CHARGE

Charge is transferred in three common ways: conduction, induction, and friction. **Conduction**, as the name implies, takes place between conductive materials. There must be a point of contact between the two materials and a potential difference, such as when a battery is connected to a circuit. **Induction also requires conductive materials. It occurs when a conductive material encounters a changing magnetic field**. The change can be the result of a changing magnetic field or the material moving within a constant magnetic field. Charge transfer due to **friction** does not require conductive materials. When two materials are rubbed together, electrons may be transferred from one to the other, leaving the two materials with equal and opposite charges. This is observed when shoes are dragged across a carpeted floor.

Review Video: Charging by Conduction
Visit mometrix.com/academy and enter code: 502661

CONDUCTORS, INSULATORS, AND SEMICONDUCTORS

In many materials, electrons are able to move freely; these are known as **conductors**. Due to their atomic structure and delocalized electrons, **metals** tend to be the best conductors, particularly copper and silver. Highly conductive wires are instrumental in creating low-resistance pathways for electrons to travel along within a circuit.

Other materials naturally inhibit the movement of charge and are known as **insulators**. Their electrons are tightly held by the individual constituent atoms. Glass, pure water, wood, and plastic are all insulators. Insulators are necessary in circuits to prevent charge from escaping to undesirable places, such as an operator's hand. For this reason, most highly conductive materials are covered by insulators.

Semiconductors, as the name suggests, are materials that only partially conduct electrical charge. The elements silicon and germanium are both common semiconductors, and are frequently used in microelectronic devices because they allow for tight control of the rate of conduction. In many cases, the conduction ability of semiconductors can be controlled by adjusting the temperature of the material.

DOPING SEMICONDUCTORS

Resistivity is the physical property of resistance of different materials: metals, which easily conduct electricity, have low resistivity; insulators have high resistivity; and the resistivity of **semiconductors** falls in between (example: silicon). **Doping** is the process of mixing different semiconductor atoms in order to control conductivity of the material. **N-type semiconductors** have an excess of electrons as a result of the doping process; when an electric field is applied, a negative pole forms due to the buildup of negatively charged electrons (example: silicon doped with antimony). **P-type semiconductors** have a shortage of electrons; when an electric field is applied, a positive pole forms (example: silicon doped with boron).

Introduction to Circuits and Current

Electric Current

Charge is a physical property of particles. For the particles of an atom, protons have a positive charge of +1, neutrons have no charge, and **electrons** have a negative charge of −1. Like charges repel each other (positive and positive or negative and negative), and opposite charges attract (negative and positive). The **net charge** of an atom or molecule can be found by adding up all the protons and electrons that it contains. When dealing with charge on the macro level, it is helpful to aggregate the charges in a material with different units. The coulomb is the SI unit for charge and is equivalent to about 6.24×10^{18} charged particles.

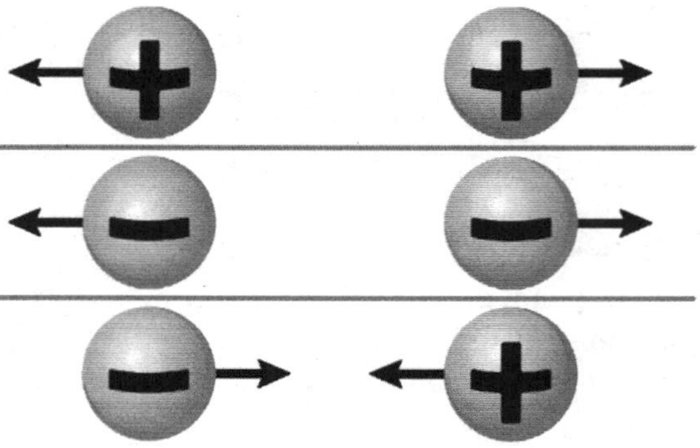

Electric current is the net rate of flow of charge (electrons) past a specific point, as in a wire or circuit. Current (represented by I in equations) is measured in amperes or amps (A). An ampere is equal to one coulomb per second $\left(A = \frac{C}{s}\right)$. Ammeters are tools that can be used to measure current.

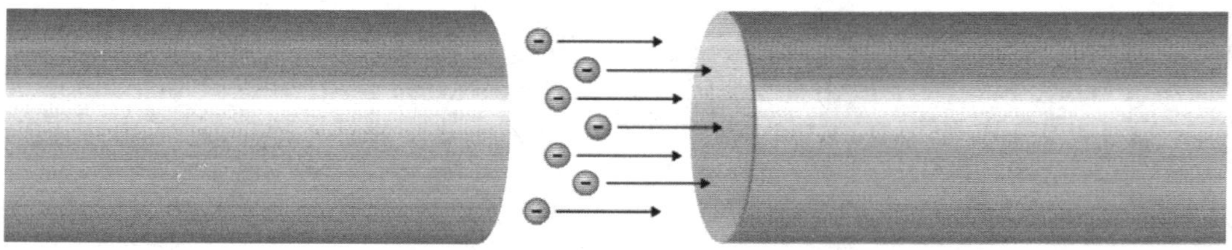

Electric current carries energy much like moving balls carry energy.

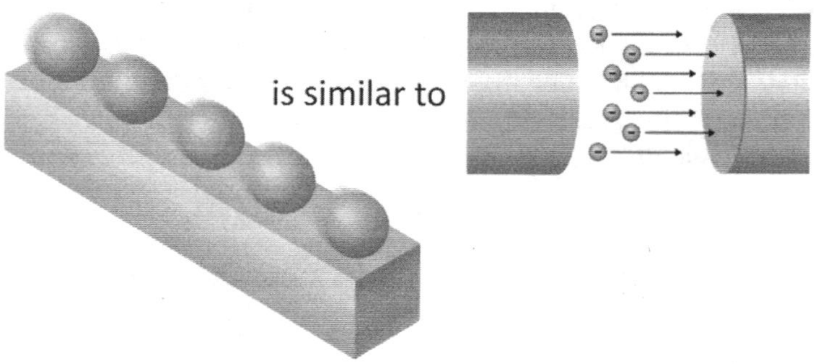

Electron flow theory states that electrons (e^-) flow from the negative terminal to the positive terminal. **Electricity** is the form of energy that exists statically (potential energy) with an accumulation of protons or electrons or dynamically with their movement (current).

Review Video: Electric Charge
Visit mometrix.com/academy and enter code: 323587

ALTERNATING AND DIRECT CURRENT

For circuits with **direct current** (DC), when current flows in only one direction, the voltage and current are constant. Direct current is supplied by batteries and is used in cell phones, ships, and planes. **Alternating current** (AC), in which current periodically reverses direction, can be produced using generators and is used for land-based applications (including in homes) because less power is lost when electricity travels long distances. In the United States, AC electricity is supplied most commonly at 120 V and 240 V.

ELECTRIC POTENTIAL

Electric potential energy is the energy stored in a charge by virtue of its proximity to other charged regions. It can be calculated in the same way as calculating the amount of work required to move it to that location from an infinite distance away. The work required to move a charge of magnitude q from infinity to a distance r from another charge of magnitude Q is calculated to be $PE_e = W = \frac{kQq}{r}$, where k is the **electrostatic constant**.

Electric potential, V, is closely related to electric potential energy. The potential due to a charge Q can be found by dividing the electric potential energy of another charge q by its magnitude, $V = \frac{PE_e}{q}$, or by the equation $V = \frac{kQ}{r}$.

The difference between the electric potential of two points is known as **voltage**. It is measured in volts, or joules per coulomb. Since it is impractical to find a point of zero absolute electric potential, for each system a reference point or ground is defined, to which all other points in the system may be related. Voltage is similar to gravitational potential energy.

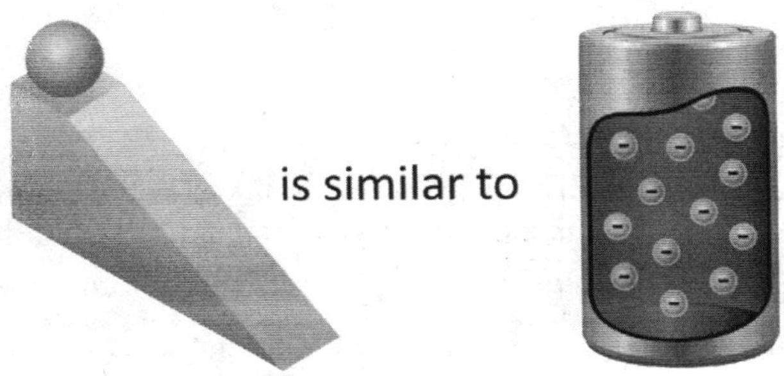

ELECTROMOTIVE FORCE AND COMMON EMF DEVICES

A force that maintains a potential difference between two locations in a circuit is known as an **electromotive force (emf)**. A device that creates this force is referred to as an **emf device**. The most common emf device is the battery. **Batteries** operate by converting chemical energy stored in the electrolyte, the internal chemical material, into electrical energy. The reaction causes a lack of electrons on the cathode, and when the circuit is connected, they flow from the anode, creating a flow of current. The electrolyte's composition also determines whether the battery is classified as acidic or alkaline, and wet or dry. Another emf device is the **photocell**, also commonly called the solar cell, since most photocells are powered by the sun. These operate by absorbing photons, which cause the electrons to be excited and flow in a current, a process of converting light energy into electrical energy. A third type of emf device is the **generator**. This device converts mechanical energy to electrical energy. A generator may be powered by such diverse sources as gasoline engines, flowing water, or even manually powered cranks. These devices utilize a rotating shaft to spin a coil within a magnetic field, creating a potential difference by induction.

OHM'S LAW

If we were to apply the exact same potential difference between the ends of two geometrically similar rods, one made of copper and one made of glass, we would create vastly different currents. This is because these two substances have different **resistances**. **Ohm's Law** describes the relation between applied voltage and induced current, $V = IR$. This is one of the most important tools of circuit analysis. Resistance, then, can be calculated as $R = \frac{V}{I}$. The SI unit for resistance is the **ohm** (Ω), equal to a volt per ampere. When a component is placed into a circuit to provide a specific resistance, it is known as a **resistor**. For a given potential difference, the greater the resistance is to the current, the smaller the current will be. Electrical resistance is much like friction, resisting flow and dissipating energy.

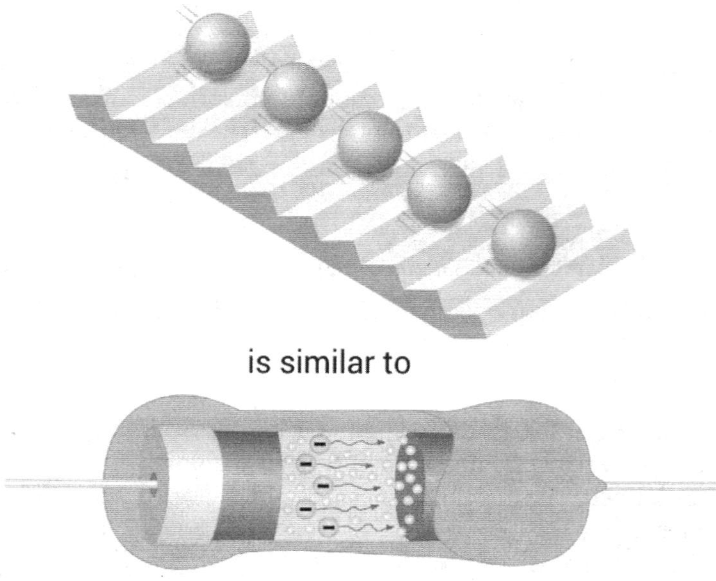

If we wish to look instead at the quality of the material of which the resistor is made, then we must consider resistivity. **Resistivity**, ρ, is a physical property of every material, which, if known, can be used to size a resistor for a specific resistance. Resistance is dictated by both the material and the dimensions of the resistor, given by the relation $R = \frac{\rho L}{A}$, where L is the effective length of the resistor and A is the effective cross-section. Alternatively, an unknown resistivity may be calculated by rearranging the equation as $\rho = \frac{RA}{L}$.

Resistivity will often change with temperature. In these cases, the relevant resistivity may be calculated $\rho = \rho_{ref}\left(1 + \alpha(T - T_{ref})\right)$, where α is the resistivity proportionality constant and T is the material temperature.

Review Video: Resistance of Electric Currents
Visit mometrix.com/academy and enter code: 668423

GROUND

Grounding is the process of neutralizing the charge of an object by removal of excess electrons to or donation of additional electrons by a much larger object (example: the Earth). This ground or large object can seemingly infinitely donate or accept electrons without mathematically significant changes to its net voltage. Examples of grounds include lighting rods and the round component of a three-pronged plug, as used for home appliances. Current does not usually flow through air, but lightning is the visible current that results when charge builds up in clouds; lightning rods provide a safe, low-resistance ground so the high-voltage current is less likely to be destructive. The round component of three-pronged plugs serves as one of the residential applications of this concept.

ENERGY AND POWER

Electric circuits operate by **transferring** electrical energy from one location in the circuit to another. Some devices in a circuit can store and release energy while other devices, like resistors, dissipate energy. **Power** is a measure of the rate at which energy is stored, released, transferred, or dissipated. It is measured in watts (W), or joules per second. Power is calculated by $P = VI$. The amount of power being released by a 9-V battery producing a current of 5 A is 45 W. When calculating the amount of power dissipated by a resistor, Ohm's Law can be combined with the power equation to form two other equations for power, $P = I^2R$ and $P = \frac{V^2}{R}$.

When power consumption over long periods of time needs to be measured, it will often be measured in units of kilowatt-hours, which is the amount of energy consumed at a rate of 1 kW over the course of an hour. One kilowatt-hour is equal to 3,600 kJ.

CAPACITORS AND DIELECTRICS

Capacitors are devices used in circuits to store energy in the form of electric fields. They are most often composed of two oppositely charged parallel plates separated by a medium, generally air. This medium is referred to as the capacitor's **dielectric.**

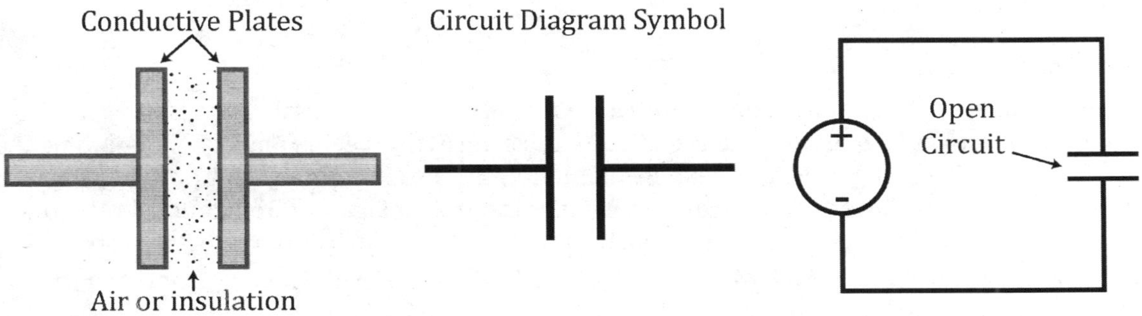

The dielectric material dictates the amount of energy in the electric field and, consequently, the amount of energy that can be stored by the capacitor. The measurable quality of a capacitor is known as its **capacitance**, which is defined as the amount of charge that it can store per volt of potential difference. This is given by the equation $C = \frac{Q}{V}$, with capacitance having units of farads or coulombs per volt. Physically, the capacitance depends on three things: the **area** of the parallel plates, the **separation distance** between them, and the **dielectric** material. For cases in which the separation distance is insignificant compared to the area, the capacitance can be found by the equation $C = \frac{\varepsilon A}{d}$, where ε is the permittivity of the dielectric material. Often, instead of being given the permittivity, we will be given the dielectric constant, κ, which is the ratio of the permittivities of the material and air, $\kappa = \frac{\varepsilon}{\varepsilon_{air}}$. This yields an obvious result of $\kappa_{air} = 1$.

The energy stored in a capacitor can be calculated in three different ways: $E = \frac{CV^2}{2} = \frac{Q^2}{2C} = \frac{VQ}{2}$. Another quantity associated with capacitors is the electric field energy density, η. This energy density is found by $\eta = \frac{\varepsilon E^2}{2}$.

INDUCTORS

When current passes through a wire coil, a magnetic field develops. An **inductor** is an electrical component made of a coil of wire that can store energy and opposes the rate of change of alternating current flowing through it; however, direct current passes through easily. They can be used as filters, sensors, motors, and transformers.

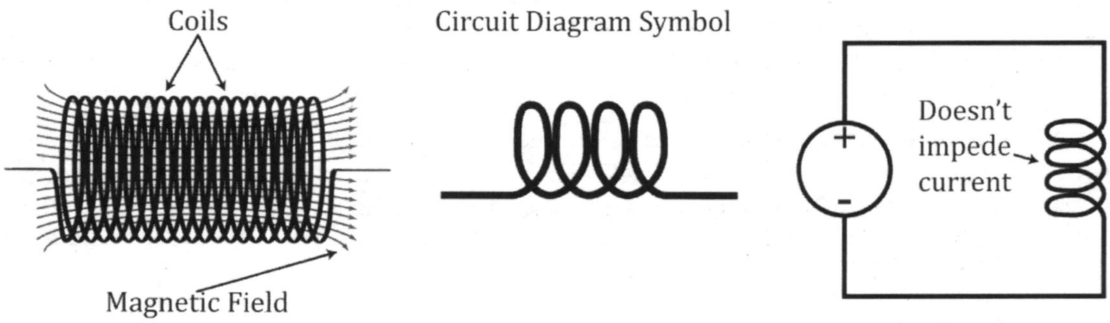

Inductance is the measure of ability of an inductor to resist changes in current. **Faraday's law of induction describes the ways voltage** or electromagnetic frequency can be generated by changing the magnetic environment in a coil of wire by moving a magnet within it, changing the external magnetic field of the magnet, or changing the area of the coil.

Capacitors and Inductors in AC Circuits

Capacitors and inductors both oppose immediate acceptance of the flow reversal of alternating current. This opposition is referred to as **impedance** and is similar to resistance, also having units of ohms, but unlike resistance, impedance is a complex value, meaning that it may have an **imaginary component** as well as a **real component**. For ideal capacitors and inductors, impedance is purely imaginary, and for ideal resistors, impedance is purely real. It is only when combining the effects of these devices that the full expression for impedance, Z, is necessary: $Z = R + X_i$, where $i = \sqrt{(-1)}$. X is a quantity known as reactance. For capacitors, $X_c = \frac{1}{\omega C}$, where ω is the angular frequency of the current, and for inductors, $X_L = \omega L$.

Other Electrical Components

Diodes

Diodes are a basic component of circuits, but they can't be described using Ohm's law; they operate as an electrical "valve", only allowing current to pass in one direction. This allows them to rectify alternating current by converting it to direct current, which is preferred or necessary for some applications. A common example is the light-emitting diode (LED) bulb, which emits light when powered more efficiently than regular light bulbs.

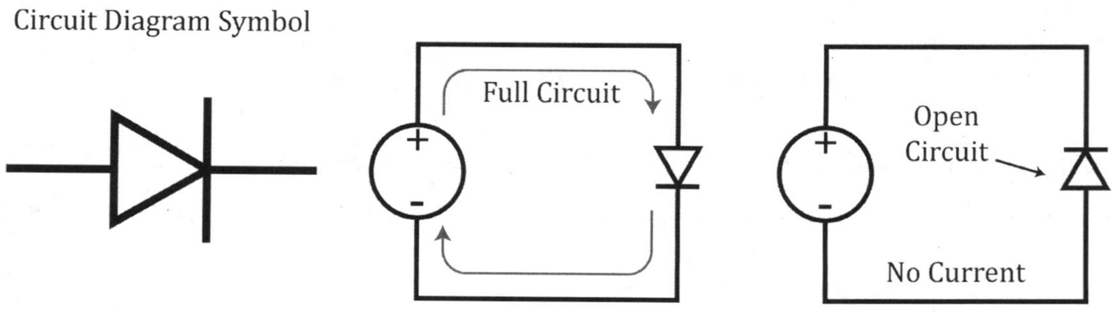

A p-n junction diode is formed by fusing a p-type semiconductor and an n-type semiconductor. It is considered a solid-state device because electricity flows through solid material rather than a vacuum tube. The p-region of the junction is positively charged and the n-region is negatively charged. Reverse bias occurs when the diode is connected such that the positive voltage is applied to the n-region; forward bias occurs when the positive voltage is applied to the p-region.

TRANSISTORS

A bipolar junction transistor, p-n-p or n-p-n, consists of two p-n junction diodes arranged back-to-back with three electrical leads or terminals: the emitter, the collector, and the base. Transistors are used to boost electrical signals or switch them on or off at high speeds. A large current flows from the emitter to the collector, and a smaller current entering through the base lead can be used to control the larger collector current.

TRANSFORMERS

Transformers are devices made of two or more coils of wire that use induction to transfer electricity between circuits. A **step-up transformer**'s input (primary) voltage is lower than its output (secondary) voltage; and a **step-down transformer**'s input voltage is higher than its output voltage. This allows for electricity to be to be generated safely at a lower voltage (example: 12 kV), passed through a step-up transformer for transport through power lines at high voltage (example: 400 kV), and passed through step-down transformers for distribution and use (example: 240 V residential use).

MOTORS AND GENERATORS

Motors use electromagnetic induction to convert electrical energy (electricity) to mechanical energy (motion). In a **DC motor**, torque is produced by magnetic force, which results from current passing through coil located in a magnetic field. They have been around for more than 100 years and are simple, inexpensive, and easy to maintain. In **AC (synchronous) motors**, torque is produced the same way as in DC motors, but much higher current is required, and they are inefficient. **Induction (asynchronous) motors** are more common, and they rotate a magnetic field in order to induce alternating current.

Generators use electromagnetic induction to convert mechanical energy to electrical energy. **AC generators** mechanically turn a coil in a magnetic field to produce voltage output and induce alternating current.

SIMPLE CIRCUITS

THE USE OF OHM'S LAW AND KIRCHHOFF'S LAWS

Circuit analysis is the process of determining the **current** or **voltage drop** across devices of interest in a circuit. Ohm's Law is useful in doing this since it definitively relates the current to the voltage drop for resistors, $V = IR$. Kirchhoff's voltage law (KVL) states that if you sum the voltage drops across all devices in any closed loop of a circuit, the sum will always be zero, $V_1 + V_2 + \cdots + V_n = 0$. This law is particularly useful if there are multiple closed-loop pathways in a circuit. Kirchhoff's current law (KCL) states that the amount of current entering a point must equal the amount of current leaving, $I_{in} = I_{out}$. This law may also be expanded to apply to the current entering and leaving a larger region of a circuit. In any given circuit analysis, it may be necessary to use all three of these laws.

Another important principle to remember in an ideal circuit is that any two points connected by only wire are at equal voltage. Only devices on the circuit may change the voltage. In actual practice, however, all wire has some amount of resistance. A battery that provides an EMF of V_B is only able to deliver a voltage to the circuit of $V = V_B - IR_B$, where R_B is the internal resistance of the battery. To express this concept in an ideal circuit, we would need to add a small resistor in series after the battery.

MEASURING DEVICES

There are several devices that allow various quantifiable properties of a circuit to be measured to a great degree of accuracy. An **ammeter** is a device placed in series with a circuit to measure the current through that location. Ideally, an ammeter has as little internal resistance as possible to prevent altering the current it is trying to measure. A **voltmeter** measures the voltage or potential difference between two locations in a circuit. It has two leads that are connected in parallel with the circuit and consists of a very high resistance and an ammeter in series. This allows only a very small amount of current to be diverted through the voltmeter, but enough to determine the voltage by Ohm's Law. A **galvanometer** is the primary working component of an ammeter. It operates based on the idea that a wire in a magnetic field will experience a force proportional to the amount of current it is carrying. It converts the observed current into a dial reading. A **potentiometer** is a variable resistor, often controlled by a knob, that allows an operator to control the amount of voltage or current provided to a given circuit. They are commonly used in volume-control knobs. Potentiometers can also be called voltage dividers. Their use in circuit measurement is for finding voltages by comparing them to known voltages. A **multimeter** is a device that combines the functions of all the above devices into one. In addition to voltage, current, resistance and capacitance, they can typically measure inductance, frequency, and other quantities.

Resistance in Series Circuits

A **series circuit** is a loop through which charge can flow along only one path. Resistance of resistors (labeled R_n) lined up in series is additive, so $R_{total} = R_1 + R_2 + R_3 + \cdots$ for all resistors in that series. Current (I) is consistent in all locations throughout a closed series circuit, so $I_{battery} = I_{R_1} = I_{R_2} = I_{R_3} = \cdots$, regardless of the number of elements in the series. Charge at the positive terminal of the battery experiences a **voltage drop** (ΔV), or loss of potential energy, as it passes through each resistor, such that its voltage will be zero at the negative terminal of the battery. Therefore, $\Delta V_{battery} = \Delta V_1 + \Delta V_2 + \Delta V_3 + \cdots$, where each ΔV_n represents the voltage drop across each resistor in series.

Problem Solving with Series Circuits

Using the labeled diagram of a series circuit, solve the following problems:

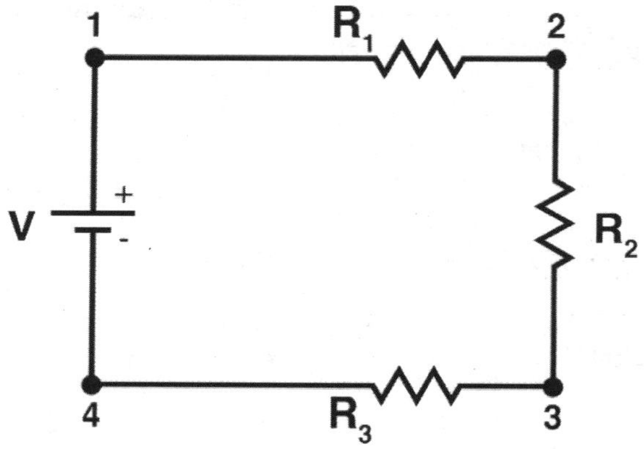

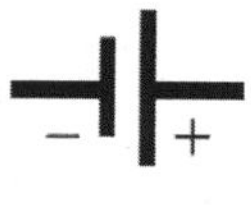

V = Voltage source (battery)

R = Resistor

Example 1: If each resistor is 3 Ω and the battery is 9 V, what is the current at each of the indicated corners?

<u>Step 1:</u>
Given: $R_1 = R_2 = R_3 = 3\ \Omega$
Equation: $R_{total} = R_1 + R_2 + R_3$
Solve: $\text{R}_{\text{total}} = 3\ \Omega + 3\ \Omega + 3\ \Omega = 9\ \Omega$

<u>Step 2:</u>
Given: $V_{battery} = 9\text{ V}$
Equation: $I = \frac{V}{R}$
Solve: $I_{battery} = \frac{9\text{ V}}{9\ \Omega} = 1\text{ A}$

<u>Step 3:</u>
Because current is the same throughout the circuit, current at each corner is the same:
$I_{total} = I_1 = I_2 = I_3 = I_4 = 1\ A$

Example 2: If the current at point 3 is 4 Amps, and each resistor is 1 Ω, what is the battery voltage?

Step 1:	Step 2:	Step 3:
Given: $I_3 = 4\text{ A}$ The circuit is in series so current is the same throughout: $I_{total} = 4\text{ A}$	Given: $R_1 = R_2 = R_3 = 1\ \Omega$ Equation: $R_{total} = R_1 + R_2 + R_3$ Solve: $R_{total} = 1\ \Omega + 1\ \Omega + 1\ \Omega = 3\ \Omega$	Equation: $V_{total} = I_{total}(R_{total})$ Solve: $V_{total} = (4\text{ A})(3\ \Omega) = 12\text{ V}$

Resistance in Parallel Circuits

Parallel circuits provide multiple pathways for current to follow, which adjusts the way that current, voltage, and resistance interact when compared to series circuits. Because current (I) can follow multiple pathways, it is divided among those pathways at each branch, so $I_{total} = I_1 + I_2 + I_3 + \cdots$, where 1, 2, and 3 represent each unique branch. In this example, there are 3.

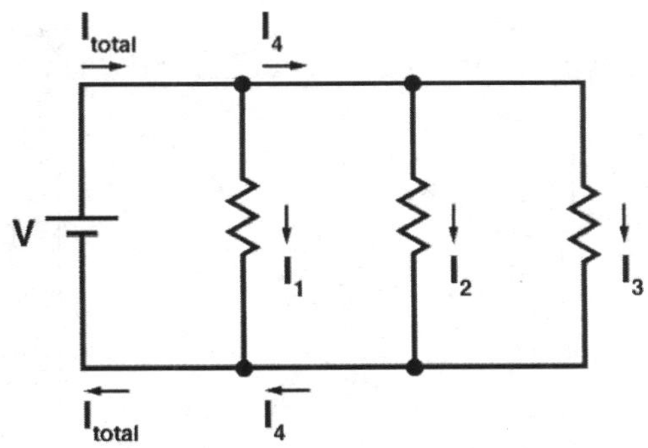

Equivalent resistance (R_{eq}) is the amount of resistance in a parallel circuit, represented as if there was only one resistor in series. All of the resistors in parallel can be simplified using the following equation:

$$\frac{1}{R_{eq}} = \frac{1}{R_1} + \frac{1}{R_2} + \frac{1}{R_3}$$

Because a charge will only pass through one resistor in the parallel circuit and not all three, the voltage drop across each resistor will be the same as that of the battery. Therefore, voltage drops for parallel circuits follow this rule:

$$\Delta V_{battery} = \Delta V_1 = \Delta V_2 = \Delta V_3 = \cdots$$

Note: If multiple resistors exist on a branch of a parallel circuit, they are in series and should be added together ($R_{total} = R_1 + R_2 + R_3 + \cdots$) before dealing with them as part of a parallel circuit.

Problem Solving with Parallel Circuits

Using the labeled diagram of a parallel circuit, solve the following problems:

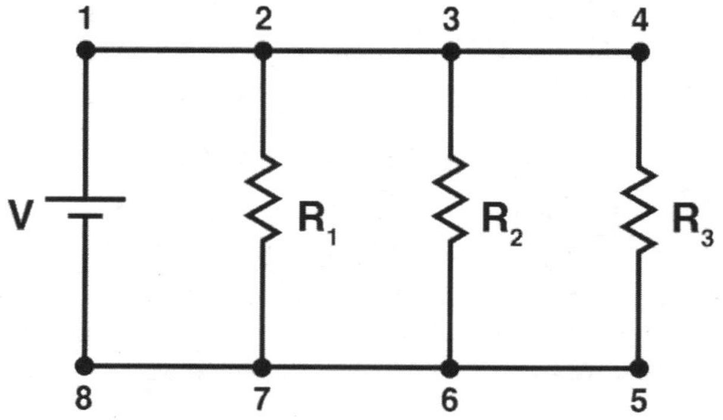

Example 1: If each resistor is 3 Ω and the battery is 9 V, what is the current at each of the indicated points (1-8) and each resistor?

Step 1:
Given: $R_1 = R_2 = R_3 = 3\ \Omega$
Equation: $\frac{1}{R_{eq}} = \frac{1}{R_1} + \frac{1}{R_2} + \frac{1}{R_3}$
Solve: $\frac{1}{R_{eq}} = \frac{1}{3\ \Omega} + \frac{1}{3\ \Omega} + \frac{1}{3\ \Omega}$
$\frac{1}{R_{eq}} = \frac{3}{3\ \Omega}$
$R_{eq} = 1\ \Omega$

Step 2:
Given: $V_{batt} = 9\ \text{V}$
Equation: $I_{total} = \frac{V_{batt}}{R_{eq}}$
Solve: $I_{total} = \frac{9\ \text{V}}{1\ \Omega} = 9\ \text{A}$

Step 3:
Equation: $\Delta V_n = I_{R_n}(R_n)$
Solve: $I_{R_1} = \frac{9\ \text{V}}{3\ \Omega} = 3\ A$
Current is the same for each branch in this example because $R_1 = R_2 = R_3 = 3\ \Omega$

Using this information and the additive properties of current in parallel circuits, the current through the following points and resistors is:

$$I_1 = I_2 = I_7 = I_8 = I_{total} = 9\ \text{A}$$
$$I_3 = I_6 = 6\ \text{A}$$
$$I_4 = I_5 = 3\ \text{A}$$
$$I_{R_1} = I_{R_2} = I_{R_3} = 3\ \text{A}$$

Example 2: If the current at point 4 is 4 Amps, and $R_1 = 3\ \Omega$; $R_2 = 2\ \Omega$; $R_3 = 6\ \Omega$, what is the total current?

Step 1:
Given: $R_3 = 6\ \Omega$; $I_4 = I_{R_3} = 4\ A$
Equation: $\Delta V_3 = I_{R_3}(R_3)$
Solve: $\Delta V_3 = (4\ \text{A})(6\ \Omega) = 24\ \text{V}$

Step 2:
Given: $R_1 = 3\ \Omega$; $R_2 = 2\ \Omega$
Equation: $I_n = \frac{V}{R_n}$
Solve: $I_1 = \frac{24\ \text{V}}{3\ \Omega} = 8\ \text{A}$
$I_2 = \frac{24\ \text{V}}{2\ \Omega} = 12\ \text{A}$

Step 3:
Equation: $I_{total} = I_1 + I_2 + I_3$
Solve: $I_{total} = 8\ \text{A} + 12\ \text{A} + 4\ \text{A}$
$I_{total} = 24\ \text{A}$

Capacitors and Inductors in Circuits

Capacitors have combination rules opposite to those of resistors. **Capacitors in series** have an equivalent value of:

$$C_{eq} = \left(\frac{1}{C_1} + \frac{1}{C_2} + \cdots + \frac{1}{C_n}\right)^{-1}$$

Capacitors in parallel have equivalence of:

$$C_{eq} = C_1 + C_2 + \cdots + C_n$$

Inductors follow the same combination rules as resistors. **Inductors in series** have an equivalent value of:

$$L_{eq} = L_1 + L_2 + \cdots + L_n$$

Inductors in parallel have equivalence of

$$L_{eq} = \left(\frac{1}{L_1} + \frac{1}{L_2} + \cdots + \frac{1}{L_n}\right)^{-1}$$

RC CIRCUITS

An RC circuit consists of a battery wired in series with a **resistor** and a **capacitor**. Since a capacitor in steady state allows no current flow, it makes no sense to analyze a steady-state RC circuit. Instead, we will look at an RC circuit that has only just been connected, with the capacitor uncharged. The battery supplies voltage V_B to the circuit, and since the capacitor's voltage is initially zero, the voltage across the resistor is initially V_B, giving an initial current of $I = \frac{V_B}{R}$. As current flows, the charge on the capacitor increases, which in turn creates an opposing voltage that **lowers the voltage drop** across the resistor. Combining Ohm's Law with the KVL gives the voltage relation as $V_B = IR + \frac{Q}{C}$, where Q is the charge on the capacitor. Since the current is simply the transfer rate of the charge, this becomes a differential equation. Solving for charge and current yields the expressions $Q(t) = CV_B\left(1 - e^{-t/RC}\right)$ and $I(t) = \left(\frac{V_B}{R}\right)e^{-t/RC}$. The factor RC in the exponent is referred to as the circuit's time constant. It is the amount of time required for the capacitor to charge up to 63.2% capacity.

If the battery is removed from the circuit after the capacitor is charged and the circuit is reconnected with just the resistor and capacitor, the capacitor will begin to drain at the same rate that it was charged. The current magnitude will follow the same equation as before, though it will be in the opposite direction. The new expression for the charge will be $Q(t) = CV_Be^{-t/RC}$.

POWER IN AC CIRCUITS

Unlike DC circuits, the power provided by an AC voltage source is not constant over time. Generally, an AC source will provide voltage in a sinusoidal pattern, $V(t) = V_{max}\sin(\omega t)$. Similarly, the current will be given by $I(t) = I_{max}\sin(\omega t)$. From our known equations for power, this yields a power of $P(t) = R{I_{max}}^2\sin^2(\omega t)$. However, if we wish to find the average power or the amount of energy transmission after a given period of time, we need to find some way to average voltage and current. The root-mean-square (rms) method, as the name suggests, takes the square root of the time average of the squared value. For sinusoidal functions such as the voltage and current here, the rms value is the maximum value divided by the square root of 2. For voltage and current, $V_{rms} = \frac{V_{max}}{\sqrt{2}}$, and $I_{rms} = \frac{I_{max}}{\sqrt{2}}$. In this way, the average power can be found as $P_{avg} = V_{rms}I_{rms}$, which can also be stated $P_{avg} = \frac{V_{max}I_{max}}{2}$. A DC source with supplied voltage V_B will provide the same power over time as an AC source if $V_B = V_{rms}$.

Properties of Magnets

Magnets and Magnetism

A **magnet** is any object or material, such as iron, steel, or magnetite (lodestone), that can affect another substance within its **field of force** that has like characteristics. Magnets can either attract or repel other substances. Magnets have two **poles**: north and south. Like poles repel and opposite poles (pairs of north and south) attract. The magnetic field is a set of invisible lines representing the paths of attraction and repulsion.

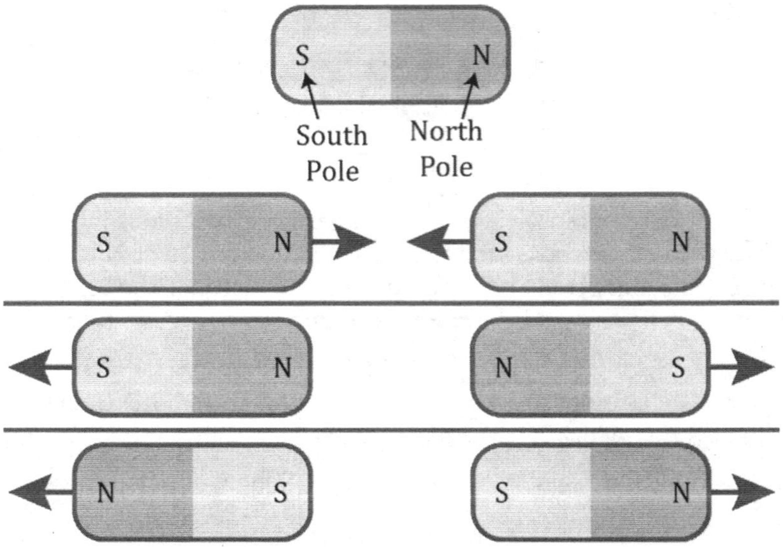

Magnetism can occur naturally, or ferromagnetic materials can be magnetized. Certain matter that is magnetized can retain its magnetic properties indefinitely and become a permanent magnet. Other matter can lose its magnetic properties. For example, an iron nail can be temporarily magnetized by stroking it repeatedly in the same direction using one pole of another magnet. Once magnetized, it can attract or repel other magnetically inclined materials, such as paper clips. Dropping the nail repeatedly will cause it to lose its magnetic properties.

Review Video: Magnets
Visit mometrix.com/academy and enter code: 570803

Magnetic Fields and Atomic Structure

Motion of a charge produces a **magnetic field**. Within an atom, the negatively-charged electrons moving around the nucleus each generate a magnetic field. In most materials, these fields all perfectly oppose and cancel each other, but in certain elements (e.g., iron, cobalt, nickel) the fields are not completely canceled, which makes each atom a tiny magnet. The strength and direction of a magnetic field is known as the magnetic moment.

Pairs of electrons moving in opposite directions cancel each other out, creating a **net magnetic field** of zero. Materials that have an unpaired electron are magnetic. Those with a weak attractive force are referred to as **paramagnetic materials**, while **ferromagnetic materials** have a strong attractive force. A **diamagnetic material** has electrons that are paired, and therefore does not typically have a magnetic moment. There are, however, some diamagnetic materials that have a weak magnetic field.

A magnetic field can be formed not only by a magnetic material, but also by electric current flowing through a wire. When a coiled wire is attached to the two ends of a battery, for example, an **electromagnet** can be formed by inserting a ferromagnetic material such as an iron bar within the coil. When electric current flows through the wire, the bar becomes a magnet. If there is no current, the magnetism is lost. A **magnetic domain** occurs when the magnetic fields of atoms are grouped and aligned. These groups form what can be thought of as miniature magnets within a material. This is what happens when an object like an iron nail is temporarily magnetized. Prior to magnetization, the organization of atoms and their various polarities are somewhat random with respect to where the north and south poles are pointing. After magnetization, a significant percentage of the poles are lined up in one direction, which is what causes the magnetic force exerted by the material.

Magnetic Fields

Magnetism and Magnetic Fields

Magnetism and magnetic attraction are similar in many ways to electrical charge and electrostatic force. Magnets have two distinct **polarities**, of which like polarities repel and opposite polarities attract. Just as an object that holds an electric charge will produce a vector field, so will a charged magnet. Like the electric field lines, magnetic field lines are drawn as **originating** from north poles and **terminating** on south poles. Magnetic field is typically represented with the letter $\boldsymbol{B}$, and has SI units of teslas (T), which are equivalent to newtons per Ampere-meter (N/A-m). Unlike electric charge, however, an isolated magnetic pole cannot exist. Magnets must exist as **dipoles**, meaning that if there is a north pole, the other end of the magnet, no matter how small, will be a south pole. Most common magnets can be demagnetized simply by heating the material or subjecting it to repeated impact. This is because magnets are composed of many tiny dipoles that, when aligned, create a large unified magnet. Some materials are permanently aligned in the manner and are known as permanent magnets. Ferromagnets are iron-based materials that can be magnetized if their dipoles are aligned by a sufficiently strong magnetic field.

Magnetic and **electric fields** are quite interrelated. It is believed that magnetic fields are set up by electric currents, and it has also been observed that magnetic fields can **induce electric current**. If we were to place a moving charge or a wire carrying current into a magnetic field, a magnetic force would act on it.

Forces Exerted by a Magnetic Field

We will define $\boldsymbol{B}$, the magnetic field, by measuring the magnetic force exerted on a moving electric charge within the field. This is generally done by firing a test charge into the area where $\boldsymbol{B}$ is to be defined. After a time, we will find that force $\boldsymbol{F}_{\mathrm{B}}$ acting on a test charge of velocity $\boldsymbol{v}$ and charge q can be written $\boldsymbol{F}_{\mathrm{B}} = q\boldsymbol{v} \times \boldsymbol{B}$, in which q can be either positive or negative. If q is negative, the direction of the force will be opposite to that shown by the right-hand rule from this cross product. From this equation, we will discover that the magnetic force always acts perpendicular to the velocity vector. This means a magnetic field can neither speed up nor slow down a charged particle; it can only deflect it. Also, a magnetic field will exert no force on a stationary charge or a charge that moves parallel to the field. We can see from this equation that the magnitude of the deflecting force will be $\boldsymbol{F}_{\mathrm{B}} = q\boldsymbol{v}\boldsymbol{B}\sin(\varphi)$, where φ is the angle between the particle velocity vector and the magnetic field vector.

Cyclotrons and Mass Spectrometers

Cyclotrons are particle accelerators that operate by using a magnetic field to create a deflection force on a fast-moving charged particle. The field strength is designed to cause the particle to move in a **circular pattern**. An electric field provides a force for the particle to accelerate tangentially as well. Once the particle has achieved sufficient velocity, it will exit the magnetic field and continue on in a straight line. One big advantage of the cyclotron over other types of particle accelerators is its relatively small size. Particles can achieve incredible velocities without having to travel a great distance.

Mass spectrometers are used to find the charge-to-mass ratio of ionized materials. An ionized particle of known mass, but unknown charge, is sent at a known velocity into a perpendicular magnetic field of known magnitude. Since the magnetic field is perpendicular, the **tangential speed** of the particle is constant. The force on a particle with constant tangential speed is equal to $\frac{mv^2}{r}$, where r is the radius of curvature of the particle's path. The force exerted by the magnetic field can be calculated as $q\boldsymbol{v}\boldsymbol{B}$, since it is perpendicular to the particle's direction of motion. Equating these two expressions gives us $\frac{q}{m} = \frac{v}{rB}$, allowing us to find the charge-to-mass ratio if we measure the radius of curvature.

Lorentz Force Law

The **Lorentz force law** describes the force exerted on a charged particle in an electromagnetic field. The force exerted on the particle with charge q can be found $\boldsymbol{F} = q(\boldsymbol{E} + \boldsymbol{v} \times \boldsymbol{B})$, where $\boldsymbol{v}$ is the particle's velocity vector and $\boldsymbol{E}$ and $\boldsymbol{B}$ are the electric and magnetic field vectors, respectively. Essentially, this law states that a positively charged particle will be accelerated in the same linear direction as the electric field, but will curve perpendicularly to the magnetic field according to the right-hand rule. The Lorentz force law is used in a number of devices currently employed by physicists, like the cyclotron, magnetron, mass spectrometer, motor, generator, and rail gun.

Gauss's Law for Magnetic Flux

Gauss's law for magnetism solidifies the assertion that **magnetic monopoles cannot exist**. It does so by making statements about magnetic flux, which is defined in much the same way as electric flux, $\Phi_m = \boldsymbol{B} \cdot \boldsymbol{A}$, where $\boldsymbol{A}$ is the surface's normal vector. Magnetic flux has SI units of webers (Wb). If the surface is taken to be an enclosing surface, or a Gaussian surface, Gauss's law states that the total flux through the surface will equal zero. Unlike the case with electric flux, which allows for contained net charge, there can be no net magnetic poles inside of a closed surface. For every north pole, there must be a south pole of equal magnitude. If, for instance, we envision our Gaussian surface as enclosing one end of a short solenoid (which will set up a magnetic field resembling that of a magnetic dipole), we will notice that the magnetic field $\boldsymbol{B}$ will enter the Gaussian surface inside the solenoid (at the north pole) and will leave it outside the solenoid. No lines will begin or end in the interior of the surface, so the total flux for the surface is zero.

Magnetic Force on a Current-Carrying Wire

A magnetic field will exert a **sideways force** on the conduction electrons in a wire. Since the conduction electrons cannot escape sideways out of the wire, we know that this force must be transmitted bodily to the wire itself. So, if we have a wire carrying current I, and we know that the longitudinal axis of the wire is perpendicular to a magnetic field $\boldsymbol{B}$, then we know that a force equal to $(-e)\boldsymbol{vB}$ will act on each conduction electron. Taken as a whole, the wire will experience a force of $IL\boldsymbol{B}$, where L is the length of wire in the field. If we were to reverse either the magnetic field or the direction of the current, then the force on the wire would reverse as well. If the magnetic field is not perpendicular to the wire, then we can find the magnetic force as $F_{\boldsymbol{B}} = IL\boldsymbol{B}\sin(\varphi)$, where φ is the angle between the direction of current and the magnetic field vector. The torque on a current-carrying loop is a result of the same phenomenon, except that with a loop, the current travels in opposite directions on opposite sides of the loop. This causes a result of zero net force since all the current exits the field from the same direction that it entered. There is, however, a net torque since the current going in opposite directions is separated by a distance. The torque on the loop can be found by $\boldsymbol{\tau} = IA\boldsymbol{n} \times \boldsymbol{B}$, where A is the area enclosed by the loop and $\boldsymbol{n}$ is the unit vector perpendicular to the plane of the loop. The loop may be any shape so long as it does not cross itself and is a closed shape.

Relationship Between Magnetism and Electricity

Ampere's Law

Ampere's law is a mathematical equation that relates current flowing to the magnetic field it generates. It is expressed by the closed-loop line integral:

$$\oint_C \boldsymbol{B} \cdot d\boldsymbol{L} = \mu_0 I$$

For a straight length of wire, the magnetic field encircles the wire in the direction indicated by the right-hand rule (with the thumb pointed in the direction of current and the fingers curling to indicate the magnetic field). For a very long wire where end effects may be ignored, the magnetic field is given as $\boldsymbol{B} = \frac{\mu_0 I}{2\pi r}$, where r is the distance from the wire.

For a loop of current-carrying wire, the magnetic field direction can still be determined from the right-hand rule. However, the field magnitude at most points around and inside the loop is difficult to determine. The field magnitude at the center of the loop is found to be $\boldsymbol{B} = \frac{\mu_0 I}{2r}$.

For a solenoid, a long coil of current-carrying wire that is sometimes wrapped around a metal core, the magnetic field direction may again be determined by the right-hand rule. At all points inside the solenoid, the field has magnitude $\boldsymbol{B} = \frac{\mu_0 n I}{h}$, where n is the number of loops in the solenoid and h is its height. For a long solenoid, it can be shown that the field magnitude outside the solenoid is negligible.

Biot-Savart Law

Any current-carrying wire will produce a magnetic field that circles the wire in the direction indicated by the right-hand rule (with the thumb pointing in the direction of the current). The **Biot-Savart law** gives the **magnitude** and **direction** of the magnetic field created by each infinitesimal element of current. The equation form of this law is given as $d\boldsymbol{B} = \left(\frac{\mu_0 I}{4r^3\pi}\right) \times d\boldsymbol{L} \times \boldsymbol{r}$, where μ_0 is a physical constant called the permeability of free space, $d\boldsymbol{L}$ is an infinitesimal vector pointing along the length of the wire in the direction of current, and $\boldsymbol{r}$ is the vector pointing from the wire element to the location where the field is to be calculated. Integrating this expression along the full length of wire gives the total resultant field.

The primary shortcoming of Ampere's law is that it is only applicable for a **constant steady-state current**. For transient cases, such as RC circuits, it is necessary to take into account what is known as the displacement current. **Displacement current** is found by the equation $I_d = \varepsilon_0 \left(\frac{\partial \Phi_e}{\partial t}\right)$, where ε_0 is the permittivity of free space and $\left(\frac{\partial \Phi_e}{\partial t}\right)$ is the instantaneous rate of change of electric flux. It is not actually a current, but for use in Ampere's law, it is treated like one. Thus, for transient cases, the I in Ampere's law is calculated as $I = I_{actual} + I_d$.

Transformers, Generators, and Electric Motors

Transformers are devices that allow power to be exchanged between two circuits through electromagnetic induction. They generally consist of a pair of coils wrapped around a single metal core. The magnetic field induced by the current in one coil in turn induces a current in the second coil. The amount of current induced in the second coil is dependent on the inducing current and the number of loops in each coil: $\frac{I_2}{I_1} = \frac{N_1}{N_2}$, where N is the number of loops in the given coil. Since the power given up by the one circuit is the same as that received by the second circuit, we may also say that $V_1 I_1 = V_2 I_2$, or equivalently $\frac{I_2}{I_1} = \frac{V_1}{V_2}$.

Generators operate by using mechanical energy to turn a coil in a magnetic field, thus converting it to electrical energy. Often, large generators will require gasoline combustion engines to provide the necessary power to operate, though some are able to tap natural power sources such as flowing water. Smaller generators may be powered by hand cranks or stationary bicycles.

Electric motors are basically the reverse of generators. They operate by using an alternating current source connected to an electromagnet to create an oscilating magnetic field that causes a current-carrying coil to rotate, thus generating a torque. DC motors require additional parts to direct the flow of current in such a way that the coil will be continuously rotating.

Faraday's Law and Lenz's Law

Electromagnetic induction is the process by which current is induced due to a change in magnetic flux. The magnetic flux through one or more loops of wire in a magnetic is $\Phi_m = \boldsymbol{B}A\cos(\theta)$, where A is the area enclosed by the loop and θ is the angle between a vector normal to the plane of the loop and the magnetic field vector. The produced electromotive force (emf) can be found by **Faraday's law**, stated in equation form as $V_{emf} = -N\left(\frac{\Delta\Phi_m}{\Delta t}\right)$, where N is the number of loops in the coil. So, this induced voltage will exist only as long as Φ_m is changing. A change in any of the variables ($\boldsymbol{B}$, A, or θ) can cause a change in magnetic flux. Generators operate by rotating a coil in a constant magnetic field.

The contribution to this concept by Lenz's law is the negative sign in the equation of Faraday's law. **Lenz's law** states that the induced emf will try to counter the changing magnetic flux by creating a current to produce a magnetic field that opposes the change in magnetic flux.

Chapter Quiz

Ready to see how well you retained what you just read? Scan the QR code to go directly to the chapter quiz interface for this study guide. If you're using a computer, simply visit the online resources page at **mometrix.com/resources719/texesphysc6-12** and click the Chapter Quizzes link.

Chemistry

Structure of Matter

Historical Models of the Atom

Atomic Models and Theories

There have been many theories regarding the **structure** of atoms and their particles. Part of the challenge in developing an understanding of matter is that atoms and their particles are too small to be seen. It is believed that the first conceptualization of the atom was developed by **Democritus** in 400 B.C. Some of the more notable models are the solid sphere or billiard ball model postulated by **John Dalton**, the plum pudding or raisin bun model by **J.J. Thomson**, the planetary or nuclear model by **Ernest Rutherford**, the Bohr or orbit model by **Niels Bohr**, and the electron cloud or quantum mechanical model by **Louis de Broglie** and **Erwin Schrödinger**. Rutherford directed the alpha scattering experiment that discounted the plum pudding model. The shortcoming of the Bohr model was the belief that electrons orbited in fixed rather than changing elliptical orbits.

Review Video: Atomic Models
Visit mometrix.com/academy and enter code: 434851

Review Video: John Dalton
Visit mometrix.com/academy and enter code: 565627

Thomson "Plum Pudding" Model

J.J. Thomson, the discoverer of the electron, suggested that the arrangement of protons and electrons within an atom could be approximated by dried fruit in a **plum pudding**. Thomson, whose discovery of the electron preceded that of the proton or neutron, hypothesized that an atom's electrons, the dried plums, were **positioned uniformly** inside the atom within a cloud of positive charge, the pudding. This model was later disproved.

Rutherford Scattering

Ernest Rutherford concluded from the work of Geiger and Marsden that the majority of the atom's mass was concentrated in a minute, positively charged region, the **nucleus**, which was surrounded by **electrons**. When a positive alpha particle approached close enough to the nucleus, it was strongly repelled, enough so that it had the ability to rebound at high angles. The small nucleus size explained the small number of alpha particles that were repelled in this fashion. The scattering led to development of the **planetary model of the atom**, which was further developed by Niels Bohr into what is now known as the Bohr model.

Bohr Model

Niels Bohr postulated that the electrons orbiting the nucleus must occupy **discrete orbits**. These discrete orbits also corresponded to discrete levels of energy and angular momentum. Consequently, the only way that electrons could move between orbits was by making nearly instantaneous jumps between them. These jumps, known as **quantum leaps**, are associated with the absorption or emission of a quantum of energy, known as a

photon. If the electron is jumping to a higher energy state, a photon must be absorbed. Similarly, if the electron is dropping to a lower energy state, a photon must be emitted.

Review Video: Structure of Atoms
Visit mometrix.com/academy and enter code: 905932

Atomic and Subatomic Structure

Basic Organization of Matter

An **element** is the most basic type of matter. It has unique properties and cannot be broken down into other elements. The smallest unit of an element is the **atom**. Most elements are found somewhere in nature in single-atom form, but a few elements only exist naturally in pairs. These are called diatomic elements, and some of the most common of these are hydrogen, nitrogen, and oxygen. A chemical combination of two or more types of elements is called a compound. **Compounds** often have properties that are very different from those of their constituent elements. The smallest independent unit of an element or compound of two or more atoms is known as a **molecule**. Elements and compounds are represented by chemical symbols, one or two letters, most often the first in the element name. More than one atom of the same element in a compound is represented with a subscript number designating how many atoms of that element are present. Water, for instance, contains two hydrogens and one oxygen. Thus, the chemical formula is H_2O. Methane contains one carbon and four hydrogens, so its formula is CH_4.

Review Video: Molecules
Visit mometrix.com/academy and enter code: 349910

Protons, Neutrons, and Electrons

The three major subatomic particles are the proton, neutron, and electron. The **proton**, which is located in the nucleus, has a relative charge of +1. The **neutron**, which is located in the nucleus, has a relative charge of 0. The **electron**, which is located outside the nucleus, has a relative charge of -1. The proton and neutron, which are essentially the same mass, are much more massive than the electron and make up the mass of the atom. The electron's mass is insignificant compared to the mass of the proton and neutron.

Orbits and Orbitals

An orbit is a definite path, but an orbital is a region in space. The Bohr model described electrons as orbiting or following a definite path in space around the nucleus of an atom. But, according to **Heisenberg's uncertainty principle**, it is impossible to determine the location and the momentum of an electron simultaneously. Therefore, it is impossible to draw a definite path or orbit of an electron. An **orbital**, as described by the quantum-mechanical model or the electron-cloud model, is a region in space that is drawn in such a way as to indicate the probability of finding an electron at a specific location. The distance an orbital is located from the nucleus corresponds to the principal quantum number. The orbital shape corresponds to the subshell or azimuthal quantum number. The orbital orientation corresponds to the magnetic quantum number.

Quantum Numbers

The **principal quantum number** (n) describes an electron's shell or energy level and actually describes the size of the orbital. Electrons farther from the nucleus are at higher energy levels. The **subshell** or azimuthal quantum number (l) describes the electron's sublevel or subshell (s, p, d, or f) and specifies the shape of the orbital. Typical shapes include spherical, dumbbell, and clover leaf. The **magnetic quantum number** (m_l) describes the orientation of the orbital in space. The spin or magnetic moment quantum number (m_s) describes the direction of the spin of the electron in the orbital.

Atomic Number and Mass Number

The **atomic number** of an element is the number of protons in the nucleus of an atom of that element. This is the number that identifies the type of an atom. For example, all oxygen atoms have eight protons, and all carbon atoms have six protons. Each element is identified by its specific atomic number.

The **mass number** is the number of protons and neutrons in the nucleus of an atom. Although the atomic number is the same for all atoms of a specific element, the mass number can vary due to the varying numbers of neutrons in various isotopes of the atom.

Isotopes

Isotopes are atoms of the same element that vary in their number of neutrons. Isotopes of the same element have the same number of protons and thus the same atomic number. Because isotopes vary in the number of neutrons, they are identified by their mass numbers. For example, two naturally occurring carbon isotopes are carbon-12 and carbon-13, which have mass numbers 12 and 13, respectively. The symbols ${}^{12}_{6}C$ and ${}^{13}_{6}C$ also represent the carbon isotopes. The general form of the symbol is ${}^{M}_{A}X$, where X is the element symbol, M is the mass number, and A is the atomic number.

Average Atomic Mass

The **average atomic mass** is the weighted average of the masses of all the naturally occurring isotopes of an atom in comparison to the carbon-12 isotope. The unit for average atomic mass is the atomic mass unit (u). Atomic masses of isotopes are measured using a mass spectrometer by bombarding a gaseous sample of the isotope and measuring its relative deflections. Atomic masses can be calculated if the percent abundances and the atomic masses of the naturally occurring isotopes are known.

Cathode Ray Tube (CRT)

Electrons were discovered by Joseph John Thomson through scientific work with cathode ray tubes (CRTs). **Cathode rays** had been studied for many years, but it was Thomson who showed that cathode rays were **negatively charged particles**. Although Thomson could not determine an electron's charge or mass, he was able to determine the ratio of the charge to the mass. Thomson discovered that this ratio was constant regardless of the gas in the CRT. He was able to show that the cathode rays were actually streams of negatively charged particles by deflecting them with a positively charged plate.

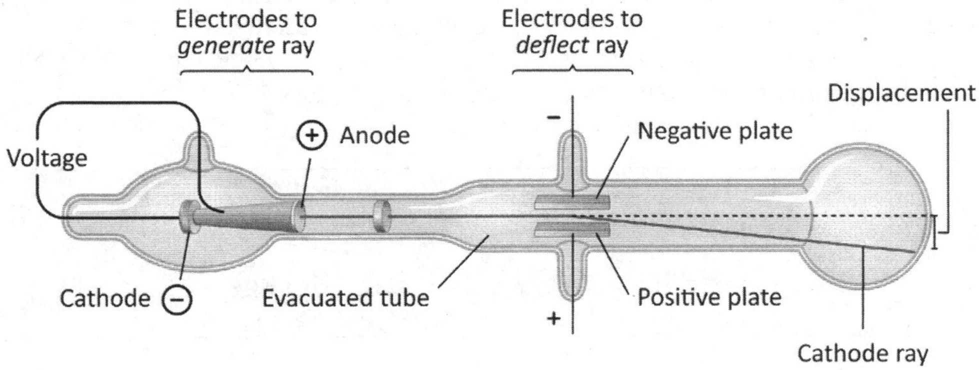

Gold Foil Experiment

After Thomson determined the ratio of the charge to the mass of an electron from studying cathode rays, he proposed the plum pudding model, in which he compared electrons to the raisins embedded in plum pudding. This model of the atom was disproved by the gold foil experiment. The gold foil experiment led to the discovery of the nucleus of an atom. Scientists at Rutherford's laboratory bombarded a thin gold foil with high-speed helium ions. Much to their surprise, some of the ions were reflected by the foil. The scientists concluded that the atom has a **hard central core**, which we now know to be the **nucleus**.

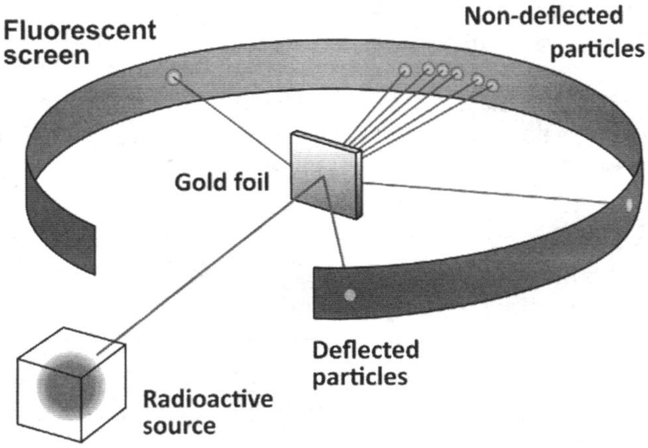

Problems that Rutherford's Model Had with Spectral Lines

Rutherford's model allowed for the electrons of an atom to be in an **infinite number of orbits** based on Newton's laws of motion. Rutherford believed that electrons could orbit the nucleus at any distance from the nucleus and that electrons could change velocity and direction at any moment. But, according to Rutherford's model, the electrons would lose energy and spiral into the nucleus. Unfortunately, if this was in fact true, then every atom would be **unstable**. Rutherford's model also does not correspond to the spectral lines emitted from gases at low pressure. The **spectral lines** are discrete bands of light at specific energy levels. These spectral lines indicate that electrons must be at specific distances from the nucleus. If electrons could be located at any distance from the nucleus, then these gases should emit continuous spectra instead of spectral lines.

Electron Configuration and the Periodic Table

Electron Configuration

The chemical and physical properties of atoms are related to the number of **valence electrons** the atom possesses. Atoms (except hydrogen and helium) seek to have **eight electrons in their outer shell** as stated in the octet rule. A full octet corresponds to full *s* and *p* orbitals. Noble gases have full *s* and *p* orbitals and are inert. To fulfill the octet rule, elements in groups 1A (alkali metals) and 2A (alkaline earth metals) tend to lose one or two electrons, respectively, forming cations. Elements in group 6A (chalcogens) and group 7A (halogens) tend to gain one or two electrons, respectively, forming anions. Other elements such as carbon (group 4A) tend to form covalent bonds to satisfy the octet rule.

Review Video: Electron Configuration
Visit mometrix.com/academy and enter code: 565113

Review Video: Anion, Cation, and Octet Rule
Visit mometrix.com/academy and enter code: 303525

Aufbau Principle

The **Aufbau principle** is named from the German word for "building up," and it describes how electrons fill the energy levels or **shells of an atom**. In general, electrons will fill the $n = 1$ energy level before filling the $n = 2$ energy level, and electrons will fill the $n = 2$ energy level before filling the $n = 3$ energy level. The *s* subshell of an energy level will fill before the *p* subshell, which fills before the *d* and *f* subshells.

Hund's Rule

Hund's rule describes how electrons fill the orbitals in a sublevel. Less energy is required for an electron to occupy an orbital alone than the energy needed for an electron to pair up with another electron in an orbital.

Therefore, electrons will occupy each orbital in a subshell before electrons will begin to pair up in those orbitals. For example, in the $2p$ subshell, one electron will occupy each of the three orbitals before pairing begins. In the $3d$ subshell, one electron will occupy each of the five orbitals before pairing begins.

Pauli Exclusion Principle

The **Pauli exclusion principle** describes the unique address or location of each electron in an atom. Each electron has a unique or exclusive set of four quantum numbers indicating the electron's energy level, subshell, orbital orientation, and magnetic moment. Every orbital can hold a maximum of two electrons, but even if two electrons occupy the same orbital resulting in identical energy levels, subshells, and orbital orientations, they must have opposite spins, which means that their magnetic moment quantum numbers will differ.

Correlation Between the Electron Configuration and the Periodic Table

Electron configurations show a direct correlation to the periodic table. The periodic table can be divided into blocks representing *s*, *p*, *d*, and *f* subshells. The **energy level** corresponds to the row or period of the periodic table. The **subshells**, *s*, *p*, *d*, or *f* are related to the block's group numbers. The *s* block corresponds to groups 1A and 2A. The *p* block corresponds to groups 3A–8A. The *d* block corresponds to the 10 groups of transition metals, and the *f* block corresponds to the two rows of inner transition metals (14 groups) located at the bottom of the table.

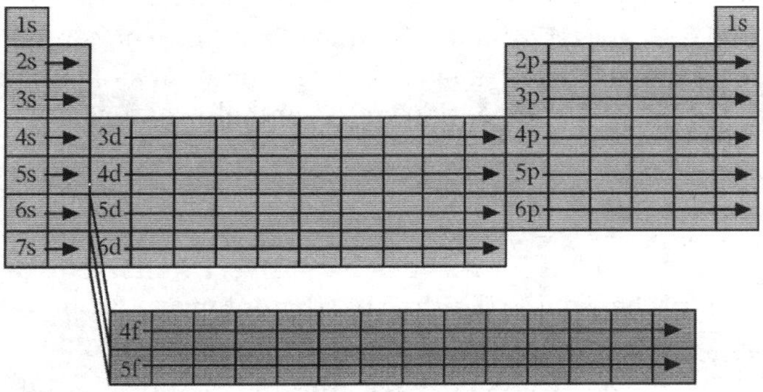

Pure Substances and Mixtures

Pure Substances

Pure substances are substances that cannot be further broken down into simpler components or pieces and still retain their characteristics. Pure substances are categorized as either **elements** or **compounds**. Elements consist of only one type of atom may be monatomic, diatomic, or polyatomic. For example, helium (He) and copper (Cu) are monatomic elements, and hydrogen (H_2) and oxygen (O_2) are diatomic elements. Phosphorus (P_4) and sulfur (S_8) are polyatomic elements. Compounds consist of molecules of more than one type of atom. For example, pure water (H_2O) is made up of molecules consisting of two atoms of hydrogen bonded to one atom of oxygen, and glucose ($C_6H_{12}O_6$) is made up of molecules of six carbon atoms and twelve hydrogen atoms bonded together with six oxygen atoms.

Mixtures

Mixtures can be classified as either homogeneous or heterogeneous. The molecules of a **homogeneous mixture** are distributed uniformly throughout the mixture, whereas the molecules of a **heterogeneous mixture** are not. Air is an example of a homogeneous mixture, and a pile of sand and rock is an example of a heterogeneous mixture. Solutions are homogeneous mixtures consisting of a **solute** (the substance that is dissolved) and a **solvent** (the substance doing the dissolving).

Suspensions

Suspensions are heterogeneous mixtures in which the particle size of the substance **suspended** is too large to be kept in suspension by Brownian motion. Once left undisturbed, suspensions will settle out to form layers.

An example of a suspension is sand stirred into water. Left undisturbed, the sand will fall out of suspension and the water will form a layer on top of the sand.

Mixtures with Compounds

Mixtures are similar to compounds in that they are produced when two or more substances are combined. However, there are some key differences as well. Compounds require a chemical combination of the constituent particles, while mixtures are simply the interspersion of particles. Unlike compounds, mixtures may be **separated** without a chemical change. A mixture retains the chemical properties of its constitutent particles, while a compound acquires a new set of properties. Given compounds can exist only in specific ratios, while mixtures may be any ratio of the involved substances.

Chemical and Physical Properties and Changes

Chemical and Physical Properties

Matter has both physical and chemical properties. **Physical properties** can be seen or observed without changing the identity or composition of matter. For example, the mass, volume, and density of a substance can be determined without permanently changing the sample. Other physical properties include color, boiling point, freezing point, solubility, odor, hardness, electrical conductivity, thermal conductivity, ductility, and malleability.

Chemical properties cannot be measured without changing the identity or composition of matter. Chemical properties describe how a substance reacts or changes to form a new substance. Examples of chemical properties include flammability, corrosivity, oxidation states, enthalpy of formation, and reactivity with other chemicals.

Intensive and Extensive Properties

Physical properties are categorized as either intensive or extensive. **Intensive properties** *do not* depend on the amount of matter or quantity of the sample. This means that intensive properties will not change if the sample size is increased or decreased. Intensive properties include color, hardness, melting point, boiling point, density, ductility, malleability, specific heat, temperature, concentration, and magnetization.

Extensive properties *do* depend on the amount of matter or quantity of the sample. Therefore, extensive properties do change if the sample size is increased or decreased. If the sample size is increased, the property increases. If the sample size is decreased, the property decreases. Extensive properties include volume, mass, weight, energy, entropy, number of moles, and electrical charge.

Atomic Properties of Neutral Atoms, Anions, and Cations

Neutral atoms have the same number of protons as electrons. **Cations** are positively-charged ions that are formed when atoms lose electrons. For example, the alkali metals sodium and potassium form the cations Na^+ and K^+, and the alkaline earth metals magnesium and calcium form the cations Mg^{2+} and Ca^{2+}. These elements easily lose electrons because the resulting ion is left with a full valence shell.

Anions are negatively-charged ions that are formed when atoms gain electrons. For example, the halogens fluorine and chlorine form the anions F^- and Cl^-. These elements easily gain electrons because the resulting ion has a full valence shell.

Chemical and Physical Changes

Physical changes do not produce new substances. The atoms or molecules may be rearranged, but no new substances are formed. **Phase changes**—changes of state such as melting, freezing, and sublimation—are physical changes. For example, physical changes include the melting of ice, the boiling of water, sugar dissolving into water, and the crushing of a piece of chalk into a fine powder.

Chemical changes involve a **chemical reaction** and do produce new substances. When iron rusts, iron oxide is formed, indicating a chemical change. Other examples of chemical changes include baking a cake, burning wood, digesting food, and mixing an acid and a base.

Energy in Chemistry

Conservation of Energy and Matter

Law of Conservation of Energy

The **law of conservation of energy** states that in a closed system, energy cannot be created or destroyed but only changed from one form to another. This is also known as the first law of thermodynamics. Another way to state this is that the **total energy in an isolated system is constant**. Energy comes in many forms that may be transformed from one kind to another, but in a closed system, the total amount of energy is conserved or remains constant. For example, potential energy can be converted to kinetic energy, thermal energy, radiant energy, or mechanical energy. In an isolated chemical reaction, there can be no energy created or destroyed. The energy simply changes forms.

Law of Conservation of Mass

The **law of conservation of mass** is also known as the **law of conservation of matter**. This law states that for a chemical reaction in a closed system, the total mass of the products must equal the total mass of the reactants. This could also be stated that in a closed system, mass never changes. A consequence of this law is that matter is never created or destroyed during a typical chemical reaction. The atoms of the reactants are only rearranged to form the products. The number and type of each specific atom involved in the reactants is identical to the number and type of atoms in the products. This is the key principle used when balancing chemical equations. In a balanced chemical equation, the number of moles of each element on the reactant side equals the number of moles of each element on the product side.

Review Video: Balancing Chemical Equations
Visit mometrix.com/academy and enter code: 341228

Conversion of Energy Within Chemical Systems

Chemical energy is the energy stored in molecules in the bonds between the atoms of those molecules and the energy associated with the intermolecular forces. This stored **potential energy** may be converted into **kinetic energy** and then into heat. During a chemical reaction, atoms may be rearranged and chemical bonds may be formed or broken accompanied by a corresponding absorption or release of energy, usually in the form of heat. According to the first law of thermodynamics, during these energy conversions, the **total amount of energy must be conserved**.

Kinetic and Potential Energy in Chemistry

Kinetic and Potential Energy

The internal energy of a system may be categorized as kinetic energy or potential energy. **Kinetic energy** is the energy of a system associated with movement. In chemical systems, this movement is described by the **kinetic theory of matter** and is due to the random movement of the particles that make up the system. The kinetic energy of a particle may be calculated by the following formula: $KE = \frac{1}{2}mv^2$, where KE is the kinetic energy in joules, m is the mass of the particle in kilograms, and v is the velocity of the particle in meters per second.

Potential energy is the stored energy in a system associated with position or configuration. In chemical systems, this energy is the energy associated with the chemical bonds and intermolecular forces of the matter contained in the system.

Basics of Radioactivity

Radioactivity

Radioisotopes: Also known as radionuclides or radioactive isotopes, radioisotopes are atoms that have an unstable nucleus. This is a nucleus that has excess energy and the potential to undergo radioactive decay, which most often results in the emission of alpha, beta, or gamma radiation. Many radionuclides occur naturally but others have only been produced artificially.

Radioactive decay: This occurs when an unstable atomic nucleus spontaneously loses energy by emitting ionizing particles and radiation. Decay is a form of energy transfer, as the energy lost by the nucleus is given to the particles or radiation emitted. It also results in products that are different from the initial atoms. Before decay there is one type of atom, called the **parent nuclide**. After decay there are one or more different products, called the **daughter nuclide(s)**.

Radioactivity: This refers to particles or energy that are emitted from nuclei as a result of nuclear instability.

Review Video: Radioactivity
Visit mometrix.com/academy and enter code: 537142

Radiation is the term for energy emitted or transmitted as waves or particles. Radiation is classified as either ionizing (able to detach an electron from an atom) or non-ionizing. Nuclear weapons, nuclear reactors, and radioactive substances are all examples of things that involve ionizing radiation. Acoustic radiation and electromagnetic radiation (with wavelength greater than 125 nm) are types of non-ionizing radiation.

Radioactive half-life is the time it takes for half of the radioactive nuclei in a sample to undergo radioactive decay. Radioactive decay rates are usually expressed in terms of half-lives. The different types of radioactivity lead to different decay paths, which transmute the nuclei into other chemical elements. **Decay products** (or daughter nuclides) make radioactive dating possible. **Decay chains** are a series of decays that result in different products. For example, uranium-238 is often found in granite. Its decay chain includes 14 daughter products. It eventually becomes a stable isotope of lead, which is why lead is often found with deposits of uranium ore. Its first half-life is equivalent to the approximate age of the earth, about 4.5 billion years. One of its products is radon, a radioactive gas.

Isotopes that have not been observed to decay are **stable**, or non-radioactive, isotopes. It is not known whether some stable isotopes may have such long decay times that observing decay is not possible. Currently, 80 elements have one or more stable isotopes. There are 256 known stable isotopes in total. Carbon, for example, has three isotopes. Two (carbon-12 and carbon-13) are stable and one (carbon-14) is radioactive.

Ionizing radiation comes in three types: alpha (α), beta (β), and gamma (γ). Alpha particles are positive, beta particles are negative, and gamma rays are neutral. **Alpha particles** are larger than beta particles and can cause severe damage if a source of alpha particles is ingested. Because of their large mass, however, they can be easily stopped. Even paper can protect against this type of radiation. **Beta particles** can be beta-minus or beta-plus. Beta-minus particles contain an energetic electron, while beta-plus particles are emitted by positrons. Beta particles can be stopped with a thin sheet of metal. **Gamma rays** are a type of high energy electromagnetic radiation. Gamma radiation is one of the ways a decaying nucleus emits excess energy after it has emitted either alpha or beta radiation. Gamma rays can cause serious damage when absorbed by living tissue, and it takes a lot of shielding (typically lead) to stop them. Alpha, beta, and gamma radiation can also have positive applications.

Nuclear fission and nuclear fusion are similar in that they occur in the nucleus of an atom, can release great amounts of energy, and result in the formation of different elements (nuclear transmutation). They are different in that **nuclear fission** is the splitting of a nucleus into smaller particles, and **nuclear fusion** is the joining of nuclei to form a heavier nucleus. It requires immense pressures and temperatures, but when fusion occurs, energy can either be absorbed or released, depending on the resultant nucleus. Fusion occurs naturally in stars, and is thought to be the process responsible for the generation of all naturally occurring elements (stellar nucleosynthesis).

Radioactive waste is a waste product that is considered dangerous because of either low levels or high levels of radioactivity. Radioactive waste could include discarded clothing that was used as protection against radiation, or decay products of substances used to create electricity through nuclear fission. Small amounts of radioactive material can be ingested as a method of tracing how the body distributes certain elements. Other radioactive materials are used as light sources because they glow when heated. Uncontrolled radiation or even small amounts of radioactive material can cause sickness and cancer in humans. **Gamma wave radiation** is fast-moving radiation that can cause cancer and damage genetic information by crashing into DNA molecules or other cells. Low-level radiation also occurs naturally. When related to everyday occurrences, radiation is measured in millirems per hour (mrem/hr). Humans can be exposed to radiation from stone used to build houses, cosmic rays from space, x-rays and other medical devices, and nuclear energy products.

Nuclear Chemistry and Radioactivity

Alpha Particles

Alpha particles are the products of **alpha decay**. They are identical to helium nuclei. An alpha particle consists of two protons and two neutrons. Because they have two protons but zero electrons, alpha particles have a net +2 charge. They are represented by the Greek letter alpha as α, α^{2+}, or ${}^{4}_{2}\alpha^{2+}$. Because they are identical to helium nuclei, they may also be written as He^{2+}, ${}^{4}_{2}He$, or ${}^{4}_{2}He^{2+}$. Because alpha particles have a strong charge and travel slowly, they interact significantly with matter that they pass through and may therefore be stopped by a sheet of paper or a few inches of air. Alpha particles cannot penetrate the skin.

Beta Particles

Beta particles are the products of **beta decay**. Beta particles may be high-speed electrons or high-speed positrons. These two forms of beta decay are designated by the Greek letter beta as β^- and β^+ or ${}^{0}_{-1}e$ and ${}^{0}_{+1}e$, respectively. Negative beta particles are created during radioactive decay when a neutron changes into a proton and an electron. Positive beta particles are created when a proton changes into a neutron and a positron. Beta particles have a greater penetrating ability than alpha particles. Beta particles can be stopped by thin plywood or metal or several feet of air.

Gamma Radiation

Gamma radiation (represented by the Greek letter gamma γ) is released during **gamma decay**. Often, atoms that have just undergone alpha or beta decay then undergo gamma decay. An atom produced during alpha or beta decay may still be in an excited state. The atom then releases this energy in a burst of gamma rays as high-energy photons. Gamma radiation is part of the electromagnetic spectrum and consists of electromagnetic waves that travel at the speed of light with frequencies higher than x-rays. Because gamma radiation has no charge, it easily penetrates solid substances. Gamma decay is useful in medical procedures, including cancer treatment.

Energy, Frequency, and Wavelength

The properties of energy, frequency, and wavelength can be used to describe electromagnetic waves. These properties also have a mathematical relationship with each other. Energy (E) is directly related to frequency (f) as given by $E = hf$, where h represents Planck's constant (6.626×10^{-34} J-s). As the frequency increases, the energy increases. For example, gamma rays, which have the highest frequency of the electromagnetic spectrum, also have the highest energy. The speed (v) of the wave is equal to the product of wavelength (λ) and frequency (f). Because the speed of light (c) is constant in a vacuum at 3.00×10^8 m/s, wavelength and frequency are inversely related. As wavelength decreases, frequency increases. For example, gamma rays have the shortest wavelength of the electromagnetic spectrum and the highest frequency.

Radioactive Decay and Half-Life

Radioactivity or **radioactive decay** occurs when an unstable atom splits to form a new atom and emits some type of radiation. An atom's nucleus contains protons and neutrons. The protons have positive charges and repel each other, but with the help of neutrons the repulsive force between protons is overcome by the strong nuclear force, which holds the nucleus together. With elements of greater atomic number, the repulsive force is increasingly a match for the strong force. All atoms with atomic number greater than 83 are unstable. The three basic types of **radioactive decay** are alpha decay, beta decay, and gamma decay. The **half-life** of an isotope is the length of time it takes for one-half of the atoms of a radioactive substance to decay into a new type of atom.

Typical Fission Reaction

A typical fission reaction is the fission of uranium-235 from neutron bombardment:

$${}^{235}_{92}\text{U} + {}^{1}_{0}\text{n} \rightarrow {}^{139}_{56}\text{Ba} + {}^{94}_{36}\text{Kr} + 3[{}^{1}_{0}\text{n}]$$

The uranium-235 atom $\left({}^{235}_{92}\text{U}\right)$ is bombarded by a neutron $({}^{1}_{0}\text{n})$. This neutron is absorbed, forcing the uranium-235 atom into an excited, unstable state. This excited, unstable uranium-235 atom splits into smaller more stable pieces, which consist of a barium-139 atom $({}^{139}_{56}\text{Ba})$, a krypton-94 atom $({}^{94}_{36}\text{Kr})$, and three neutrons $({}^{1}_{0}\text{n})$. These neutrons in turn may bombard other uranium-235 atoms causing the nuclear fission to continue.

Review Video: Reading Nuclear Equations
Visit mometrix.com/academy and enter code: 688890

Nuclear Fusion

Nuclear fusion is the process in which the nuclei of atoms that are light and unstable will unite or fuse to form a heavier, more stable atom. Fusion requires extremely high temperatures and often pressures that force the atoms into a plasma state. In this high-energy state, the atoms collide frequently and are able to fuse together. In this process, some mass is lost and released as large quantities of energy. The Sun's heat and light are produced by a fusion reaction in the Sun's core, in which four hydrogen atoms fuse into a helium nucleus.

Review Video: Nuclear Fusion
Visit mometrix.com/academy and enter code: 381782

Alpha Emission

In alpha emission, the parent nuclide splits into **two parts** consisting of the daughter nuclide and an alpha particle. The alpha particle is identical to a helium nucleus and consists of two protons and two neutrons, represented by ${}^{4}_{2}\text{He}$ or ${}^{4}_{2}\text{He}^{2+}$. The daughter nuclide has a mass number that is four less than the parent nuclide and an atomic number that is two less than the parent nuclide. An example of alpha emission is the decay of a uranium-238 atom into a thorium-234 atom and an alpha particle, as shown below:

$${}^{238}_{92}\text{U} \rightarrow {}^{234}_{90}\text{Th} + {}^{4}_{2}\text{He}$$

Positive and Negative Beta Decay

In **positive beta decay**, also known as **positron emission**, the parent nuclide splits into two parts consisting of the daughter nuclide and a positron. The positron is represented by ${}^{0}_{+1}\text{e}$ because its mass is negligible compared to a neutron or proton, and its charge is +1. The daughter nuclide has the same mass number as the parent nuclide and an atomic number of one less than the parent nuclide. An example of positive beta decay is when a carbon-11 atom splits into a boron-11 atom and a positron, as given by the equation shown here:

In **negative beta decay**, also simply called **beta decay**, the parent nuclide splits into two parts consisting of the daughter nuclide and an electron. The electron is represented by ${}_{-1}^{0}e$ because its mass is negligible compared to a neutron or proton, and its charge is −1. An example of negative beta decay is when a carbon-14 atom splits into a nitrogen-14 atom and an electron, as given by the following equation:

$${}_{6}^{14}C \rightarrow {}_{7}^{14}N + {}_{-1}^{0}e$$

Electron Capture

In electron capture, an electron from an atom's own electron cloud impacts the atom's nucleus and causes a **decay reaction**. The parent nuclide absorbs the electron, and a proton is converted to a neutron. A neutrino is emitted from the nucleus. Gamma radiation is also emitted. The daughter nuclide has the same mass number as the parent nuclide, and the atomic number of the daughter nuclide is one lower than the atomic number of the parent nuclide. An example of electron capture is when a nitrogen-13 atom absorbs an electron and converts to a carbon-13 atom while emitting a neutrino (${}_{0}^{0}\nu$) and gamma radiation (γ), as shown by the following equation:

$${}_{7}^{13}N + {}_{-1}^{0}e \rightarrow {}_{6}^{13}C + {}_{0}^{0}\nu + \gamma$$

Transmutation

Transmutation is a type of nuclear decay in which an atom is bombarded by **high-speed particles** to cause it to convert from one type of atom to another type of atom. Ernest Rutherford was the first to accomplish this, with the transmutation of the nitrogen-14 atom into an oxygen-17 atom by bombardment with a beam of high-speed helium ions. In this transmutation, the helium-4 ion is also converted to a hydrogen-1 ion:

$${}_{7}^{14}N + {}_{2}^{4}He \rightarrow {}_{8}^{17}O + {}_{1}^{1}H$$

Neutron Radiation

Neutron radiation is a type of **transmutation** that is used to create many isotopes that do not occur naturally. In neutron radiation, an atom is bombarded by high-speed neutrons (${}_{0}^{1}n$) to cause nuclear decay. In neutron radiation, the daughter nuclide has a mass number one higher than the parent nuclide, but the atomic number remains the same. The daughter is an atom of the same element as the parent nuclide, but it has one more neutron, which makes it a different isotope of that element. An example of neutron radiation is when a cobalt-59 atom is bombarded by a high-speed neutron and converts to a cobalt-60 atom, as shown in the following equation:

$${}_{27}^{59}Co + {}_{0}^{1}n \rightarrow {}_{27}^{60}Co$$

Balancing a Nuclear Reaction

When balancing a nuclear reaction, two key principles must be applied. First, the **mass number must be conserved**. Second, the **atomic number must be conserved**. To determine the products formed, the mass numbers and atomic numbers of the particles emitted or absorbed must be known. Alpha decay emits alpha particles (${}_{2}^{4}He$). Beta decay emits electrons (${}_{-1}^{0}e$). Positron decay emits positrons (${}_{+1}^{0}e$). Neutron radiation absorbs neutrons (${}_{0}^{1}n$). In alpha decay, the mass number decreases by four, and the atomic number decreases by two. In negative beta decay, the mass number stays the same, and the atomic number increases by one. In positive beta decay, the mass number stays the same, and the atomic number decreases by one. In neutron radiation, the mass number increases by one, and the atomic number stays the same.

Complete or Balance the Following Nuclear Reactions:

The key principles to completing or balancing nuclear reactions are that the mass number is conserved and the atomic number is conserved.

$$^{230}_{90}\text{Th} \leftrightarrow {}^{4}_{2}\text{He} + \_\_\_$$

In this reaction, thorium-230 under goes alpha decay and emits an alpha particle with a mass number of 4 and an atomic number of 2. Balancing the atomic numbers $(90 - 2)$ yields an atomic number of 88, which corresponds to radium. Balancing the mass numbers $(230 - 4)$ yields 226. Therefore, the missing product is $^{226}_{88}\text{Ra}$.

$$^{40}_{19}\text{K} \leftrightarrow {}^{0}_{-1}\text{e} + \_\_\_$$

In this reaction, potassium-40 undergoes beta decay and emits an electron with an assigned mass number of 0 and an assigned atomic number of −1. Balancing the atomic numbers $\big(19 - (-1)\big)$ yields an atomic number of 20, which indicates calcium. Balancing the mass numbers $(40 - 0)$ yields a mass number of 40. Therefore, the missing product is $^{40}_{20}\text{Ca}$.

Conversions between Forms of Energy

Conversion of Energy

There are many different types of energy that exist. These include mechanical, sound, magnetic, electrical, light, heat, and chemical. From the **first law of thermodynamics**, we know that no energy can be created or destroyed, but it may be **converted** from one form to another. This does not mean that all forms of energy are useful. Indeed, the **second law** states that net useful energy **decreases** in every process that takes place. Most often this occurs when other forms of energy are converted to heat through means such as friction. In these cases, the heat is quickly absorbed into the surroundings and becomes unusable. There are many examples of energy conversion, such as in an automobile. The chemical energy in the gasoline is converted to mechanical energy in the engine. Subsequently, this mechanical energy is converted to kinetic energy as the car moves. Additionally, the mechanical energy is converted to electrical energy to power the radio, headlights, air conditioner, and other devices. In the radio, electrical energy is converted to sound energy. In the headlights, it is converted to heat and light energy. In the air conditioner, it does work to remove heat energy from the car's interior. It is important to remember that a portion of the energy is lost from its intended purpose in all of these processes.

Electronic Absorption and Emission Spectra

Electronic Energy Transition (Emission/Absorption of Energy) in Atoms

An electron must gain or absorb energy to **transition** to a higher or excited state, and the electron will emit that energy when it transitions back to the ground state. The **ground state** of an electron is the electron's lowest state of energy or when the electron is in the energy level that it normally occupies. An electron can gain energy if it absorbs a photon or collides with another particle. When an electron occupies an energy level higher that its normal level or ground state, it is in an excited state. The excited state is an unstable state, and the electron will return to the ground state as quickly as possible.

Absorption Spectroscopy and Emission Spectroscopy

When an electron makes a **quantum leap** from one electron shell to another, a **photon** is either **absorbed** or **emitted**. Because the energy levels of these shells are discrete, the energy of an absorbed or emitted photon is unique to a particular pair of shells. Thus, any element can be positively identified by the energy levels of the photons it emits.

Absorption Spectroscopy

Spectroscopy is most commonly used to determine the **composition of unknown compounds**. In absorption spectroscopy, a compound is bombarded with a full spectrum of photons, causing the compound to absorb those photons corresponding to its constituent elements' electron shell energy levels. By capturing and measuring the wavelengths of the photons **not absorbed**, it can be determined which wavelengths, and thus which energy levels, were absorbed, giving the identity of the elements contained in the compound. The resulting visible spectrum consists of color from red to violet with black bands at the wavelength of the absorbed photons.

EMISSION SPECTROSCOPY

Emission spectroscopy works in a similar fashion. The compound's electrons are excited by an application of energy and allowed to decay back down to lower energy levels. This decay is necessarily accompanied by an emission of photons, whose wavelengths are measured to determine the identity of the elements. The resulting visible spectrum consists of colored bands at the wavelengths of the emitted photons.

Nomenclature

NOMENCLATURE FOR INORGANIC COMPOUNDS

BINARY MOLECULAR COMPOUNDS

The names of binary molecular compounds follow this pattern:

prefix + first element name (space) prefix + root of second element name + -ide.

If a prefix ends with *a* or *o* and the element name begins with *a* or *o*, the ending *a* or *o* of the prefix is dropped. For example, N_2O_5 is named dinitrogen pentoxide. The prefix *mono-* is usually dropped unless more than one binary compound may be formed from the two elements involved.

Numeric Prefixes			
#	**Prefix**	**#**	**Prefix**
1	*mono-*	6	*hexa-*
2	*di-*	7	*hepta-*
3	*tri-*	8	*octa-*
4	*tetra-*	9	*nona-*
5	*penta-*	10	*deca-*

NAMING BINARY IONIC COMPOUNDS

The names of binary ionic compounds follow this pattern: cation name (space) anion name.

The name of **simple cations** is usually the element name. For example, the K^+ cation is named potassium. Some cations exist in more than one form. In those cases, the charge of the ion follows the element as a Roman numeral in parentheses. For example, the Cu^+ ion is named copper(I), and the Cu^{2+} ion is named copper(II). **Simple anions** are named with the root of the element name followed by the suffix *-ide.* For example, the O^{2-} anion is named oxide, and the F^- ion is named fluoride. The following are some examples of names of binary ionic compounds: KI is named potassium iodide, and FeO is named iron(II) oxide.

NAMING BINARY COMPOUNDS EXAMPLES

$$N_2O_4$$

The example above is a binary molecular compound. Using the prefixes *di-* for 2 and *tetra-* for 4, this compound is named dinitrogen tetroxide. Note that the entire element name is retained for the cation, but the root plus *-ide* is used for the anion name.

$$S_2F_{10}$$

This is a binary molecular compound. Using the prefixes *di-* for 2 and *deca-* for 10, this compound is named disulfur decafluoride. Note that the entire element name is retained for the cation, but the root plus *-ide* is used for the anion name.

$$Fe_2O_3$$

This is a binary ionic compound. Iron forms two types of cations Fe^{2+} and Fe^{3+}, but because the anion is O^{2-}, this must be the Fe^{3+} ion in order to balance the charges. This compound is named iron(III) oxide.

$$CuCl_2$$

This is a binary ionic compound. Copper forms two types of cations Cu^+ and Cu^{2+}, but because the anion is Cl^-, this must be the Cu^{2+} ion in order to balance the charges. This compound is named copper(II) chloride.

NAMING ACIDS

Acids are generally categorized as binary acids or oxyacids. **Binary acids** are named by the pattern: *hydro-* + root of element + *-ic* (space) acid. For example, HI is named hydroiodic acid, and HCl is named hydrochloric acid. One exception is that in hydrosulfuric acid (H_2S), the entire element name *sulfur* is used. The names of **oxyacids** depend on the endings of their polyatomic anions. If the polyatomic anions end in *-ate*, then the acid names end in *-ic*. If the anions end in *-ite*, the acid names end in *-ous*. The naming pattern for an oxyacid is as follows: anion root + ending (space) acid. For example, H_2CO_3 is named carbonic acid because the carbonate ion ends in *-ate*, and H_2SO_3 is named sulfurous acid because the sulfite ion ends in *-ite.*

NAMING HYDRATES

Hydrates form from salts (ionic compounds) that attract water. Hydrates are named from their salt (ionic compound) name and the number of water molecules involved, in the following pattern:

For example, the name of $CuSO_4 \cdot 5H_2O$ is copper(II) sulfate pentahydrate, and the name of $CoCl_2 \cdot 6H_2O$ is cobalt(II) chloride hexahydrate.

Hydrates			
#	**Prefix**	**#**	**Prefix**
1	mono-	6	hexa-
2	di-	7	hepta-
3	tri-	8	octa-
4	tetra-	9	nona-
5	penta-	10	deca-

NAMING SALTS

Salts are ionic compounds with any cation except H^+ from an aqueous base and any anion except OH^- from an aqueous acid. Salts are named like regular ionic compounds, with the name of the cation followed by the name of the anion. Examples of salts include sodium chloride (NaCl), potassium fluoride (KF), magnesium iodide (MgI_2), sodium acetate ($NaC_2H_3O_2$), and ammonium carbonate ($(NH_4)_2CO_3$).

NAMING BASES

Bases are typically ionic compounds with a hydroxide anion and are named following the conventions of naming ionic compounds. For example, NaOH is named sodium hydroxide, and $Mg(OH)_2$ is named magnesium hydroxide.

Nomenclature for Organic Compounds

Alkanes, Alkenes, and Alkynes

Alkanes, alkenes, and alkynes are organic compounds called **hydrocarbons**, which consist only of carbon and hydrogen. **Alkanes** have only single bonds between their carbon atoms. Alkanes are saturated hydrocarbons because they contain as many hydrogen atoms as possible due to their single bonds. Alkanes include methane (CH_4), ethane (C_2H_6), propane (C_3H_8), and butane (C_4H_{10}).

Alkenes have at least one double bond between two of their carbon atoms. Alkenes are unsaturated hydrocarbons. Alkenes include ethene or ethylene (C_2H_4), propene (C_3H_6), 1-butene (C_4H_8), and 1-pentene (C_5H_{10}).

Alkynes have at least one triple bond between two of their carbon atoms. Like alkenes, alkynes are unsaturated hydrocarbons. Alkynes include ethyne or acetylene (C_2H_2), 1-propyne (C_3H_4), 1-butyne (C_4H_6), and 1-pentyne (C_5H_8).

Review Video: Properties of Alkanes
Visit mometrix.com/academy and enter code: 903333

Review Video: Basics for Alkenes
Visit mometrix.com/academy and enter code: 916284

Review Video: Basics of Alkynes
Visit mometrix.com/academy and enter code: 963837

Naming Alkanes, Alkenes, and Alkynes

The prefixes of alkanes, alkenes, and alkynes are based on the number of carbon atoms. These prefixes are given by the table below. For example, an alkane with one carbon atom is named methane. An alkane with two carbon atoms would be named ethane. An alkene with two carbon atoms is named ethene. An alkene with five carbon atoms is named pentene. An alkyne with four carbon atoms is named butyne. An alkyne with eight carbon atoms is named octyne.

Hydrocarbons

#	Prefix	#	Prefix
1	meth-	6	hexa-
2	eth-	7	hepta-
3	prop-	8	octa-
4	but-	9	nona-
5	penta-	10	deca-

Review Video: Rules for Naming Alkanes, Alkenes, and Alkynes
Visit mometrix.com/academy and enter code: 441567

Alcohol

An **alcohol** is a substituted hydrocarbon compound with a hydroxyl group (—OH) bound to a saturated carbon. To name an alcohol, drop the *-e* from the name of the hydrocarbon and add *-ol.* For example, when the functional group for an alcohol replaces one hydrogen in methane, then the name is changed to methanol (left). Likewise, ethane becomes ethanol (right).

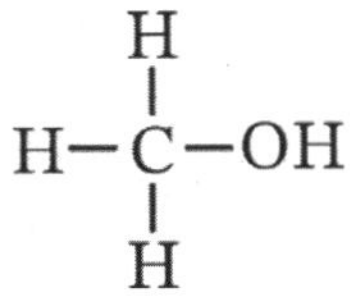

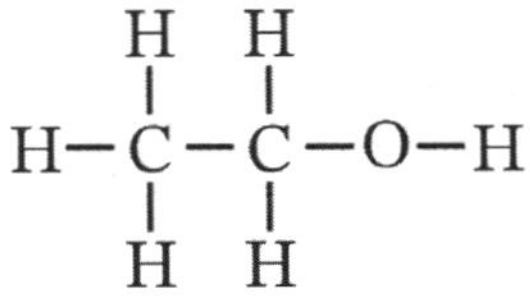

Review Video: Naming of Alcohols
Visit mometrix.com/academy and enter code: 737321

Ether

An **ether** is a substituted hydrocarbon compound containing an oxygen molecule linking two hydrocarbon groups. Ethers are named for the two hydrocarbons that flank the functional group. The root of the shorter of the two chains is named first. This is followed by *-oxy-*, which is then followed by the name of the longer chain. For example, $CH_3OCH_2CH_3$ (below) is named methoxyethane.

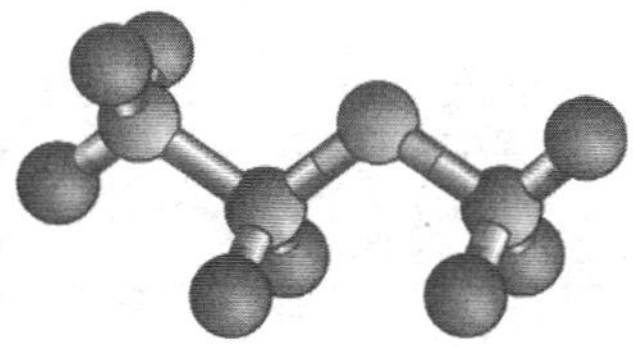

Aldehyde

An **aldehyde** is a substituted hydrocarbon compound with an oxygen molecule that is double bonded to the CH group at an end of a hydrocarbon chain. To name an aldehyde, drop the *-e* from the name of the hydrocarbon and add *-al*. For example, when the functional group for an aldehyde is substituted into methane, the aldehyde name would be methanal (below).

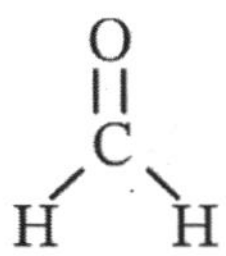

Ketone

A **ketone** is a substituted hydrocarbon compound containing an oxygen that is double bonded to a carbon atom somewhere within the hydrocarbon chain. The difference between a ketone and an aldehyde is that in an aldehyde the $= O$ will be at one or both ends of the hydrocarbon molecule, whereas in a ketone the $= O$ will be somewhere other than the end of the hydrocarbon molecule. To name a ketone, drop *-e* from the name of the hydrocarbon and add *-one.* For example, when the functional group for a ketone is inserted into propane, the name is changed to propanone, which is commonly known as acetone (below).

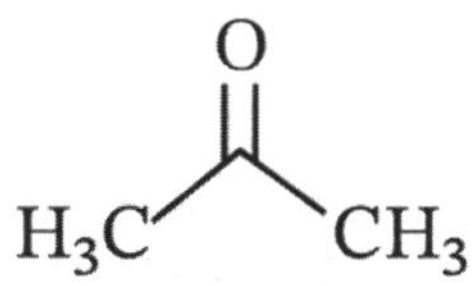

Carboxylic Acids

Carboxylic acids are organic compounds that contain a carboxyl functional group that consists of a carbon atom double-bonded to an oxygen and single-bonded to a hydroxyl ($-OH$). For example, the simplest carboxylic acid is formic acid, HCO_2H (left). Acetic acid or ethanoic acid, CH_3CO_2H (right), is commonly known as vinegar. Fatty acids and amino acids are also examples of carboxylic acids.

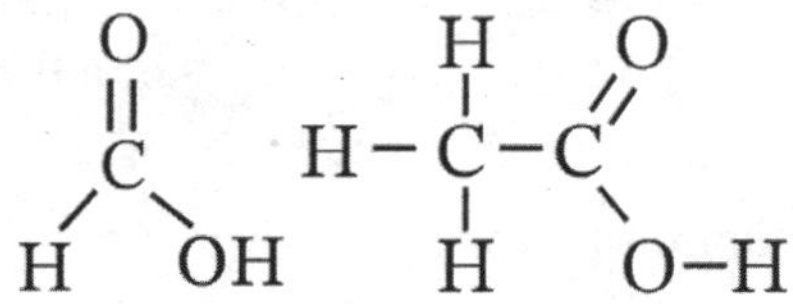

BENZENE

Benzene is an organic compound that is an aromatic hydrocarbon. Benzene has a molecular formula of C_6H_6, where the six carbon atoms are arranged in a "ring" shaped like a hexagon. Each carbon is single-bonded to two other carbons and single-bonded to one hydrogen. The remaining valence electrons from the six carbon atoms are delocalized electrons that are shared among all the carbons in the molecule.

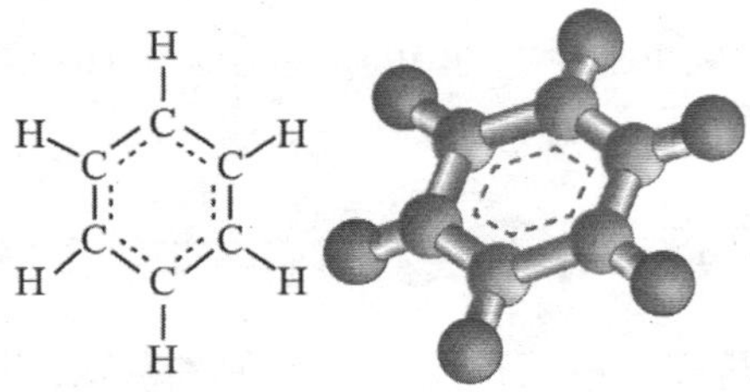

Derivatives of benzene include phenol, which is used in producing carbonates; toluene, which is used as a solvent and an octane booster in gasoline; and aniline, which is used in the production of polyurethane.

AMINE

An **amine** is a compound with a nitrogen atom that contains a lone pair of electrons and is bound to one or more hydrocarbon groups. Amines may be named in more than one way. The two most common ways are either with the prefix *amino-* or the suffix *-amine.* Two simple amines are methylamine (CH_3NH_2) and ethylamine ($CH_3CH_2NH_2$).

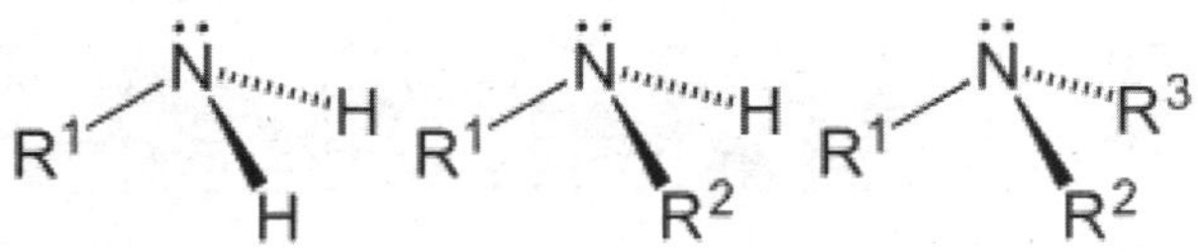

Molarity

MOLARITY

AVOGADRO'S NUMBER, MOLAR MASS, AND THE MOLE

Avogadro's number is equivalent to the number of atoms in 12 g of the carbon-12 isotope and is the definition of the quantity 1 mole. Avogadro's number is numerically equal to approximately 6.022×10^{23}. Just like a dozen eggs represents 12 eggs and a pair of shoes represents 2 shoes, a **mole** of atoms represents 6.022×10^{23} atoms. **Molar mass** is the mass of one mole of a substance in grams. As such, molar mass has units of grams per mole (g/mol).

Review Video: The Mole Concept
Visit mometrix.com/academy and enter code: 593205

Explain How to Determine the Mass of 2.50 moles of O_2. (The Atomic Mass of Oxygen is 16.0 u.)

To convert from moles of O_2 to mass in grams of O_2, use the dimensional analysis method with the molar mass of O_2. The molar mass of O_2 is 2(16.0 g/mol) or 32.0 g/mol. This molar mass can be written as the conversion factor $\left(\frac{32.0 \text{ g } O_2}{\text{mol } O_2}\right)$. Then, using dimensional analysis, multiply $(2.50 \text{ mol } O_2)\left(\frac{32.0 \text{ g } O_2}{\text{mol } O_2}\right)$. The "mol O_2" cancels from the numerator of the first factor and the denominator of the second factor, resulting in 80.0 g O_2.

Explain How to Determine the Number of Moles of $C_{12}H_{22}O_{11}$ in 100.0 g of This Substance. (The Atomic Masses of C, H, and O are 12.0 u, 1.0 u, and 16.0 u, Respectively.)

To find the number of moles in a sample of $C_{12}H_{22}O_{11}$, first calculate the molar mass to be used in dimensional analysis. The molar mass of $C_{12}H_{22}O_{11}$:

$$12(12.0 \text{ g}) + 22(1.0 \text{ g}) + 11(16.0 \text{ g}) = 144.0 \text{ g} + 22.0 \text{ g} + 176.0 \text{ g} = 342 \text{ g}$$

This means that every mole of $C_{12}H_{22}O_{11}$ has a molar mass of 342 g. To convert from grams to moles, use dimensional analysis as follows:

$$(100.0 \text{ g } C_{12}H_{22}O_{11})\left(\frac{1 \text{ mol } C_{12}H_{22}O_{11}}{342 \text{ g}}\right) = 0.292 \text{ mol}$$

Given the Reaction $3H_2(g) + N_2(g) \rightarrow 2NH_3(g)$, Determine How Many Grams of Nitrogen Gas Are Needed to Produce 100.0 g of Ammonia. (The Molar Mass of $N_2 = 28.0$ g; the Molar Mass of $NH_3 = 17.0$ g.)

One approach to working out this problem is to use the dimensional analysis method all the way through the work of the problem. Conversion factors using the molar masses of NH_3 and N_2 are used, as well as a mole ratio from the balanced chemical equation. The approach is to convert from grams of NH_3 to moles of NH_3, then to convert moles of NH_3 to moles of N_2, and finally to convert the moles of N_2 to grams of N_2.

$$\left(\frac{100.0 \text{ g } NH_3}{1}\right)\left(\frac{1 \text{ mol } NH_3}{17.0 \text{ g}}\right)\left(\frac{1 \text{ mol } N_2}{2 \text{ mol } NH_3}\right)\left(\frac{28.0 \text{ g } N_2}{1 \text{ mol } N_2}\right) = 82.4 \text{ g } N_2$$

Review Video: Concept of a Mole Ratio
Visit mometrix.com/academy and enter code: 747963

Calculating the Empirical Formula and the Molecular Formula of a Compound

To find the **empirical formula of a compound**, first, calculate the masses of each element in the compound based on the percent composition that is given. Then, convert these masses to moles by dividing by the molar masses of those elements. Next, divide these amounts in moles by the smallest calculated value in moles and round to the nearest tenth. These calculations provide the subscripts for each element in the empirical formula. To find the **molecular formula**, divide the actual molar mass of the compound by the molar mass of the empirical formula.

Show How to Find the Empirical Formula and the Molecular Formula for Hydrogen Peroxide Given That It Has a Composition of 5.94% Hydrogen and 94.1% Oxygen. (The Atomic Mass for Hydrogen is 1.008 u; The Atomic Mass of Oxygen is 16.00 u.)

To find the empirical formula, calculate the masses of each element in hydrogen peroxide for a sample size of 100.0 g. Calculating 5.94% of 100.0 g yields 5.94 g of hydrogen. Calculating 94.1% of 100.0 g yields 94.1 g of oxygen. Next, convert the masses of these elements to moles.

For hydrogen:

$$(5.94\text{ g})\left(\frac{\text{mol}}{1.008\text{ g}}\right) = 5.89\text{ mol}$$

For oxygen:

$$(94.1\text{ g})\left(\frac{\text{mol}}{16.00\text{ g}}\right) = 5.88\text{ mol}$$

Now, divide these amounts by the smallest value of moles that was calculated and round to the nearest tenth. For hydrogen, $\left(\frac{5.89}{5.88}\right) = 1.00$, and for oxygen, $\left(\frac{5.88}{5.88}\right) = 1.00$. These calculations are the subscripts for the empirical formula. Therefore, the empirical formula of hydrogen peroxide is HO. To find the molecular formula, find the molar mass of the empirical formula (HO) by adding $1.008\text{ g} + 16.00\text{ g} = 17.008\text{ g}$. To perform the calculation, the molar mass of hydrogen peroxide would need to be given. If the problem states that the actual molar mass of hydrogen peroxide is 34.016 g, divide this molar mass by the molar mass of the empirical formula: $\frac{34.016}{17.008} = 2$. Multiply each subscript of the empirical formula by 2. The molecular formula for hydrogen peroxide is H_2O_2.

Calculating Percent Composition When Given the Molecular Formula

Percent composition of a substance is a measure of the contibution of each element by mass to the total mass of the compound. To find the **percent composition** of a compound when given the molecular formula, start by finding find the molar mass of the compound. Then, find the percent contribution of each element of the compound by dividing the molar mass of the element (remembering to multiply through by the subscripts of the molecular formula) by the molar mass of the compound. Finally, check the calculations by totaling these individual percentages to ensure their combined total is 100%. This may be slightly off if any of the numbers used were rounded, but it should be very close.

Explain How to Find the Percent Composition of Methane (CH_4). (The Atomic Mass of Carbon = 12.01 u; the Atomic Mass of Hydrogen = 1.008 u.)

To find the percent composition of methane, first find the molar mass of methane. The molar mass of methane is given by $12.01\text{ g} + 4(1.008\text{ g}) = 16.042\text{ g}$. Next, find the percent contributed by the carbon and the percent contributed by the hydrogen. For the carbon, $\frac{12.01\text{ g/mol}}{16.042\text{ g/mol}} \times 100\% = 74.87\%$. For the hydrogen, $\frac{4(1.008)\text{ g/mol}}{16.042\text{ g/mol}} \times 100\% = 25.13\%$. Finally, check to see that the total of the calculated percentages sum to approximately 100%. For methane, $74.87\% + 25.13\% = 100\%$.

Thermodynamics

Chemical Reactions and Energy

Exothermic and Endothermic Reactions

Exothermic reactions **release** heat energy, whereas endothermic reactions **absorb** energy. Exothermic reactions can be represented by $reactants \rightarrow products + heat$. Endothermic reactions can be represented by $reactants + heat \rightarrow products$. The change in enthalpy for exothermic reactions is negative, whereas the change in enthalpy for endothermic reactions is positive. An example of an exothermic reaction is the burning of propane. An example of an endothermic reaction is the reaction that takes place in a first-aid cold pack.

Hess's Law

Bond energy is the energy needed to **break** or **form** a bond. Hess's law can be used to calculate bond energy. Usually, Hess's law is used to state the relationship between the enthalpies of formations of the reactants and the enthalpies of formation of the products of a reaction. Basically, Hess's law states that when reactants are converted to products, the total sum of the energy required to break the bonds of the reactants minus the total sum of energy required to form the bonds of the products is equal to the heat of the reaction. Enthalpies of formation are generally used in place of the actual bond energies because enthalpies of formation have been standardized whereas the bond energies of individual molecules vary. Hess's law is given by the equation $\Delta H^{\circ}_{reaction} = \sum \Delta H^{\circ}_{f(products)} - \sum \Delta H^{\circ}_{f(reactants)}$. It is important to note that in these equations the state of the components is important. The superscript ° means they are in the state of standard temperature and pressure.

Review Video: Standard Temperature and Pressure (STP)
Visit mometrix.com/academy and enter code: 995054

Explain How to Calculate the $\Delta H°$ for the Following Reaction: $3H_2(g) + N_2(g) \rightarrow 2NH_3(g)$ (Ammonia: $\Delta H^{\circ}_f = -46.19 \frac{kJ}{mol}$).

To calculate the ΔH° for the following reaction: $3H_2(g) + N_2(g) \rightarrow 2NH_3(g)$ given that for ammonia $\Delta H^{\circ}_f = -46.19 \frac{kJ}{mol}$, use the equation given by Hess's law:

$$\Delta H^{\circ}_{reaction} = \sum \Delta H^{\circ}_{f(products)} - \sum \Delta H^{\circ}_{f(reactants)}$$

Recall that the enthalpy of formation (ΔH°_f) of an element in its uncombined state is zero. The number of moles of each reactant and product is the coefficients from the balanced chemical equation. Substituting this information and the given information into the equation yields:

$$\begin{aligned}\Delta H^{\circ}_{reaction} &= \sum \Delta H^{\circ}_{f(products)} - \sum \Delta H^{\circ}_{f(reactants)} \\ &= \left[(2\text{ mol})\left(-46.19\ \frac{\text{kJ}}{\text{mol}}\right)\right] - \left[(3\text{ mol})\left(0\,\frac{\text{kJ}}{\text{mol}}\right) + (1\text{ mol})\left(0\ \frac{\text{kJ}}{\text{mol}}\right)\right] \\ &= -92.38\text{ kJ}\end{aligned}$$

Periodicity

Periodic Table Layout

Groups and Periods in the Periodic Table

A **group** is a vertical column of the periodic table. Elements in the same group have the same number of **valence electrons**. For the representative elements, the number of valence electrons is equal to the group number. Because of their equal valence electrons, elements in the same groups have similar physical and chemical properties. A **period** is a horizontal row of the periodic table. Atomic number increases from left to right across a row. The period of an element corresponds to the **highest energy level** of the electrons in the atoms of that element. The energy level increases from top to bottom down a group.

↓ Period / Group →	1	2	3	4	5	6	7	8	9	10	11	12	13	14	15	16	17	18
1	1 H																	2 He
2	3 Li	4 Be											5 B	6 C	7 N	8 O	9 F	10 Ne
3	11 Na	12 Mg											13 Al	14 Si	15 P	16 S	17 Cl	18 Ar
4	19 K	20 Ca	21 Sc	22 Ti	23 V	24 Cr	25 Mn	26 Fe	27 Co	28 Ni	29 Cu	30 Zn	31 Ga	32 Ge	33 As	34 Se	35 Br	36 Kr
5	37 Rb	38 Sr	39 Y	40 Zr	41 Nb	42 Mo	43 Tc	44 Ru	45 Rh	46 Pd	47 Ag	48 Cd	49 In	50 Sn	51 Sb	52 Te	53 I	54 Xe
6	55 Cs	56 Ba	*	72 Hf	73 Ta	74 W	75 Re	76 Os	77 Ir	78 Pt	79 Au	80 Hg	81 Tl	82 Pb	83 Bi	84 Po	85 At	86 Rn
7	87 Fr	88 Ra	**	104 Rf	105 Db	106 Sg	107 Bh	108 Hs	109 Mt	110 Ds	111 Rg	112 Cn	113 Uut	114 Fl	115 Uup	116 Lv	117 Uus	118 Uuo

*	57 La	58 Ce	59 Pr	60 Nd	61 Pm	62 Sm	63 Eu	64 Gd	65 Tb	66 Dy	67 Ho	68 Er	69 Tm	70 Yb	71 Lu
**	89 Ac	90 Th	91 Pa	92 U	93 Np	94 Pu	95 Am	96 Cm	97 Bk	98 Cf	99 Es	100 Fm	101 Md	102 No	103 Lr

Review Video: Periodic Table
Visit mometrix.com/academy and enter code: 154828

Atomic Number and Atomic Mass in the Periodic Table

The elements in the periodic table are arranged in order of **increasing atomic number**, first left to right and then top to bottom across the periodic table. The **atomic number** represents the number of protons in the atoms of that element. Because of the increasing numbers of protons, the atomic mass typically also increases from left to right across a period and from top to bottom down a row. The **atomic mass** is a weighted average of all the naturally occurring isotopes of an element.

Atomic Symbols

The **atomic symbol** for many elements is simply the first letter of the element name. For example, the atomic symbol for hydrogen is H, and the atomic symbol for carbon is C. The atomic symbol of other elements is the first two letters of the element name. For example, the atomic symbol for helium is He, and the atomic symbol for cobalt is Co. The atomic symbols of several elements are derived from Latin. For example, the atomic symbol for copper (Cu) is derived from *cuprum,* and the atomic symbol for iron (Fe) is derived from *ferrum.* The atomic symbol for tungsten (W) is derived from the German word *wolfram*.

ARRANGEMENT OF METALS, NONMETALS, AND METALLOIDS IN THE PERIODIC TABLE

The **metals** are located on the left side and center of the periodic table, and the **nonmetals** are located on the right side. The **metalloids** or **semimetals** form a zigzag line between the metals and nonmetals as shown below. Metals include the alkali metals, such as lithium, sodium, and potassium, and the alkaline earth metals, such as beryllium, magnesium, and calcium. Metals also include the transition metals, such as iron, copper, and nickel, and the inner transition metals, such as thorium, uranium, and plutonium. Nonmetals include the chalcogens, such as oxygen and sulfur; the halogens, such as fluorine and chlorine; and the noble gases, such as helium and argon. Carbon, nitrogen, and phosphorus are also nonmetals. Metalloids or semimetals include boron, silicon, germanium, antimony, and polonium.

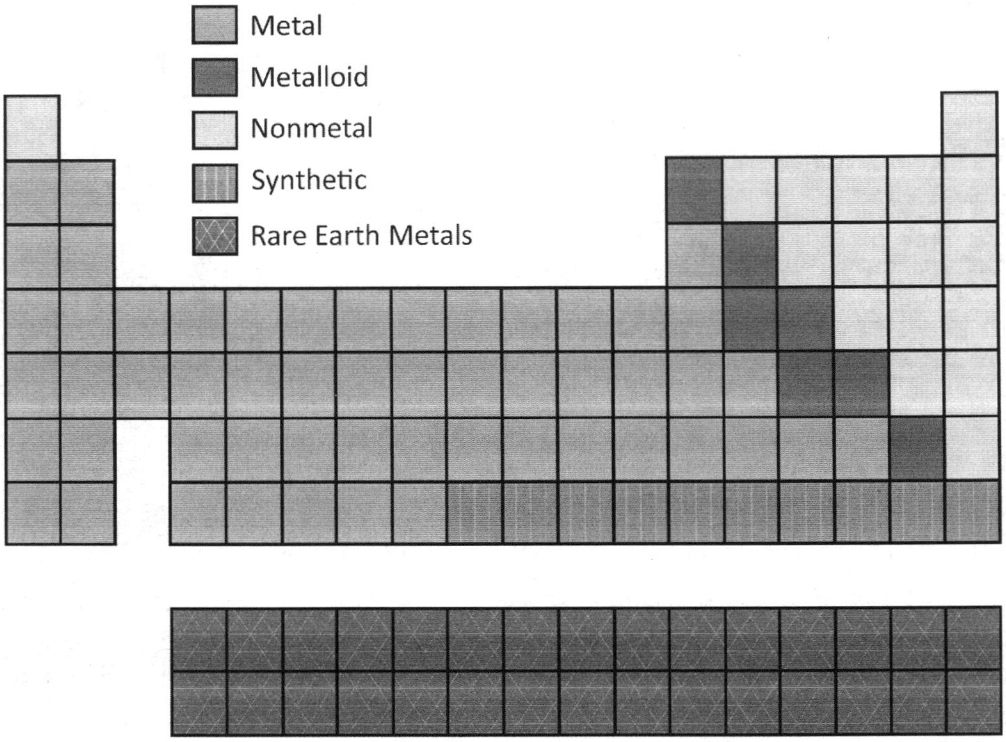

ARRANGEMENT OF TRANSITION ELEMENTS

The **transition elements** belong to one of two categories—transition metals or inner transition metals. The **transition metals** are located in the middle of the periodic table, and the inner transition metals are typically set off as two rows by themselves at the bottom of the periodic table. The transition metals correspond to the "*d* block" for orbital filling, and the inner transition metals correspond to the "*f* block" for orbital filling. Examples of transition metals include iron, copper, nickel, and zinc. The **inner transition metals** consist of the lanthanide or rare-earth series, which corresponds to the first row, and the actinide series, which corresponds to the second row of the inner transition metals. The **lanthanide series** includes lanthanum, cerium, and praseodymium. The **actinide series** includes actinium, uranium, and plutonium.

Periodic Trends

Atomic Radius Size

Atomic radius size decreases across a period from left to right and increases down a group from top to bottom. The atomic radius decreases across a period due to the increasing number of protons and the attraction between those protons and the orbiting electrons. The atomic radius increases down a group due to the increasing energy levels. Atoms in the top-right corner of the periodic table (including hydrogen) have the smallest atomic radii, and atoms in the bottom-left corner of the periodic table have the largest atomic radii. Helium has the smallest atomic radius, and cesium has the largest confirmed atomic radius.

Ionic Radius Size

The **ionic radius size** increases down a group of the periodic table. This is due to the increasing energy levels and the fact that electrons are orbiting farther and farther from the nucleus. The trend seen across the periods of the periodic table is due to the formation of cations or anions. Metals form cations or positive ions. Cations are smaller than their neutral atoms due to the loss of one or more electrons. Nonmetals except the noble gases form anions or negative ions. Anions are larger than their neutral atoms due to the gain of one or more electrons.

Ionization Energy

Ionization energy is the amount of energy needed to remove an electron from an isolated atom. Ionization energy decreases down a group of the periodic table because the electrons get farther and farther from the nucleus, making it easier for the electron to be removed. Ionization energy increases across a period of the periodic table due to the decreasing atomic size, which is due to the increasing number of protons attracting the electrons towards the nucleus. These trends of ionization energy are the opposite of the trends for atomic radius.

Electron Affinity

Electron affinity is the energy required to add an electron to a neutral atom in the gaseous phase of an element. If electrons are added to a halogen such as fluorine or chlorine, energy is released and the electron affinity is negative. If electrons are added to an alkaline earth metal, energy is absorbed and the electron affinity is positive. In general, electron affinity becomes more negative from left to right across a period in the periodic table. Electron affinity becomes less negative from the top to the bottom of a group of the periodic table.

Electronegativity

Electronegativity is a measure of the ability of an atom that is chemically combined to at least one other atom in a molecule to attract electrons to it. The Pauling scale is commonly used to assign values to the elements, with fluorine, which is the most electronegative element, being assigned a value of 4.0. Electronegativity increases from left to right across a period of the periodic table and decreases from top to bottom down a group of the periodic table.

Review Video: Electron Configuration
Visit mometrix.com/academy and enter code: 565113

Review Video: Electronegativity
Visit mometrix.com/academy and enter code: 823348

Physical Properties of the Elements in Relation to the Periodic Table

The **boiling point**, **melting point**, and **conductivity** of the elements depend partially on the number of valence electrons of the atoms of those elements. For the representative elements in groups 1A–8A, the number of valence electrons matches the group number. Because all of the elements in each individual group contain the same number of valence electrons, elements in the same groups tend to have similar boiling points, melting points, and conductivity. Boiling points and melting points tend to decrease moving down the column of groups 1A–4A and 8A but increase slightly moving down the column of groups 5A–7A.

Chemical Reactivity in Relation to the Periodic Table

Atoms of elements in the same **group** or **family** of the periodic table tend to have **similar chemical properties** and **similar chemical reactions**. For example, the alkali metals, which form cations with a charge of +1, tend to react with water to form hydrogen gas and metal hydroxides. The alkaline earth metals, which form cations with a charge of +2, react with oxygen gas to form metal oxides. The halogens, which form anions with a charge of –1, are highly reactive and toxic. The noble gases are unreactive and never form compounds naturally.

Bonds

Properties of Bonds

Relative Bond Length and Strength of Covalent Bonds

The **bond length of a covalent bond** is the distance between the nuclei of two covalently bonded atoms. The higher the bond order, the shorter the bond length. **Single bonds** are between one pair of electrons, and they are the weakest. Because single bonds (bond order 1) are the weakest, they are the longest of the three types of covalent bonds. **Double bonds** are between two pairs of electrons. Because double bonds (bond order 2) are stronger than single bonds, double bonds are shorter than single bonds. **Triple bonds** are between three pairs of electrons. Because triple bonds (bond order 3) are stronger than double bonds and single bonds, triple bonds have the shortest bond length.

Bond Types

Bonds

Chemical bonds are the attractive forces that bind atoms together into molecules. Atoms form chemical bonds in an attempt to satisfy the octet rule. These bond types include covalent bonds, ionic bonds, and metallic bonds. **Covalent bonds** are formed from the sharing of electron pairs between two atoms in a molecule. **Ionic bonds** are formed from the transferring of electrons between one atom and another, which results in the formations of cations and anions. **Metallic bonding** results from the sharing of delocalized electrons among all of the atoms in a molecule.

Ionic Bonding

Ionic bonding results from the transfer of electrons between atoms. A **cation** or positive ion is formed when an atom loses one or more electrons. An **anion** or negative ion is formed when an atom gains one or more electrons. An ionic bond results from the electrostatic attraction between a cation and an anion. One example of a compound formed by ionic bonds is sodium chloride or NaCl. Sodium (Na) is an alkali metal and tends to form Na^+ ions. Chlorine (Cl) is a halogen and tends to form Cl^- ions. The Na^+ ion and the Cl^- ion are attracted to each other. This electrostatic attraction between these oppositely charged ions is what results in the ionic bond between them.

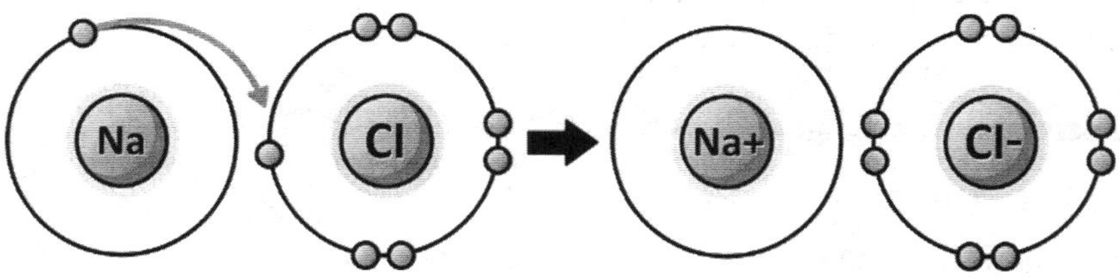

Review Video: Ionic Bonds
Visit mometrix.com/academy and enter code: 116546

COVALENT BONDING

Covalent bonding results from the sharing of electrons between atoms. Atoms seek to fill their valence shell and will share electrons with another atom in order to have a full octet (except hydrogen and helium, which only hold two electrons in their valence shells). **Molecular compounds** have covalent bonds. **Organic compounds** such as proteins, carbohydrates, lipids, and nucleic acids are molecular compounds formed by covalent bonds. Methane (CH_4) is a molecular compound in which one carbon atom is covalently bonded to four hydrogen atoms as shown below.

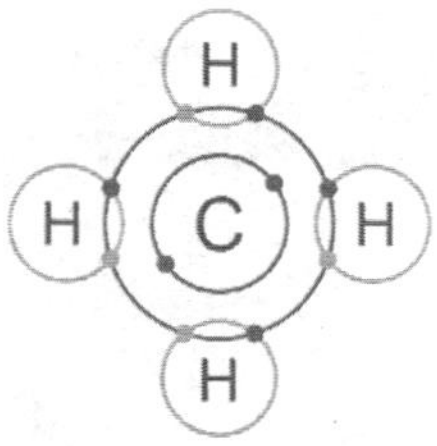

POLAR COVALENT BONDS, NONPOLAR COVALENT BONDS, AND HYBRIDIZATION

Polar covalent bonds result when electrons are shared unequally between atoms. **Nonpolar covalent bonds** result when electrons are shared equally between atoms. The unequal sharing of electrons is due to the differences in the electronegativities of the two atoms sharing the electrons. Partial charges develop due to this unequal sharing of electrons. The greater the difference in electronegativities between the two atoms, the stronger the dipole is. For example, the covalent bonds formed between the carbon atom and the two oxygen atoms in carbon dioxide are polar covalent bonds because the electronegativities of carbon and oxygen differ slightly. If the electronegativities are equal, then the covalent bonds are nonpolar. For example, the covalent double bond between two oxygen atoms is nonpolar because the oxygen atoms have the same electronegativities.

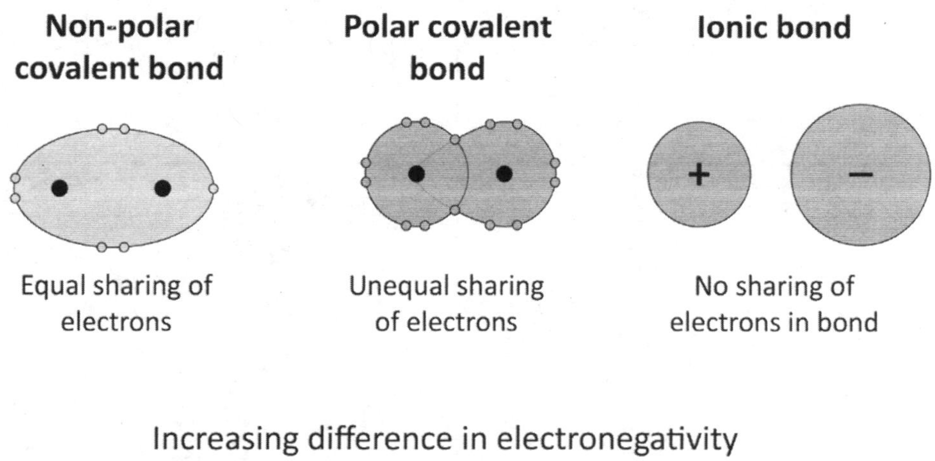

Review Video: Nonpolar Covalent Bonds
Visit mometrix.com/academy and enter code: 986465

Review Video: Covalent Bonds
Visit mometrix.com/academy and enter code: 482899

Metallic Bonding

Metallic bonding is a type of bonding between metals. Metallic bonds are similar to covalent bonds in that they are a type of sharing of electrons between atoms. However, in covalent bonding, the electrons are shared with only one other atom. In metallic bonding, the electrons are shared with all the surrounding atoms. These electrons are referred to as delocalized electrons. Metallic bonding is responsible for many of the characteristics in metals including conductivity, malleability, and ductility. An example of metallic bonding is the metallic bond between the copper atoms in a piece of copper wire.

Review Video: Metallic Bonds
Visit mometrix.com/academy and enter code: 230855

Shape of Bonds

Drawing a Lewis Structure

In order to draw a **Lewis structure** for a molecule, determine the number of **valence electrons** for each atom in the molecule and the number of valence electrons each atom needs in order to have a full outer shell. All atoms except hydrogen and helium seek to have eight electrons in their outer shells. Hydrogen and helium only have room for two valence electrons. Next, determine the **central atom**. Usually, the central atom is the atom with the largest number of valence openings. Draw the skeletal structure with the central atom. Each single bond represents two electrons. Each double bond represents four electrons. Each triple bond represents six electrons. Start with single bonds and change to double or triple bonds as needed to satisfy the octet rule. But remember, atoms may only share what they have available. For example, elements in group IIIA have three valence electrons and need an additional five electrons to make eight, but they may only share the three that they have available. Add the remaining valence electrons to all the atoms. Check to make sure that each atom (except hydrogen, helium, and boron) satisfies the octet rule.

Examples of Lewis Structures:

NH_3	H_2O
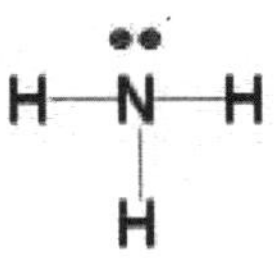	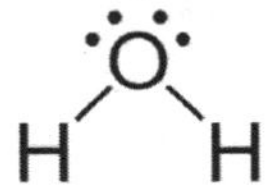
CCl_4	BF_3
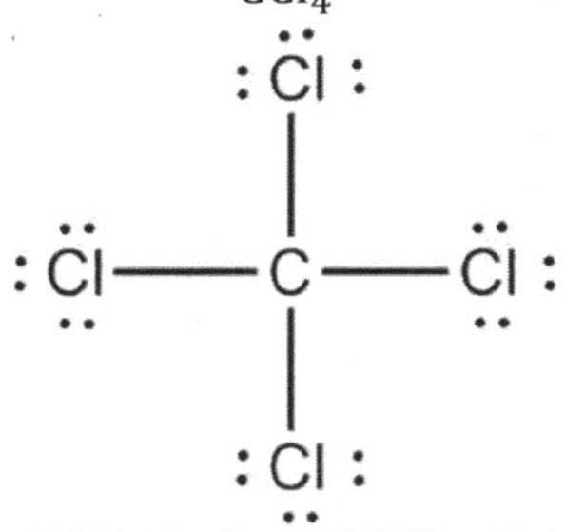	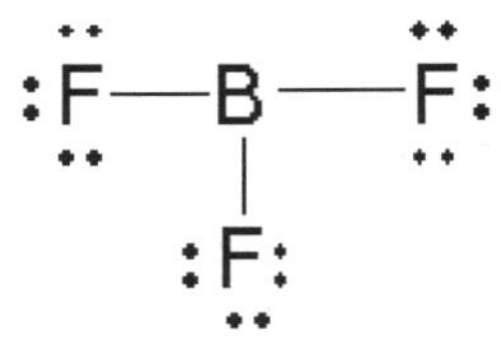

Resonance Structures

For some molecules, more than one Lewis structure may be drawn due to the delocalization of electrons. In order to determine which resonance structure is the most stable, calculate the formal charge of each structure. The structure with the lowest formal charge is the most stable. The actual molecule is a hybrid of all the possible Lewis structures. An example of resonance occurs in benzene, C_6H_6. The two possible Lewis structures for benzene are shown below. The only difference between the two Lewis structures is the placement of the single and double bonds between the carbon atoms.

Studies show that in reality, **neither Lewis structure is correct**. In fact, all the bonds between the carbon atoms are exactly the same. The structure of the resonance hybrid of benzene is often represented by the drawing shown below. The circle inside the ring of carbons represents the delocalized electrons that are shared among all the carbon atoms of the ring.

Possible Lewis Structures Resonance Hybrid

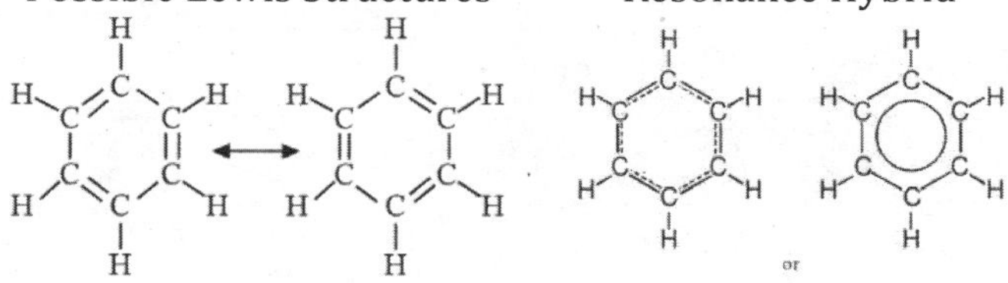

LINEAR MOLECULAR GEOMETRY

Linear: All diatomic molecules are linear molecules. Also, molecules with two bonding groups and two nonbonding pairs of electrons are linear. The bond angle measurement for linear molecules is 180°. Nitric oxide (also called nitrogen monoxide) is an example of a linear molecule.

TRIGONAL PLANAR MOLECULAR GEOMETRY

Trigonal planar: For a trigonal planar molecule, the central atom has three bonding pairs of electrons and zero nonbonding pairs. These molecules are an exception to the octet rule. The bond angle measurement for trigonal planar molecules is 120°. Boron trifluoride (BF_3), which has has three bonding pairs and zero nonbonding pairs around the central atom, is an example of a trigonal planar molecule.

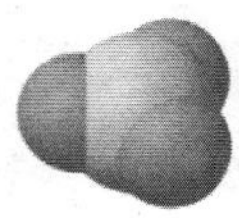

ANGULAR MOLECULAR GEOMETRY

Angular: For an angular molecule, the central atom has two bonding pairs of electrons and one or two nonbonding pairs. The bond angle measurement for angular molecules is less than 120° if there is one nonbonding pair, and less than 109° if there are two. Oxygen difluoride (OF_2), which has two bonding pairs and two nonbonding pairs around the central angle, is an example of an angular molecule.

TETRAHEDRAL MOLECULAR GEOMETRY

Tetrahedral: For a tetrahedral molecule, the central atom has four bonding pairs of electrons and zero nonbonding pairs. The bond angle measurement for tetrahedral molecules is 109.5°. Methane (CH_4), which has four bonding pairs and zero nonbonding pairs around the central angle, is an example of a tetrahedral molecule.

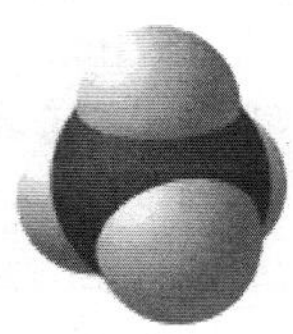

Trigonal Pyramidal Molecular Geometry

Trigonal pyramidal: For a trigonal pyramidal molecule, the central atom has three bonding pairs and one nonbonding pair. The bond angle measurement for trigonal pyramidal molecules is less than 109.5°. Ammonia (NH_3), which has three bonding pairs and one nonbonding pair around the central atom, is an example of a trigonal pyramidal molecule.

Polar and Nonpolar Molecules

Covalently bonded molecules are either **polar** or **nonpolar** depending on the type and arrangement of their covalent bonds. **Covalent bonds** are polar if the electronegativities of the two atoms sharing the pair of electrons differ. With differing electronegativities, the electrons are shared unequally, with the pair of electrons displaced more toward the more electronegative atom. This results in a polar covalent bond. **Covalent molecules** always have polar covalent bonds. If the bonds are arranged symmetrically around a central atom, the polar bonds will "cancel" each other out, resulting in a nonpolar molecule. If a molecule contains polar covalent bonds that are not arranged symmetrically in a way to "cancel" each other out, the molecule is polar. Molecules with only nonpolar covalent bonds are always nonpolar. Only molecules with polar covalent bonds can be polar.

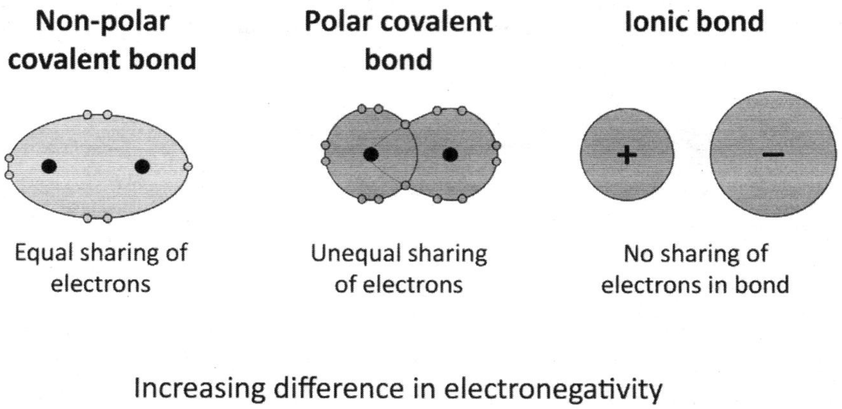

Identifying Polar or Nonpolar Examples:

CH_4

Nonpolar: Methane, or CH_4 has a tetrahedral geometry with four hydrogen atoms covalently bonded around the central carbon atom. These four bonds are polar covalent bonds, but because they are arranged symmetrically around the central carbon atom, the molecule is nonpolar.

CO_2

Nonpolar: Carbon dioxide, or CO_2, is a linear molecule with two oxygen atoms covalently double bonded to a central carbon atom. These two double bonds are polar covalent bonds, but because they are arranged symmetrically around the carbon atom, the molecule is nonpolar.

H_2S

Polar: Dihydrogen sulfide, or H_2S, is an angular molecule with the two hydrogen atoms covalently bonded to a sulfur atom. This molecule has two bonding pairs and one nonbonding pair. Because of the nonbonding pair, the molecule is bent or angular. Because the polar bonds do not cancel each other out in this arrangement, the molecule is polar.

NH_3

Polar: Ammonia, or NH_3, is a trigonal pyramidal molecule with the three hydrogen atoms bonded asymmetrically around the central nitrogen atom. The molecule has three bonding pairs and one nonbonding pair of electrons. Because the polar covalent bonds are arranged asymmetrically, the molecule is polar.

BF_3

Nonpolar: Boron trifluoride, or BF_3, is a trigonal planar molecule with three fluorine atoms bonded symmetrically around the central boron atom. Because the molecule is an exception to the octet rule and only has three bonding pairs and no nonbonding pairs around the central boron atom, these fluorine atoms are arranged symmetrically around the boron atom canceling out the effect of the polar covalent bonds and resulting in a nonpolar molecule.

INTERMOLECULAR INTERACTIONS

HYDROGEN BONDING

Hydrogen bonding is a type of intermolecular force present between molecules containing hydrogen atoms covalently bonded to oxygen, fluorine, or nitrogen. Hydrogen bonding is the strongest of the intermolecular forces. When hydrogen from one molecule is near a highly electronegative atom such as oxygen, fluorine, or nitrogen in another molecule and acts as a bridge between another highly electronegative atom, a hydrogen bond is formed. Hydrogen bonding is responsible for the high boiling point in water and for the crystalline structure of ice.

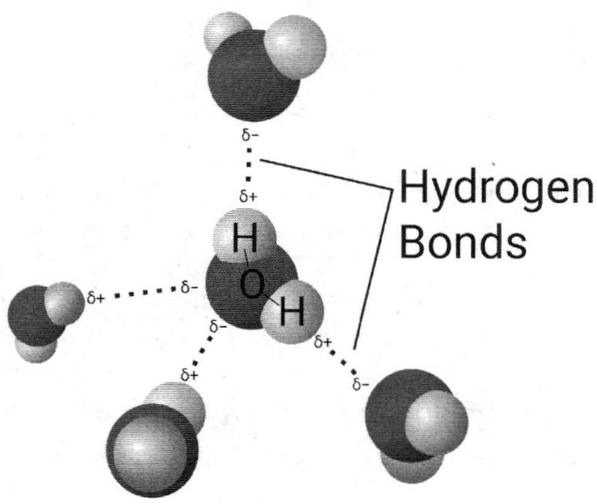

DIPOLE-INDUCED DIPOLE INTERMOLECULAR FORCES

Whereas **dipole–dipole intermolecular forces** are between two polar molecules, **a dipole-induced intermolecular force** is between a polar molecule and a nonpolar molecule. Dipole-induced dipole intermolecular forces are forces that occur when a dipole induces a temporary dipole in a molecule that is nonpolar. The electron cloud of the nonpolar molecule is distorted when it comes near the electron cloud of a dipole. This is typically a weak intermolecular force. However, this dipole-induced dipole intermolecular force is responsible for the stability of hydrates formed from hydrocarbons and some of the noble gases.

Dipole–Dipole Intermolecular Forces

Dipole-dipole forces are intermolecular forces that occur only between polar molecules. Polar molecules have positive and negative ends because of an unequal sharing of electrons due to differences in electronegativities between the atoms of the molecules. The positive end of one molecule is attracted to the negative end of the other molecules. Dipole–dipole forces are stronger than London (dispersion) forces but weaker than hydrogen bonds. In the figure below, the dipole–dipole force between the positive end of one hydrogen chloride molecule and the negative end of another hydrogen chloride molecule is indicated by the dashed line.

$$\overset{\delta+}{H}—\overset{\delta-}{Cl}\text{- - - -}\overset{\delta+}{H}—\overset{\delta-}{Cl}$$

London Forces

London forces are intermolecular forces that exist between all molecules due to the temporary instantaneous dipoles induced by an unequal distribution of electrons around a molecule. London forces are present between all molecules of liquids, solids, and gases. London forces are the weakest of the intermolecular forces and the only intermolecular forces present between nonpolar molecules. London forces are also known as London dispersion forces or dispersion forces. London forces are weaker than both dipole–dipole forces and hydrogen bonds.

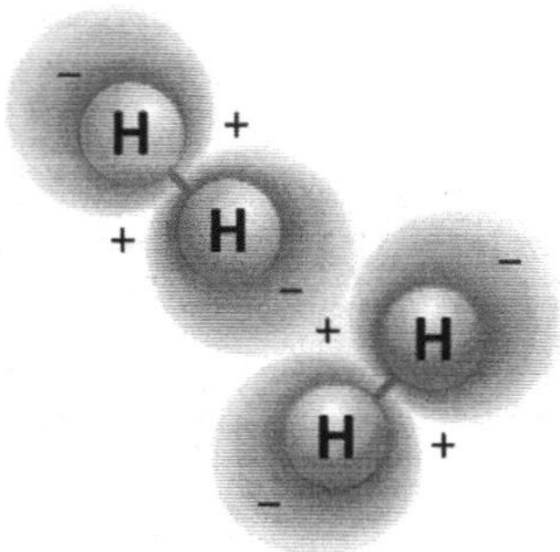

Intermolecular Interactions Examples

NH_3

The intermolecular forces present in a sample of NH_3 are London forces and hydrogen bonds. London forces are present between all molecules. Hydrogen bonds are present between molecules with hydrogen covalently bonded to nitrogen, fluorine, and oxygen.

CH_4

The intermolecular forces present in a sample of CH_4 are only London forces. London forces are present between all molecules. Because CH_4 is a nonpolar molecular molecule, no dipole–dipole forces are present.

H_2S

The intermolecular forces present in a sample of H_2S are London forces and dipole–dipole forces. London forces are present between all molecules. Dipole–dipole forces are present between polar molecules, and because H_2S is a polar molecule, dipole–dipole forces are present.

Effect of Bonds on Physical Properties

Bonding and Structure

Properties Affected by Bonding and Structure

Bonding and structure determine whether a substance exists naturally as a solid, liquid, or gas. Properties that are affected by bonding and structure include boiling point, freezing point, and vapor pressure. Bonding and structure determine if a substance is soluble in water or in nonpolar solvents. Also affected are the viscosity of liquids, whether a solid material is hard or soft, and whether or not a substance forms crystals or is amorphous. Bonding affects the conductivity of heat and electricity and thus whether a substance is a good insulator or conductor.

Effect of Bonding and Structure on Boiling Points and Melting Points

The types of bonds within molecules affect boiling and melting points. **Compounds with ionic bonds** typically have high melting and boiling points, whereas **compounds with covalent bonds** typically have low melting and boiling points. Intermolecular forces also affect these points. Substances with hydrogen bonds typically have high boiling and melting points. For example, hydrogen bonds are responsible for the high boiling and melting points of water.

Review Video: Differences in Boiling Points
Visit mometrix.com/academy and enter code: 810110

Effect of Bonding and Structure on Solubility

Bonding and structure affect **solubility**. The basic idea behind solubility is *like dissolves like.* This means that solutes with polar molecules typically dissolve in solvents with polar molecules. The polarity of the molecules is determined by the type of bonds and the arrangement of those bonds in the molecules. For example, both salt and table sugar (sucrose) dissolve in water because salt, table sugar, and water are all polar molecules. Solutes with nonpolar molecules typically dissolve in solvents with nonpolar molecules. For example, a grease stain will not rinse out with water because water consists of polar molecules and grease is a nonpolar lipid.

Effect of Bonding and Structure on Equilibrium Vapor Pressure

Vapor pressure is related to the **boiling point** of a substance. The boiling point of a substance is the temperature at which the vapor pressure equals the atmospheric pressure. In general, as the vapor pressure increases, the boiling point decreases. Compounds with ionic bonds typically have high boiling points and low vapor pressures. Compounds with covalent bonds typically have low boiling points and high vapor pressures. Substances with the strongest intermolecular forces, hydrogen bonds, typically have high boiling points and low vapor pressures.

Chemical Reactions

Balancing Chemical Equations

Balancing a Chemical Equation

According to the law of conservation of mass, the **mass of the products** must always equal the **mass of the reactants** in a **chemical reaction**. Because mass is conserved and it is a chemical reaction (as opposed to a nuclear reaction), the number of each type of atom in the products must equal the number of each type of atom in the reactants. The key to balancing a chemical reaction is balancing the number of atoms of each element on both sides of the equation. Only the coefficients in front of the reactants and products may be changed to accomplish this, not the subscripts in the molecules themselves. Try balancing the largest number of a type of atom first. Also, check if any odd numbers need to be changed to even. Always leave the uncombined elements to balance until the end.

Review Video: Balancing Chemical Equations
Visit mometrix.com/academy and enter code: 341228

Balance the Equation $KNO_3(s) \rightarrow KNO_2(s) + O_2(g)$.

First, determine the types and numbers of each type of atom on each side of the equation:

Element	Reactants	Products
K	1	1
N	1	1
O	3	4

"Oxygen" needs to be balanced. Add a coefficient of "2" to the left side to force "oxygen" to be even and update the counts:

Element	Reactants	Products
K	2	1
N	2	1
O	6	4

Now, balance the potassium and nitrogen by placing a coefficient of "2" in front of the KNO_2 and update the counts:

Element	Reactants	Products
K	2	2
N	2	2
O	6	6

The equation is now balanced: $2KNO_3(s) \rightarrow 2KNO_2(s) + O_2(g)$.

Balance the Equation $C_2H_2(g) + O_2(g) \rightarrow CO_2(g) + H_2O(g)$.

First, determine the types and numbers of each type of atom on each side of the equation:

Element	Reactants	Products
C	2	1
H	2	2
O	2	3

Oxygen needs to be balanced, but remember to leave the uncombined oxygen reactant until the end. Carbon also needs to be balanced. Add a coefficient of "4" to the CO_2 on the right side and a coefficient of "2" in front of the C_2H_2 and update the counts:

Element	Reactants	Products
C	4	4
H	4	4
O	2	9

Balance the hydrogen by adding a "2" in front of the H_2O and update the counts:

Element	Reactants	Products
C	4	4
H	4	4
O	2	10

Finally, balance the oxygen by adding a "5" in front of the O_2 on the left.

The equation is now balanced: $2C_2H_2(g) + 5O_2(g) \rightarrow 4CO_2(g) + 2H_2O(g)$.

Element	Reactants	Products
K	4	4
N	4	4
O	10	10

Chemical Equation Balancing Practice

Given the Following Equation at Standard Temperature and Pressure (STP): $4Fe(s) + 3O_2(g) \rightarrow 2Fe_2O_3(s)$, Determine the Volume of $O_2(g)$ Needed to Produce 10.0 mol of $Fe_2O_3(s)$.

One method to determine the volume of $O_2(g)$ needed to produce 10.0 mol of $Fe_2O_3(s)$ is to use dimensional analysis with the mole ratio for the balanced chemical equation. Because 3 mol of $O_2(g)$ produce 2 mol of $Fe_2O_3(s)$, the needed mole ratio is $\left(\frac{3 \text{ mol } O_2}{2 \text{ mol } Fe_2O_3}\right)$. Also, at STP, one mole of a gas has a volume of 22.4 L. This can be written as a conversion factor of $\left(\frac{22.4 \text{ L}}{1 \text{ mol } O_2}\right)$. Using dimensional analysis:

$$(10.0 \text{ mol } Fe_2O_3)\left(\frac{3 \text{ mol } O_2}{2 \text{ mol } Fe_2O_3}\right)\left(\frac{22.4 \text{ L}}{1 \text{ mol } O_2}\right) = 336 \text{ L}$$

Given the Following Equation at STP: $C_3H_8(l) + 5O_2(g) \rightarrow 3CO_2(g) + 4H_2O(g)$, Determine the Volume of $O_2(g)$ Needed to Burn 1.00 kg of $C_3H_8(l)$.

One method to determine the volume of $O_2(g)$ needed to burn 1.0 kg of $C_3H_8(l)$ is to use dimensional analysis with conversion factors for the molar mass, number of moles, and liters of gas at STP. The conversion factor for the molar mass of C_3H_8 can be written as $\left(\frac{1 \text{ mol } C_3H_8}{44.1 \text{ grams } C_3H_8}\right)$. Because 1 mol of $C_3H_8(l)$ requires 5 mol of $O_2(g)$, the needed mole ratio is $\left(\frac{5 \text{ mol } O_2}{1 \text{ mol } C_3H_8}\right)$.

Also, at STP, one mole of a gas has a volume of 22.4 L. This can be written as the conversion factor $\left(\frac{22.4 \text{ L}}{1 \text{ mol } O_2}\right)$. Using dimensional analysis:

$$(1.0 \text{ kg } C_3H_8)\left(\frac{1000 \text{ g}}{1 \text{ kg}}\right)\left(\frac{1 \text{ mol } C_3H_8}{44.1 \text{ g } C_3H_8}\right)\left(\frac{5 \text{ mol } O_2}{1 \text{ mol } C_3H_8}\right)\left(\frac{22.4 \text{ L } O_2}{1 \text{ mol } O_2}\right) = 2.54 \times 10^3 \text{ L } O_2$$

Given the Following Equation: $2Na(s) + Cl_2(g) \rightarrow 2NaCl(s)$, Determine the Amount in Grams of $Na(s)$ Needed to Produce 500.0 g of $NaCl(s)$.

One method to determine the amount in grams of $Na(s)$ needed to produce 500.0 g of $NaCl(s)$ is to use dimensional analysis with conversion factors for the molar mass and number of moles. The conversion factor for the molar mass of NaCl can be written as $\left(\frac{1 \text{ mol NaCl}}{58.44 \text{ g NaCl}}\right)$. Because 2 mol of $Na(s)$ produce 2 mol of $NaCl(s)$, the needed mole ratio is $\left(\frac{2 \text{ mol Na}}{2 \text{ mol NaCl}}\right)$. The conversion factor for the molar mass of $Na(s)$ can be written as $\left(\frac{22.99 \text{ g Na}}{1 \text{ mol Na}}\right)$. Using dimensional analysis:

$$(500.0 \text{ g NaCl})\left(\frac{1 \text{ mol NaCl}}{58.44 \text{ g NaCl}}\right)\left(\frac{2 \text{ mol Na}}{2 \text{ mol NaCl}}\right)\left(\frac{22.99 \text{ g Na}}{1 \text{ mol Na}}\right) = 196.7 \text{ g Na(s)}$$

Given the Following Equation at STP: $2Na(s) + Cl_2(g) \rightarrow 2NaCl(s)$, Determine the Volume in whole Liters of $Cl_2(g)$ Needed to Produce 1.00 kg of NaCl(s).

One method to determine the volume of $Cl_2(g)$ needed to produce 1.00 kg of NaCl(s) is to use dimensional analysis with conversion factors for the molar mass, number of moles, and liters of gas at STP. The conversion factor for the molar mass of NaCl can be written as $\left(\frac{1 \text{ mol NaCl}}{58.44 \text{ g NaCl}}\right)$. Because 1 mol of $Cl_2(g)$ produces 2 mol of NaCl(s), the needed mole ratio is $\left(\frac{1 \text{ mol } Cl_2}{2 \text{ mol NaCl}}\right)$. Also, at STP, one mole of a gas has a volume of 22.4 L. This can be written as a conversion factor $\left(\frac{22.4 \text{ L}}{1 \text{ mol } Cl_2}\right)$. Using dimensional analysis:

$$(1.00 \text{ kg NaCl})\left(\frac{1000 \text{ g}}{1 \text{ kg}}\right)\left(\frac{1 \text{ mol NaCl}}{58.44 \text{ g NaCl}}\right)\left(\frac{1 \text{ mol } Cl_2}{2 \text{ mol NaCl}}\right)\left(\frac{22.4 \text{ L } O_2}{1 \text{ mol } O_2}\right) = 191.65 \text{ L } Cl_2$$

This rounds up to 192 L because 191 L will not be enough.

Given that 100.0 g of $H_2(g)$ React with 350.0 g of $O_2(g)$, Determine the Limiting Reactant and the Amount of Excess Reactant That Remains $2H_2(g) + O_2(g) \rightarrow 2H_2O(g)$.

To determine the limiting reactant, first determine the amount of H_2O that can be produced from each of the reactants:

$$(100.0 \text{ g } H_2)\left(\frac{1 \text{ mol } H_2}{2.016 \text{ g } H_2}\right)\left(\frac{2 \text{ mol } H_2O}{2 \text{ mol } H_2}\right)\left(\frac{18.016 \text{ g } H_2O}{1 \text{ mol } H_2O}\right) = 893.7 \text{ g } H_2O$$

$$(350.0 \text{ g } O_2)\left(\frac{1 \text{ mol } O_2}{32.00 \text{ g } O_2}\right)\left(\frac{2 \text{ mol } H_2O}{1 \text{ mol } O_2}\right)\left(\frac{18.016 \text{ g } H_2O}{1 \text{ mol } H_2O}\right) = 394.1 \text{ g } H_2O$$

Because O_2 produces the least amount of H_2O, O_2 is the limiting reagent. Therefore, H_2 is the reactant that is in excess. Calculating the amount of H_2 consumed in this reaction:

$$(350.0 \text{ g } O_2)\left(\frac{1 \text{ mol } O_2}{32.00 \text{ g } O_2}\right)\left(\frac{2 \text{ mol } H_2}{1 \text{ mol } O_2}\right)\left(\frac{2.016 \text{ g } H_2}{1 \text{ mol } H_2}\right) = 44.10 \text{ g } H_2 \ (consumed)$$

Subtracting this amount from the original amount yields the excess amount

$$100.0 \text{ g } H_2 - 44.10 \text{ g } H_2 = 55.91 \text{ g } H_2 \ (excess)$$

Find the Percent Yield in the Following Reaction if 200.0 g of Solid $KClO_3$. Produced 100.0 g of Solid KCl: $2KClO_3(s) \rightarrow 2KCl(s) + 3O_2(g)$.

To calculate the percent yield if 200.0 g of solid $KClO_3$ produced 100.0 g of solid KCl, first calculate the theoretical yield of KCl or the maximum amount of KCl that can be produced.

Theoretical yield:

$$(200.0 \text{ g } KClO_3)\left(\frac{1 \text{ mol } KClO_3}{122.6 \text{ g } KClO_3}\right)\left(\frac{2 \text{ mol KCl}}{2 \text{ mol } KClO_3}\right)\left(\frac{74.55 \text{ g KCl}}{1 \text{ mol KCl}}\right) = 121.6 \text{ g KCl}$$

The formula to calculate percent yield is $\frac{\text{actual yield}}{\text{theoretical yield}} \times 100\%$. Substituting in the 100.0 g of KCl for the actual yield and the 121.6 g of KCl for the theoretical yield:

$$\text{Percent yield} = \frac{100.0\text{ g}}{121.6\text{ g}} \times 100\% = 82.24\%$$

Review Video: How to Calculate Percent Yield
Visit mometrix.com/academy and enter code: 565738

WRITE A BALANCED EQUATION FOR THE COMBUSTION OF METHANE.

The molecular formula for methane is CH_4. For a combustion equation, the reactants are methane (CH_4) and oxygen gas (O_2). The products of this combustion reaction are water vapor (H_2O) and carbon dioxide (CO_2). Setting up the equation yields the following reaction:

$$CH_4(g) + O_2(g) \rightarrow CO_2(g) + H_2O(g)$$

This equation must still be balanced. Finally, the combustion of methane is given by the following reaction:

$$CH_4(g) + 2O_2(g) \rightarrow CO_2(g) + 2H_2O(g)$$

Review Video: Combustion
Visit mometrix.com/academy and enter code: 592219

WRITE A BALANCED EQUATION FOR THE NEUTRALIZATION OF HYDROCHLORIC ACID, $HCl(aq)$, WITH SODIUM HYDROXIDE, $NaOH(aq)$.

In a neutralization reaction, an acid reacts with a base to form a salt and water. The salt forms from the cation of the base and the anion of the acid. The salt formed from these reactants is NaCl with the Na^+ from the base and the Cl^- from the acid. Water forms from the remaining H^+ and OH^- ions:

$$\text{acid} + \text{base} \rightarrow \text{salt} + \text{water}$$
$$HCl(aq) + NaOH(aq) \rightarrow NaCl(aq) + H_2O(l)$$

WRITE A BALANCED EQUATION FOR THE DECOMPOSITION REACTION OF SOLID LITHIUM CARBONATE (Li_2CO_3).

The general form for a decomposition reaction is AB → A + B. However, this metal oxide has three elements and may not seem to fit the general form at first. When many metal carbonates are heated, they form the metal oxide and carbon dioxide gas. In this case, the products will also be compounds. In this decomposition reaction, when heated, solid lithium oxide decomposes to form solid lithium oxide and gaseous carbon dioxide:

$$Li_2CO_3(s) \xrightarrow{\Delta} LiO(s) + CO_2(g)$$

WRITE A BALANCED EQUATION FOR THE DEHYDRATION OF ETHANOL.

Ethanol (C_2H_5OH) can be dehydrated to produce ethene (C_2H_4). The gaseous ethanol is passed over a hot aluminum oxide catalyst to produce ethene and water.

$$\text{ethanol} \xrightarrow{\text{aluminum oxide}} \text{ethene} + \text{water}$$

$$C_2H_5OH(g) \xrightarrow{Al_2O_3} C_2H_4(g) + H_2O(l)$$

This can also be shown in the form of condensed structural formulas:

$$CH_3CH_2OH \xrightarrow{Al_2O_3} H_2C = CH_2 + H_2O$$

Balancing a Chemical Equation Involving Simple Oxidation-Reduction Reactions

One method to balance simple oxidation-reduction reactions is to split the reaction into half-reactions. First, write the oxidation half-reaction and the reduction half-reaction. Remember the phrase *"LEO the lion says GER,"* which is a reminder that the Loss of Electrons is Oxidation (LEO), and the Gain of Electrons is Reduction (GER). Next, balance the electrons by multiplying the equation(s) by the necessary factor(s). Finally, cancel the electron(s) and combine the balanced oxidation and reduction half-reactions into a balanced net chemical equation.

Balance the Following Chemical Equation Involving an Oxidation-Reduction Reaction: $Na + O_2 \rightarrow Na^+ + O^{2-}$.

In order to balance the equation $Na + O_2 \rightarrow Na^+ + O^{2-}$, first, write the individual half-reactions:

$$\text{oxidation: } Na \rightarrow Na^+ + e^-$$

$$\text{reduction: } O_2 + 4e^- \rightarrow 2O^{2-}$$

Next, balance the number of electrons by multiplying the oxidation half-reaction by 4:

$$\text{oxidation: } 4Na \rightarrow 4Na^+ + 4e^-$$

$$\text{reduction: } O_2 + 4e^- \rightarrow 2O^{2-}$$

Finally, cancel the electrons and combine the half-reactions into the net reaction:

$$4Na + O_2 \rightarrow 4Na^+ + 2O^{2-}$$

Write a Balanced Equation for the Oxidation-Reduction Reaction of Metallic Zinc Powder and Aqueous Copper(II) Sulfate.

According to the activity series, zinc is more reactive than copper. Therefore, the zinc is oxidized, and the copper is reduced. Write the half-reactions:

$$\text{oxidation: } Zn \rightarrow Zn^{2+} + 2e^-$$

$$\text{reduction: } Cu^{2+} + 2e^- \rightarrow Cu$$

Cancel the electrons and combine the two half-reactions into the net equation:

$$Zn + Cu^{2+} \rightarrow Zn^{2+} + Cu$$

Finally, add the symbols to indicate the state of each reactant and product:

$$Zn(s) + Cu^{2+}(aq) \rightarrow Zn^{2+}(aq) + Cu(s)$$

Interestingly, this equation can also be written as the following single-displacement reaction:

$$Zn(s) + CuSO_4(aq) \rightarrow ZnSO_4(aq) + Cu(s)$$

This single-displacement reaction has the same net ionic equation after canceling out the spectator ions.

Write a Balanced Equation for the Oxidation-Reduction Reaction of a Piece of Solid Copper Wire Immersed in an Aqueous Solution of Silver Nitrate.

According to the activity series, copper is more reactive than silver. Therefore, the copper is oxidized, and the silver is reduced. Write the half-reactions:

$$\text{oxidation: Cu} \rightarrow \text{Cu}^{2+} + 2\text{e}^-$$

$$\text{reduction: Ag}^+ + \text{e}^- \rightarrow \text{Ag}$$

Multiply the reduction half-reaction by 2 to balance the number of electrons:

$$\text{oxidation: Cu} \rightarrow \text{Cu}^{2+} + 2\text{e}^-$$

$$\text{reduction: 2Ag}^+ + 2\text{e}^- \rightarrow 2\text{Ag}$$

Cancel the electrons and combine the two half-reactions into the net equation:

$$\text{Cu} + 2\text{Ag}^+ \rightarrow \text{Cu}^{2+} + 2\text{Ag}$$

Finally, add the symbols to indicate the state of each reactant and product:

$$\text{Cu(s)} + 2\text{Ag}^+\text{(aq)} \rightarrow \text{Cu}^{2+}\text{(aq)} + 2\text{Ag(s)}$$

Note that this equation is also classified as a single-displacement reaction:

$$\text{Cu(s)} + 2\text{AgNO}_3\text{(aq)} \rightarrow \text{Cu(NO}_3)_2\text{(aq)} + 2\text{Ag(s)}$$

This single-displacement reaction has the same net ionic equation after canceling out the spectator ions.

Chemical Equations Involving Oxidation-Reduction

Determining the Oxidation State of an Element in a Molecule or Ion

In order to determine the **oxidation state** of an element in a molecule or ion, apply these general rules: Hydrogen is usually assigned an oxidation state of +1 except for metal hydrides. Oxygen is usually assigned an oxidation state of –2 except for peroxides. Halogens are usually assigned oxidation states of –1 unless they are combined to a more electronegative element. Alkali metals are always assigned oxidation states of +1. Alkaline earth metals are always assigned oxidation states of +2. Finally, the **sum of the oxidation states** must equal the charge of the molecule or ion.

Determining Oxidation States Examples

$$\text{H}_2\text{O}$$

Oxygen is usually assigned an oxidation state of –2, and hydrogen is usually assigned an oxidation state of +1. Check: $2(+1) + (-2) = 0$. Therefore, the oxidation states are as follows: hydrogen +1 and oxygen –2.

$$\text{MgF}_2$$

Halogens are usually assigned an oxidation state of –1, and alkaline earth metals are always assigned an oxidation state of +2. Check: $(+2) + 2(-1) = 0$. Therefore, the oxidation states are as follows: magnesium +2 and fluorine –1.

$$\text{Ca(NO}_3)_2$$

Oxygen is usually assigned an oxidation number of –2, and alkaline earth metals are always assigned an oxidation state of +2. The oxidation state of nitrogen may be found by balancing the charges of the NO_3^-. Let x

represent the charge of the nitrogen atom: $x + 3(-2) = -1$. Solving for x yields $x = +5$. Checking: $(+2) + 2[(+5) + 3(-2)] = 0$. Therefore, the oxidation states are as follows: calcium +2, nitrogen +5, and oxygen –2.

Determining if a Reaction is an Oxidation-Reduction Reaction

To determine if a reaction is an **oxidation-reduction reaction**, try to determine if one reactant is **oxidized** and the other reactant is **reduced**. First, assign oxidation states to each atom in the reaction. Remember that atoms of elements in their uncombined state are always assigned oxidation states of 0. Alkali metals are assigned +1, and alkaline earth metals are assigned +2. Oxygen is usually assigned –2, hydrogen is usually +1, and halogens are usually assigned –1. Write the half-reactions for each atom in the reactants, and determine if any are oxidized and reduced. If an oxidation reaction and a reduction reaction are present, the reaction is an oxidation-reduction reaction.

Review Video: Oxidation-Reduction Reactions
Visit mometrix.com/academy and enter code: 317289

Determining Oxidation-Reduction Reaction Examples

$$2\text{Mg(s)} + \text{O}_2\text{(g)} \rightarrow 2\text{MgO(s)}$$

Assign oxidation states to each atom in the reaction. Atoms of an element in its uncombined state are always assigned 0. Therefore, both uncombined reactants are assigned 0. Oxygen is usually assigned –2, and magnesium is always assigned +2. Write the half-reactions:

- $\text{Mg} \rightarrow \text{Mg}^{2+} + 2\text{e}^-$ oxidation state of magnesium: $0 \rightarrow +2$
- $\text{O}_2 + 2\text{e}^- \rightarrow \text{O}^{2-}$ oxidation state of oxygen: $0 \rightarrow -2$

Magnesium is oxidized. Oxygen is reduced. Therefore, this is an oxidation-reduction reaction.

$$\text{Ca(s)} + 2\text{HCl(aq)} \rightarrow \text{CaCl}_2\text{(aq)} + \text{H}_2\text{(g)}$$

The reactant Ca(s) and the product $\text{H}_2\text{(g)}$ are assigned 0. Halogens such as chlorine are usually assigned –1. Hydrogen is usually assigned +1. Alkaline earth metals such as calcium are always assigned +2. Write the half-reactions:

- $\text{Ca} \rightarrow \text{Ca}^{2+} + 2\text{e}^-$ oxidation state of calcium: $0 \rightarrow +2$
- $2\text{Cl}^- \rightarrow 2\text{Cl}^-$ oxidation state of chlorine: $-1 \rightarrow -1$
- $2\text{H}^+ + 2\text{e}^- \rightarrow \text{H}_2$ oxidation state of hydrogen: $+1 \rightarrow 0$

Calcium is oxidized. Hydrogen is reduced. Therefore, this is an oxidation-reduction reaction.

Stoichiometry

Determining the Limiting Reagent in a Reaction

The **limiting reagent**, or **limiting reactant**, is the reactant that determines or "limits" the amount of product formed. The limiting reagent is **totally consumed** in the chemical reaction. The other reactants in the chemical reaction must be present in excess amounts than what is needed. The excess reactants will be left over after the limiting reactant is consumed. To determine the limiting reagent from the balanced chemical equation, select one of the products and calculate how much of that product can be produced from each reactant. The reactant that produces the least amount of that product is the limiting reactant or limiting reagent.

Calculating the Percent Yield for a Chemical Reaction

To calculate the **percent yield** for a chemical reaction, use the formula:

$$\frac{\text{actual yield}}{\text{theoretical yield}} \times 100\ \%$$

The actual yield should be stated in the problem or determined experimentally. The theoretical yield can be calculated from the balanced chemical equation with dimensional analysis using conversion factors for molar mass and number of moles. Divide the actual yield by the theoretical yield. This is a decimal that can be converted to a percentage by multiplying by 100 and adding the percent sign.

Review Video: Stoichiometry
Visit mometrix.com/academy and enter code: 801833

Reaction Types

Types of Reactions

One way to organize chemical reactions is to sort them into two categories: **oxidation/reduction reactions** (also called redox reactions) and **metathesis reactions** (which include acid/base reactions). Oxidation/reduction reactions can involve the transfer of one or more electrons, or they can occur as a result of the transfer of oxygen, hydrogen, or halogen atoms. The species that loses electrons (or increases its oxidation state) is oxidized and is referred to as the reducing agent. The species that gains electrons (or decreases its oxidation state) is reduced and is referred to as the oxidizing agent. **Single substitution reactions** are types of oxidation/reduction reactions. In a single substitution reaction, electrons are transferred from one chemical species to another. The transfer of electrons results in changes in the nature and charge of the species.

Review Video: Understanding Chemical Reactions
Visit mometrix.com/academy and enter code: 579876

Review Video: The Process of a Reaction
Visit mometrix.com/academy and enter code: 808039

Substitution Reactions

Single substitution, **displacement**, or **replacement reactions** are when one reactant is displaced by another to form the final product ($A + BC \rightarrow AB + C$). Single substitution reactions can be cationic or anionic. When a piece of copper (Cu) is placed into a solution of silver nitrate ($AgNO_3$), the solution turns blue. The copper appears to be replaced with a silvery white material. The equation is $2AgNO_3 + Cu \rightarrow Cu(NO_3)_2 + 2Ag$. When this reaction takes place, the copper dissolves and the silver in the silver nitrate solution precipitates (becomes a solid), resulting in copper nitrate and silver. Copper and silver have switched places in the nitrate.

Double substitution reactions, also called **double displacement**, **double replacement**, **metathesis**, or **ion exchange reactions**, are those where ions or bonds are exchanged by two compounds to form different compounds ($AC + BD \rightarrow AD + BC$). An example of this is that silver nitrate and sodium chloride form two different products (silver chloride and sodium nitrate) when they react. The formula for this reaction is $AgNO_3 + NaCl \rightarrow AgCl + NaNO_3$.

Review Video: Single-Replacement Reactions
Visit mometrix.com/academy and enter code: 442975

Combination and Decomposition Reactions

Combination, or **synthesis, reactions**: In a combination reaction, two or more reactants combine to form a single product ($A + B \rightarrow AB$). These reactions are also called synthesis or **addition reactions**. An example is burning hydrogen in air to produce water. The equation is $2H_2(g) + O_2(g) \rightarrow 2H_2O(l)$. Another example is when water and sulfur trioxide react to form sulfuric acid. The equation is $H_2O + SO_3 \rightarrow H_2SO_4$.

Decomposition (or desynthesis, decombination, or deconstruction) reactions: In a decomposition reaction, a reactant is broken down into two or more products ($AB \rightarrow A + B$). These reactions are also called analysis reactions. **Thermal decomposition** is caused by heat. **Electrolytic decomposition** is due to electricity. An example of this type of reaction is the decomposition of water into hydrogen and oxygen gas. The equation is $2H_2O \rightarrow 2H_2 + O_2$.

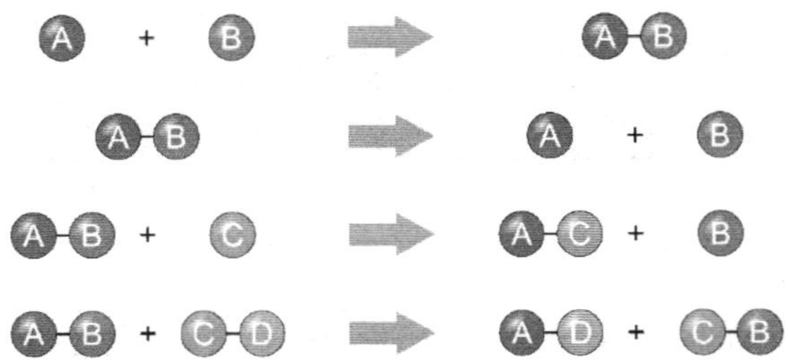

Acid/Base Reactions

In **acid/base reactions**, an **acid** is a compound that can donate a proton, while a **base** is a compound that can accept a proton. In these types of reactions, the acid and base react to form a salt and water. When the proton is donated, the base becomes water and the remaining ions form a salt. One method of determining whether a reaction is an oxidation/reduction or a metathesis reaction is that the oxidation number of atoms does not change during a metathesis reaction.

Isomerization and Neutralization Reactions

Isomerization, or **rearrangement**, is the process changing a compound to an isomer. Within a compound, bonds are reformed. The reactant and product have the same molecular formula, but different structural formulas and different properties (A → A'). For example, butane (C_4H_{10}) is a hydrocarbon consisting of four carbon atoms in a straight chain. Heating it to 100 °C or higher in the presence of a catalyst forms isobutane (methylpropane), which has a branched-chain structure. Boiling and freezing points are greatly different for butane and isobutane.

A **neutralization**, **acid-base**, or **proton transfer reaction** occurs when one compound acquires H^+ from another. These types of reactions are also usually double displacement reactions. The acid has an H^+ that is transferred to the base and the acid and base are neutralized in the form of a salt that, depending on the salt's solubility, may precipitate from the solution.

Chemical Kinetics

Chemical kinetics is the study of the **rates** of **chemical reactions** and the various factors that affect these rates. The rate of a reaction is the change in concentration of the reactants or products per unit of time. Another way to state this is that chemical kinetics is the study of the rate of change of the concentrations of the reactants and products and the factors that affect that rate of change. The study of catalysts is part of chemical kinetics. Catalysts are substances that speed up the rate of reactions without being consumed. Examples of reactions that occur at different rates include the explosion of trinitrotoluene (TNT), which occurs at a very fast rate, compared to the burning of a log, which occurs at a much slower rate.

Give the Rate Law for this General Reaction: $aA + bB + cC \rightarrow$ Products. Define Each Letter.

The rate of a chemical reaction can be defined as the following:

$$\text{rate} = \frac{\text{change in concentration}}{\text{change in time}}$$

This is usually represented by a rate law. The rate law for the general reaction $aA + bB + cC \rightarrow$ Products is given by rate $= k[A]^x[B]^y[C]^z$, where k is the rate constant; [A], [B], and [C] represent the concentrations of the reactants; and x, y, and z represent the reaction orders. The exponents x, y, and z must be experimentally determined. They do not necessarily equal the coefficients from the balanced chemical equation.

Activation Energy

Activation energy is the minimum amount of energy that must be possessed by reactant atoms or molecules in order to react. This is due to the fact that it takes a certain amount of energy to break bonds or form bonds between atoms. Reactants lacking the activation energy required will not be able to perform the necessary breaking or forming of bonds regardless of how often they collide. Catalysts lower the activation energy of a reaction and therefore increase the rate of reaction.

Reaction Mechanism

Often, when studying specific reactions, only the net reactions are given. Realistically, reactions take place in a series of steps or elementary reactions as shown in the reaction mechanism. **Reaction mechanisms** show how a reaction proceeds in a **series of steps**. Some steps are slow, and some are fast. Each step has its own reaction mechanism. The slowest step in the reaction mechanism coincides with the step with the greatest activation energy. This step is known as the rate-determining step.

Catalyst

A **catalyst** is a chemical that **accelerates** or speeds up a chemical reaction without being consumed or used up in the reaction. Although catalysts are not consumed or permanently changed during the process of the reaction, catalysts do participate in the elementary reaction of the reaction mechanisms. Catalysts lower the **activation energy** meaning more of the reactant molecules will have sufficient energy to react.

Review Video: Catalysts
Visit mometrix.com/academy and enter code: 288189

Factors That Affect Reaction Rate

Factors that affect reaction rate include concentration, surface area, and temperature. Increasing the **concentration** of the reactants increases the number of collisions between those reactants and therefore increases the reaction rate. Increasing the **surface area of contact** between the reactants also increases the number of collisions and therefore increases the reaction rate. Finally, increasing the **temperature** of the reactants increases the number of collisions but more significantly also increases the kinetic energy of the reactants, which in turn increases the fraction of molecules meeting the activation energy requirement. With more molecules at the activation energy, more of the reactants are capable of completing the reaction.

Chemical Reaction Equilibrium

Chemical Equilibrium

A **chemical equilibrium** occurs when a reaction is reversible and the rate of the forward reaction equals the rate of the reverse reaction. The forward and reverse reactions are continually occurring, but the individual concentration of the reaction and the products do not change. The concentration of the reactants and products are not necessarily equal to each other. For this to occur, the reaction must take place in a closed system in which none of the reactants or products can escape and in which no heat is added or lost.

Explain How to Write an Equilibrium Constant Expression from the Following Equilibrium Equation: $aA + bB \leftrightarrow cC + dD$.

Given the following **equilibrium reaction**: $aA + bB \leftrightarrow cC + dD$, the equilibrium constant is calculated by the expression $k = \frac{[C]^c[D]^d}{[A]^a[B]^b}$. The brackets indicate "the concentration of" each individual reactant and product. The coefficients from the balanced chemical equation are used for the exponents in the equilibrium constant expression. Pure liquids and pure solids are not represented in the equilibrium constants. The concentration of gases and the concentration of solutes do appear in the expressions for equilibrium constants. Note that the concentrations of the products are in the numerator and the concentrations of the reactant are in the denominator.

Explain How to Write Equilibrium Constant Expressions for Each of the Following Equilibriums:

2SO_2 (g) + O_2 (g) ↔ 2SO_3 (g)

All of the reactants and products are gases and need to be represented in the equilibrium constant. The concentration of the product is placed in the numerator, and the concentrations of the reactants are placed in the denominator. The coefficients from the balanced chemical equation are the exponents:

$$k = \frac{[SO_3]^2}{[SO_2]^2[O_2]}$$

$CaCO_3(s) \leftrightarrow CaO(s) + CO_2(g)$

The solid reactant $CaCO_3$ and the solid product CaO are not part of the equilibrium constant. The concentration of the gaseous product CO_2 is represented in the numerator.

$$k = [CO_2]$$

$CaH_2(s) + 2H_2O(l) \leftrightarrow Ca(OH)_2(aq) + 2H_2(g)$

The solid reactant CaH_2 and the liquid reactant H_2O are not part of the equilibrium constant. Both products should be represented. The "2" coefficient of the gaseous hydrogen is the exponent on the concentration of the gaseous H_2.

$$k = [Ca(OH)_2][H_2]^2$$

$H^+(aq) + OH^-(aq) \leftrightarrow H_2O(l)$

Pure liquids are not represented in the equilibrium constant. Aqueous solutions are included in the equilibrium constant.

$$k = \frac{1}{[H^+][OH^-]}$$

Le Châtelier's Principle

Le Châtelier's principle states that when a stressor is applied to a system in equilibrium, the system will respond in such a way to at least partially offset the stressor. Stressors include increasing or decreasing the temperature, increasing or decreasing the concentration of a reactant or product, and increasing or decreasing the pressure. Systems can be described as "shifting left" or "shifting right" when a stressor is applied. For example, if the temperature is increased in an equilibrium in which the forward reaction is endothermic, the system will "shift right" in order to "use up" the heat that was applied. Increasing or decreasing the pressure of an equilibrium will only cause the equilibrium to "shift" if the number of moles of gases of the reactants differs from the number of moles of gases of the products. If there are no gases in the equilibrium or if the number of moles of gases of the reactants and products is equal, the change in pressure will have no effect on the equilibrium.

Review Video: Le Châtelier's Principle
Visit mometrix.com/academy and enter code: 360187

Oxidation-Reduction Reactions and Oxidation States

Oxidation-Reduction Reactions

An **oxidation-reduction reaction (redox reaction)**is a reaction in which one of the reactants either loses one or more electrons or increases its oxidation state and the other reactant either gains one or more electrons or decreases in oxidation state. Oxidation cannot take place without reduction, and reduction cannot take place without oxidation. Redox reactions can be classified as either electron-transfer or atom-transfer reactions.

For **electron-transfer redox reactions**, the reactant that loses the electrons undergoes oxidation. The reactant that gains the electrons undergoes reduction. A common phrase to help remember this is *LEO the lion says GER*, where *LEO* represents *loss of electrons is oxidation* and *GER* represents *gain of electrons is reduction.*

Atom-transfer redox reactions typically involve organic compounds and the transfer of oxygen, hydrogen, or halogen atoms. While these reactions are associated with more complicated reactions, the core principle of oxidation state changes remains the same: increasing oxidation state means oxidation and decreasing oxidation state means reduction.

Review Video: Oxidation-Reduction Reactions
Visit mometrix.com/academy and enter code: 317289

Oxidation, Reduction, Oxidizing Agent, Reducing Agent, Oxidation States

- **Oxidation** can be defined as any process involving either the loss of one or more electrons or the increase of oxidation state.
- **Reduction** can be defined as any process involving either a gain of one or more electrons or the decrease of oxidation state.
- **Oxidizing agent** can be defined as the reactant in an oxidation-reduction reaction that causes oxidation. The *oxidizing agent* is reduced.
- **Reducing agent** can be defined as the reactant in an oxidation-reduction reaction that causes reduction. The *reducing agent* is oxidized.
- **Oxidation states**, also known as oxidation numbers, represent the charge that an atom has in a molecule or ion.

Biochemical Compounds

The four major classes of biochemical compounds are carbohydrates, lipids, proteins, and nucleic acids. Examples of **carbohydrates** include monosaccharides such as glucose, fructose, and ribose; disaccharides such as sucrose and lactose; and polysaccharides such as starch, cellulose, and glycogen. Examples of **lipids** include fatty acids, triglycerides, oils, lard, fat-soluble vitamins, waxes, and steroids such as cholesterol. Examples of **proteins** include enzymes, collagen, hemoglobin, histones, many hormones, and antibodies. Examples of **nucleic acids** include deoxyribonucleic acid (DNA) and ribonucleic acid (RNA).

Carbohydrates

Carbohydrates are organic compounds that produce energy. The empirical formula for most carbohydrates is CH_2O, which indicates that the ratio of carbon, hydrogen, and oxygen is always 1:2:1.The structure generally consists of aldehydes and ketones containing many hydroxyl groups. In general, carbohydrates are sugars and starches. Carbohydrates can be grouped as simple sugars or complex carbohydrates. The simple sugars include monosaccharides such as glucose and ribose and disaccharides such as sucrose and lactose. Complex carbohydrates are polymers of monosaccharides and include polysaccharides such as cellulose, starch, and glycogen.

Review Video: Carbohydrates
Visit mometrix.com/academy and enter code: 601714

Monosaccharides, Disaccharides, and Polysaccharides

Monosaccharides, disaccharides, and polysaccharides are specific types of carbohydrates. The term *saccharide* comes from the Greek word for sugar, *sákkharon*, and is synonymous with carbohydrate. **Monosaccharides** are the simplest carbohydrates. Examples of monosaccharides are glucose, fructose (fruit sugar), ribose, and galactose. **Disaccharides** consist of two monosaccharides joined together. Examples of disaccharides include sucrose (table sugar, which is a compound of glucose and fructose) and lactose (milk sugar, which is a compound of glucose and galactose). **Polysaccharides** are polymers of monosaccharides. Examples of polysaccharides include cellulose, starch, and glycogen.

Lipids

Lipids have many functions. The main function of lipids is storing energy. One type of lipid is **triglycerides**, which include fats and oils. Lipids known as **phospholipids** also form the cell membranes of all plant and animal cells. Lipids can relay messages among cells in the nervous system and in the immune system. Some lipids are **steroids**, which serve many functions. For example, cholesterol helps make cell membranes pliable, and some steroids make up hormones such as testosterone and estrogen. Fat-soluble vitamins are also steroids.

Review Video: Lipids
Visit mometrix.com/academy and enter code: 269746

Proteins

Proteins are polymers of **amino acids**. The amino acids are joined together by peptide bonds. The two major groups of proteins are fibrous proteins and globular proteins. **Fibrous proteins** provide structure in cells, bone tissue, connective tissue and line cartilage, tendons, and epidermal tissue. Examples of fibrous proteins include collage, elastin, and keratin. **Globular proteins** are folded molecules that include enzymes, hemoglobin, and some hormones. Antibodies are globular proteins that help defend the body from antigens. Some proteins such as actin and myosin are involved in muscle contraction. Some proteins act as storage containers for amino acids. Other proteins such as hemoglobin help transport materials throughout the body.

DNA

DNA, or deoxyribonucleic acid, is a two-stranded molecule in the shape of a double helix. DNA nucleotides consist of a deoxyribose (sugar), a phosphate, and a base. The bases are guanine, thymine, cytosine and adenine. Guanine always pairs with cytosine, and thymine always pairs with adenine. If the double helix is compared to a twisted ladder, the legs of the ladder are the sugars and phosphates while the rungs of the ladder consist of the bases. The bases that make up the rungs of the ladder are bound together with hydrogen bonds.

DNA Vs. RNA

Deoxyribonucleic acid (DNA) and ribonucleic acid (RNA) are both nucleic acids composed of **nucleotides**, which have three of their four bases in common: guanine, adenine, and cytosine. The sugar in DNA nucleotides is deoxyribose, whereas the sugar in RNA nucleotides is ribose. DNA contains the base thymine, but RNA replaces thymine with uracil. DNA is double-stranded, and RNA is single-stranded. DNA has the shape of a double helix, whereas RNA is complexly folded. DNA stores the genetic information of the cell, while RNA has several forms. For example, mRNA, or messenger RNA, is a working copy of DNA, and tRNA, or transfer RNA, collects the needed amino acids for the ribosomes during the assembling of proteins.

Review Video: DNA Vs. RNA
Visit mometrix.com/academy and enter code: 184871

NET EQUATION FOR PHOTOSYNTHESIS

Photosynthesis is the food-making process in green plants. Photosynthesis occurs in the chloroplasts of cells in the presence of light and chlorophyll. The reactants are **carbon dioxide** and **water**. The energy from the sunlight is absorbed and stored in the glucose molecules. The net equation for photosynthesis can be represented by the following equations:

$$\text{carbon dioxide} + \text{water} + \text{light} \xrightarrow{\text{chlorophyll}} \text{glucose} + \text{oxygen}$$

$$6CO_2 + 6H_2O + \text{light} \xrightarrow{\text{chlorophyll}} C_6H_{12}O_6 + 6O_2$$

The products of photosynthesis are glucose and oxygen gas.

RESPIRATION

Cellular respiration is the process in which energy is released from glucose in the form of adenosine triphosphate (ATP). **Cellular respiration** is the reverse process of photosynthesis. In cellular respiration, glucose is burned or combined with oxygen as shown in the following equations:

$$\text{glucose} + \text{oxygen} \rightarrow \text{carbon dioxide} + \text{water} + \text{ATP}$$

$$C_6H_{12}O_6 + 6O_2 \rightarrow 6CO_2 + 6H_2O$$

The products of cellular respiration are carbon dioxide and water. Energy is released from glucose in the form of ATP.

COMMON ORGANIC COMPOUNDS

ORGANIC COMPOUNDS

Organic compounds are compounds that contain carbon and hydrogen. Carbon has only four valence electrons and will form four covalent bonds with hydrogen and other atoms or groups of atoms in order to satisfy the octet rule. Carbon readily forms single, double, or triple bonds with other carbon atoms or with other elements. Organic compounds can form long chains, branched chains, and single- or multiple-ring structures. **Hydrocarbons** are organic compounds that contain only carbon and hydrogen. **Substituted hydrocarbons** are hydrocarbons that have a carbon backbone, but one (or more) of the hydrogen atoms has been substituted with a different atom or group of atoms called a functional group. **Functional groups** may be single atoms, such as in halocarbons where a halogen such as chlorine or fluorine is substituted for a hydrogen atom. Some functional groups consist of more than one atom; alcohols, for example, have the hydroxyl (—OH) functional group.

Acids and Bases

OVERVIEW OF ACIDS AND BASES

DIFFERENCES BETWEEN ACIDS AND BASES

There are several differences between acids and bases. While it is never a good idea to taste chemicals directly or feel chemicals without gloves, it has been done in the past and we now know that acidic solutions tend to taste sour, whereas basic solutions tend to taste bitter. Dilute bases tend to feel slippery, whereas dilute acids feel like water. Active metals such as magnesium and zinc react with acids to produce hydrogen gas, but active metals usually do not react with bases. Acids and bases form electrolytes in aqueous solutions and conduct electricity. Acids turn blue litmus red, but bases turn red litmus blue. Acidic solutions have a pH of less than 7, whereas basic solutions have a pH of greater than 7.

Review Video: Properties of Acids and Bases
Visit mometrix.com/academy and enter code: 645283

ARRHENIUS ACID AND BASE

Arrhenius acids are substances that produce hydrogen ions (H^+) when dissolved in water to form aqueous solutions. Arrhenius bases are substances that produce hydroxide ions (OH^-) when dissolved in water to form aqueous solutions. The **Arrhenius concept** is limited to acids and bases in aqueous solutions and cannot be applied to other solids, liquids, and gases. Examples of Arrhenius acids include hydrochloric acid (HCl) and sulfuric acid (H_2SO_4). Examples of Arrhenius bases include sodium hydroxide (NaOH) and magnesium hydroxide ($Mg(OH)_2$).

BRØNSTED–LOWRY ACID AND BASE

The Brønsted–Lowry concept is based on the donation or the acceptance of a proton. According to the **Brønsted-Lowry concept**, an acid is a substance that donates one or more protons to another substance and a base is a substance that accepts a proton from another substance. The Brønsted–Lowry concept can be applied to substances other than aqueous solutions. This concept is much broader than the Arrhenius concept, which can only be applied to aqueous solutions. The Brønsted–Lowry concept states that a substance cannot act like an acid (donate its proton) unless another substance is available to act as a base (accept the donated proton). In this concept, water may act as either an acid or a base. Hydrochloric acid (HCl) is an example of a Brønsted–Lowry acid. Ammonia (NH_3) is an example of a Brønsted–Lowry base.

LEWIS ACID AND BASE

A **Lewis acid** is any substance that can accept a pair of nonbonding electrons. A **Lewis base** is any substance that can donate a pair of nonbonding electrons. According to the **Lewis theory**, all cations such as Mg^{2+} and Cu^{2+} are Lewis acids. Trigonal planar molecules, which are exceptions to the octet rule such as BF_3, are Lewis acids. Molecules such as CO_2 that have multiple bonds between two atoms that differ in electronegativities are Lewis acids, also. According to the Lewis theory, all anions such as OH^- are Lewis bases. Other examples of Lewis bases include trigonal pyramidal molecules such as ammonia and nonmetal oxides such as carbon monoxide, CO. Some compounds, such as water, can act as either Lewis acids or bases depending on the context.

NEUTRALIZATION REACTION

Neutralization is a reaction of an acid and a base that yields a salt and water. The general form of the reaction is:

$$\text{acid} + \text{base} \rightarrow \text{salt} + \text{water}$$

The salt is formed from the cation of the base and the anion of the acid. The water is formed from the cation of the acid and the anion of the base.

An example is the neutralization reaction of hydrochloric acid and sodium hydroxide to form sodium chloride and water:

$$HCl(aq) + NaOH(aq) \rightarrow NaCl(s) + H_2O(l)$$

EQUIVALENCE POINT

The **equivalence point** is by definition the point in a titration at which the analyte is neutralized. When the acid–base indicator starts to change color, the equivalence point has been reached. At this point, equivalent amounts of acids and bases have reacted. Also, at this point the concentration of cations of hydrogen is equal to the concentration of hydroxide anions. On an acid–base titration curve, the slope of the curve increases dramatically at the equivalence point. For strong acids and bases, the equivalence point occurs at a pH of 7. The figures below show the equivalence points for a strong acid titrated with a strong base (a) and a strong base titrated with a strong acid (b).

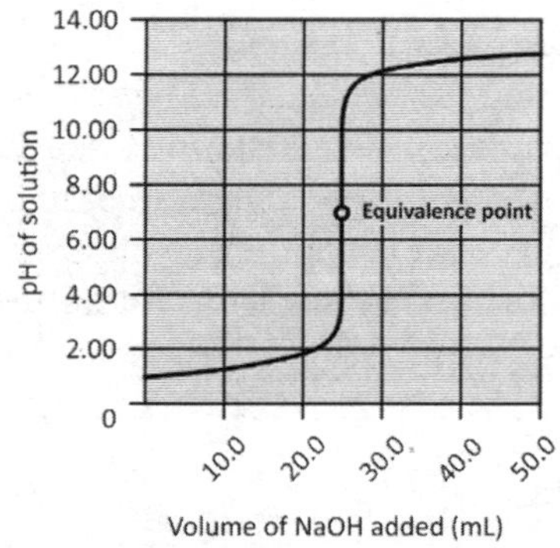

(a) Strong acid titrated with strong base

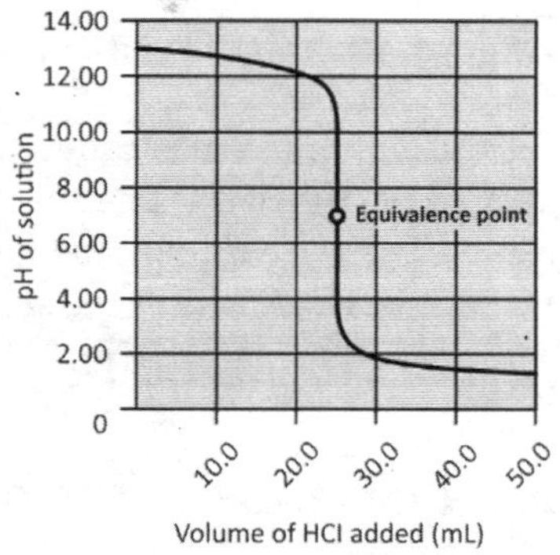

(b) Strong base titrated with strong acid

> **Review Video: Titration**
> Visit mometrix.com/academy and enter code: 550131

pH Scale and Calculations

Calculating pH, the Range of the pH Scale, and Acids and Bases on the pH Scale

The **pH scale** categorizes the **acidity** or **alkalinity** (basicity) of a solution. The pH value may be calculated by the formula $\text{pH} = -\log[\text{H}^+]$, where $[\text{H}^+]$ is the concentration of hydrogen ions. The pH scale ranges from 0 to 14 with pH values near 0 indicating the strongest acids and pH values near 14 indicating the strongest bases. With the pH scale, any solution with $\text{pH} < 7$ is considered an acid and any solution with $\text{pH} > 7$ is considered a base. Solutions with $\text{pH} = 7$ are considered to be neutral.

> **Review Video: Overview of pH Levels**
> Visit mometrix.com/academy and enter code: 187395

Relationship Between pH and pOH

The pH of a solution may be calculated using the formula $\text{pH} = -\log[\text{H}^+]$, where $[\text{H}^+]$ is the concentration of hydrogen ions. The pOH of a solution may be calculated using the similar formula $\text{pOH} = -\log[\text{OH}^-]$, where $[\text{OH}^-]$ is the concentration of hydroxide ions. The sum of the pH of a solution and the pOH of a solution is always 14. The pH of this HCl solution may be calculated using the formula $\text{pH} = -\log[0.0010\text{ M}] = 3$. The sum of the pH and pOH is always 14. Therefore, the pOH may be calculated by the formula $14 - 3 = 11$.

Calculate $[H^+]$ and $[OH^-]$ When Given the pH or pOH. Given a Solution with a pOH of 8.0, Explain How to Calculate pH, $[H^+]$, and $[OH^-]$.

Since $\text{pH} = -\log[\text{H}^+]$, $[\text{H}^+]$ may be calculated by $[\text{H}^+] = \text{antilog}(-\text{pH})$. Because $\text{pOH} = -\log[\text{OH}^-]$, $[\text{OH}^-]$ may be calculated by $[\text{OH}^-] = \text{antilog}(-\text{pOH})$. Also, because $\text{pH} + \text{pOH} = 14$, the pOH may be calculated by the formula $14 - \text{pH} = \text{pOH}$. For example, given a solution with a pOH of 8.0:

$$[\text{OH}^-] = \text{antilog}(-8.0) = 1.0 \times 10^{-8}$$

$$\text{pH} = 14 - 8.0 = 6.0$$

$$[\text{H}^+] = \text{antilog}(-6.0) = 1 \times 10^{-6}$$

K_w

Pure water dissociates to a very small extent and reaches this equilibrium:

$$H_2O(l) \leftrightarrow H_3O + (aq) + OH^-(aq)$$

The equilibrium constant for this equilibrium is called the ion product constant of water, or K_w. The constant K_w can be represented by $K_w = [H_3O^+][OH^-]$. The reactant H_2O is not represented in the equilibrium expression because it is essentially a pure liquid. The ion product constant of water K_w varies with temperature. As temperature increases, K_w increases and pH decreases. Therefore, this constant must be given at a specific temperature. At 25 °C, $[H_3O^+] = [OH^-] = 1 \times 10^{-7}$ M, which corresponds to pure water being neutral with a pH of 7.

CALCULATIONS INVOLVING ACID-BASE TITRATIONS

ACID–BASE INDICATORS

Acid–base indicators are one method to determine the range of the pH of a solution. **Acid–base indicators** change with the pH of the solution and are less precise than using a pH meter. However, acid–base indicators are used to indicate the completion of a titration to determine the concentration of an acidic or basic solution. Examples of acid–base indicators include methyl violet, litmus, and phenolphthalein. Methyl violet turns from yellow to blue with a pH range of 0.0–1.6. Litmus turns from red to blue with a pH range of 4.5–8.3. Phenolphthalein turns from colorless to reddish purple with a pH range of 8.3–10.0.

DETERMINING THE ENDPOINT IN A TITRATION

During a **titration**, when the acid–base indicator has fully changed color, the **endpoint** has been reached. If the proper acid–base indicator with the correct pH range has been used, this should also correspond to the equivalence point. For example, if trying to determine the pH of an unknown base using phenolphthalein, the solution should change from colorless to pink at the equivalence point. If trying to determine the pH of an unknown acid using methyl violet, the solution should change from yellow to blue at the equivalence point. However, the endpoint and the equivalence point are not necessarily equal. Ideally, the equivalence point is the endpoint. If the solution is overtitrated, the endpoint will be past the equivalence point.

CALCULATING THE UNKNOWN CONCENTRATION OF A BASE FROM A TITRATION

The **unknown concentration of an acid or base** may be determined by a titration. To determine the unknown concentration of a base, titrate a known volume of the base with an acid of known molarity. Use an acid–base indicator such as phenolphthalein to indicate when the titration has reached the equivalence point. If the solution is not overtitrated, the equivalence point will also be the endpoint. Then, calculate the concentration of the base using the formula $V_bN_b = V_aN_a$, where V_b represents the volume of the base, N_b represents the normality of the base, V_a represents the volume of the acid used in the titration, and N_a represents the normality of the acid used in the titration.

DURING A TITRATION, 20.0 ML OF 0.0100 M $NaOH$ IS REQUIRED TO NEUTRALIZE A 50.0 ML SAMPLE OF HCl SOLUTION. EXPLAIN HOW TO FIND THE MOLARITY OF THE HCl.

To find the **concentration of the unknown acid**, use the formula $V_bN_b = V_aN_a$, where V_b represents the volume of the base, N_b represents the normality of the base, V_a represents the volume of the acid, and N_a represents the normality of the acid used in the titration. Solving the equation for the variable N_a yields $N_a = \frac{V_bN_b}{V_a}$. Because the molarity of the NaOH is 0.0100 M, the normality of the NaOH is 0.0100 N. Substituting in the appropriate values into the formula yields $N_a = \frac{(20.0\text{ mL})(0.0100\text{ N})}{50.0\text{ mL}} = 0.00400$ N. Because HCl is monoprotic, the molarity of HCl is 0.00400 M.

Equilibrium Relationships in Acid-Base Chemistry

Strong/Weak Acids and Bases

Acids or bases are categorized as strong or weak based on how completely they ionize in an aqueous solution. **Strong** acids and bases ionize essentially completely in an aqueous solution. **Weak** acids and bases ionize incompletely in an aqueous solution. Examples of strong acids include hydrochloric acid (HCl), sulfuric acid (H_2SO_4), and nitric acid (NO_3). Examples of weak acids are acetic acid ($HC_2H_3O_2$), hydrofluoric acid (HF), and carbonic acid (H_2CO_3). Examples of strong bases include sodium hydroxide (NaOH), potassium hydroxide (KOH), and calcium hydroxide ($Ca(OH)_2$). Ammonia (NH_3) is a common weak base.

Review Video: Strong and Weak Acids and Bases
Visit mometrix.com/academy and enter code: 268930

Monoprotic and Polyprotic Acids

Monoprotic acids are acids that have only one proton available to donate. **Polyprotic acids** have two or more protons available to donate. Typically, polyprotic acids donate their available protons in stages of one at a time. Specifically, diprotic acids can donate two protons, and triprotic acids can donate three protons. Common monoprotic acids include hydrochloric acid (HCl) and nitric acid (HNO_3). Common diprotic acids include sulfuric acid (H_2SO_4) and sulfurous acid (H_2SO_3). Phosphoric acid (H_3PO_4) is a common triprotic acid.

K_a of an Acid and the K_b of a Base

Given the general form $HA(aq) + H_2O(l) \leftrightarrow H_3O^+(aq) + A^-(aq)$ for the equilibrium of an acid in an aqueous solution, the equilibrium constant expression, called the **acid dissociation constant**, K_a, is:

$$K_a = \frac{[H_3O^+][A^-]}{[HA]}$$

Strong acids have high K_a values because strong acids ionize essentially completely in aqueous solution. Weak acids have low K_a values because weak acids do not ionize completely in aqueous solution.

Given the general form $B(aq) + H_2O(l) \leftrightarrow BH^+(aq) + OH^-(aq)$ for the equilibrium of a base in an aqueous solution, the equilibrium constant expression, called the **base dissociation constant**, K_b, is:

$$K_b = \frac{[BH^+][OH^-]}{[B]}$$

Strong bases have high K_b values because strong bases ionize essentially completely in aqueous solution. Weak bases have low K_b values because weak bases do not ionize completely in aqueous solution.

Hydrolysis

Hydrolysis is a chemical reaction between water and another reactant in which both compounds split apart. The water molecules split into hydrogen ions (H^+) and hydroxide ions (OH^-). The other compound splits into a cation and anion, too. Another way to state this is that hydrolysis is a decomposition reaction of a compound that is combined with water. The general form of a hydrolysis reaction is given by $X^-(aq) + H_2O(l) \leftrightarrow HX(aq) + OH^-(aq)$.

A salt hydrolysis reaction is the reverse process of a neutralization reaction. A neutralization reaction is given by the general form: acid + base → salt + water. In general, a salt hydrolysis reaction may be thought of as salt + water → acid + base.

Buffer Solution

A **buffer solution** is an aqueous solution that helps keep the pH constant. The addition of an acid or base to a buffer solution will not greatly affect the pH of that solution. A buffer consists of a weak acid and its conjugate base or a weak base and its conjugate acid. This combination of substances can remain in solution without the substances neutralizing each other. When acids or hydrogen ions (H^+) are added to a buffer solution, they are neutralized by the base in the buffer solution. When bases or hydroxide ions (OH^-) are added to a buffer solution, they are neutralized by the acid in the buffer solution.

Review Video: Buffer
Visit mometrix.com/academy and enter code: 389183

Solutions

Terminology for Solutions and Solubility

Dilute and Concentrated

The terms *dilute* and *concentrated* have opposite meanings. In a **solution**, the **solute** is dissolved in the **solvent**. The more solute that is dissolved, the more **concentrated** is the solution. The less solute that is dissolved, the less concentrated and the more **dilute** is the solution. The terms are often associated with the preparation of a stock solution for a laboratory experiment. Stock solutions are typically acquired in a higly concentrated form. Typically, diluted forms of the solutions are used which must be prepared from the concentrated stock solutions. The desired dilutions are achieved by combining a specific amount of a solvent with a specific amount of stock solution.

Saturated, Unsaturated, and Supersaturated

Solutions can be categorized based on their saturation. In a **saturated** solution, the solute is added to the solvent until no more solute is able to dissolve. The undissolved solute will settle down to the bottom of the beaker. A solution is considered **unsaturated** as long as more solute is able to go into solution under ordinary conditions. The solubility of solids in liquids typically increases as temperature increases. If the temperature of a solution is increased as the solute is being added, more solute than is normally possible may go into solution, forming a **supersaturated** solution.

Mixture, Solution, and Colloid

A **mixture** is made of two or more substances that are combined in various proportions. The exact proportion of the constituents is the defining characteristic of any mixture. There are two types of mixtures: homogeneous and heterogeneous. **Homogeneous** means that the mixture's composition and properties are uniform throughout. Conversely, **heterogeneous** means that the mixture's composition and properties are not uniform throughout.

A **solution** is a homogeneous mixture of substances that cannot be separated by filtration or centrifugation. Solutions are made by dissolving one or more solutes into a solvent. For example, in an aqueous glucose solution, glucose is the solute and water is the solvent. If there is more than one liquid present in the solution, then the most prevalent liquid is considered the solvent. The exact mechanism of dissolving varies depending on the mixture, but the result is always individual solute ions or molecules surrounded by solvent molecules. The proportion of solute to solvent for a particular solution is its **concentration**.

A **colloid** is a heterogeneous mixture in which small particles (<1 micrometer) are suspended, but not dissolved, in a liquid. As such, they can be separated by centrifugation. A commonplace example of a colloid is milk.

Review Video: Solutions
Visit mometrix.com/academy and enter code: 995937

Calculating Molarity

Calculating Mole Fraction, Parts Per Million, Parts Per Billion, and Percent by Mass or Volume

There are applications and processes across many different fields that make use of concentration. As such, there are different methods of measuring concentration leading to many different units being used to communicate concentration. **Mole fraction** (χ) is calculated by dividing the number of moles of one component by the total number of moles of all of the components of the solution. **Parts per million** (ppm) is calculated by dividing the mass of the solute in grams by the mass of the solvent and solute in grams and then multiplying the quotient by 1,000,000 ppm. **Parts per billion** (ppb) is calculated similarly, except the quotient is multiplied by 1,000,000,000 ppb. **Percent concentration** can be calculated by mass or by volume by dividing the mass or volume of the solute by the mass or volume of the solution. This quotient is a decimal that can be converted to a percentage by multiplying by 100.

Calculating the Molarity and Molality of a Solution

Molarity and molality are measures of the concentration of a solution. **Molarity** (M) is the amount of solute in moles per the amount of solution in liters. A 1.0 M solution consists of 1.0 mol of solute for each 1.0 L of solution.

$$\text{Molarity (M)} = \frac{\text{moles of solute}}{\textbf{liters}\text{ of }\textbf{solution}} = \frac{\text{mol}}{\text{L}}$$

Molality (m) is the amount of solute in moles per the amount of solvent in kilograms. A 1.0 m solution consists of 1.0 mol of solute for each 1.0 kg of solvent.

$$\text{Molality (m)} = \frac{\text{moles of solute}}{\textbf{kilograms}\text{ of }\textbf{solvent}} = \frac{\text{mol}}{\text{kg}}$$

Often, when performing these calculations, the amount of solute is given in grams. To convert from grams of solute to moles of solute, multiply the grams of solute by the molar mass of the solute.

Calculating the Molarity of 100.0 g of $CaCl_2$ in 500.0 mL of Solution.

To use the formula molarity, you can make the necessary conversions from grams $CaCl_2$ to moles $CaCl_2$ and from 500.0 mL to liters using dimensional analysis. An alternate method of working this problem would be doing the conversions first and then substituting those values directly into the equation. Substituting the given information into the equation yields:

$$\frac{100.0\text{ grams }CaCl_2}{500.0\text{ mL of solution}}$$

Adding the necessary conversions using dimensional analysis yields:

$$\left(\frac{100.0\text{ g }CaCl_2}{500.0\text{ mL of solution}}\right)\left(\frac{\text{mol }CaCl_2}{110.98\text{ g}}\right)\left(\frac{1{,}000\text{ mL}}{\text{L}}\right) = 1.802\text{ M}$$

Preparing a Dilute Solution from a Stock Solution

In order to prepare a dilute solution from a stock solution, the molarity and the needed volume of the diluted solution as well as the molarity of the stock solution must be known. The volume of the stock solution to be diluted can be calculated using the formula $V_{stock}M_{stock} = V_{dilute}M_{dilute}$, where V_{stock} is the unknown variable, M_{stock} is the molarity of the stock solution, V_{dilute} is the needed volume of the dilute solution, and M_{dilute} is the needed molarity of the dilute solution. Solving this formula for V_{stock} yields $V_{stock} = \frac{V_{dilute}M_{dilute}}{M_{stock}}$. Then, dilute the calculated amount of stock solution to the total volume required of the diluted solution.

Factors Affecting Solubility

Temperature, Surface Area, Agitation, and Pressure on the Dissolution Rate

Temperature, surface area, agitation, and pressure affect the **dissolution rate**. Increasing the **temperature** increases the kinetic energy of the molecules, which increases the number of collisions with the solute particles. Increasing the **surface area** of contact by stirring **(agitation)** or crushing a solid solute also increases the dissolution rate and helps prevent recrystallization. Increasing the **pressure** will increase the dissolution rate for gas solutes in liquid solvents because the added pressure will make it more difficult for the gas to escape. Increasing the pressure will have virtually no effect on the dissolution rate for solid solutes in liquid solvents under normal conditions.

Effect of Temperature and Pressure on Solubility

Temperature and pressure affect **solubility**. For gas solutes in liquid solvents, increasing the **temperature** increases the kinetic energy, causing more gas particles to escape the surface of the liquid solvents and thereby decreasing the solubility of the solutes. For most solid solutes in liquid solvents, increasing the temperature increases the solubility, as shown in this solubility curve for selected salts. For gas solutes in liquid solvents, increasing the **pressure** increases the solubility. Increasing the pressure of liquid or solid solutes in liquid solvents has virtually no effect under normal conditions.

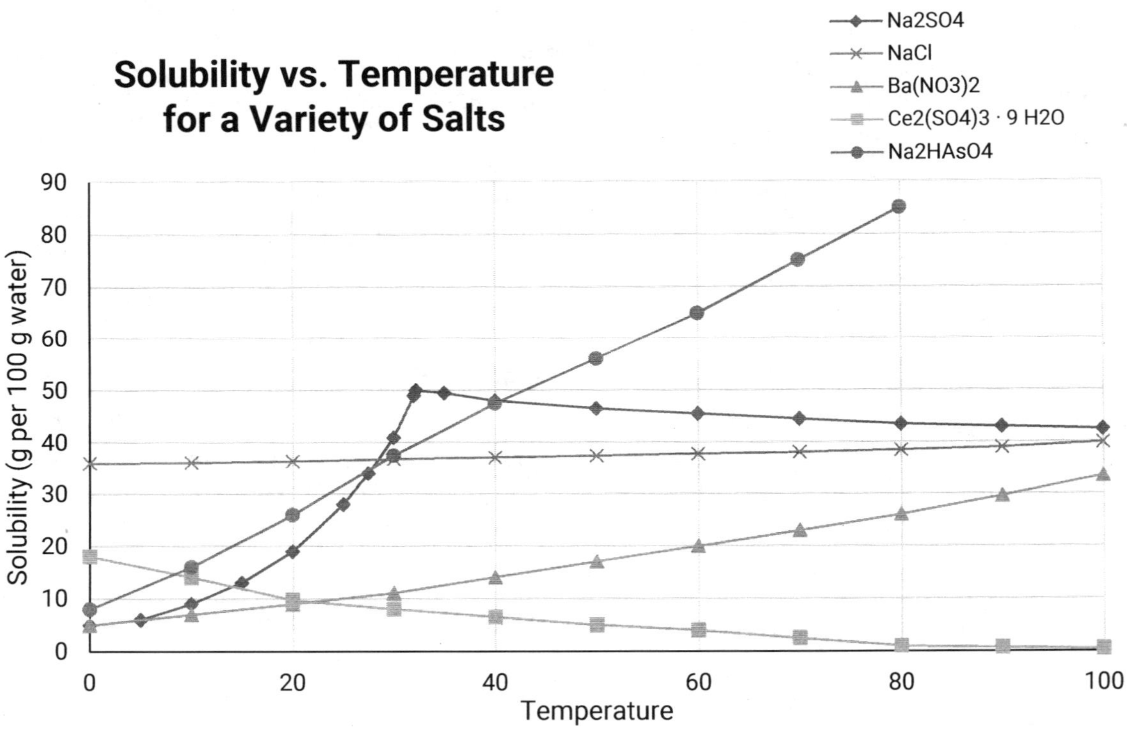

Colligative Properties of Solutions

Freezing Point Depression

Freezing point depression is a colligative property of solutions that depends only on the number of particles in the solution, not on the identity of those particles. Adding a nonvolatile solute to a solution will lower the freezing point of that solution. This decrease in temperature is known as **freezing point depression.** Basically, the particles of the nonvolatile solute occupy spaces near the surface and block or inhibit the solvent particles from escaping from the surface of the solution. As fewer particles escape, the vapor pressure lowers. This decrease in vapor pressure causes a decrease in the freezing point known as freezing point depression. The amount of depression can be calculated from the equation $\Delta T_{FP} = mk_f$, where m is the molality of the solution and k_f is the molal freezing point constant for that particular solvent.

Boiling Point Elevation

Boiling point elevation is a colligative property of solutions that depends only on the number of particles in the solution, not on the identity of those particles. Adding a nonvolatile solute to a solution will raise the boiling point of that solution. This rise in temperature is known as **boiling point elevation**. Basically, the particles of the nonvolatile solute occupy spaces near the surface and block or inhibit the solvent particles from escaping from the surface of the solution. As fewer particles escape, the vapor pressure lowers. This decrease in vapor pressure causes an increase in the boiling point known as **boiling point elevation**. The amount of elevation can be calculated from the equation $\Delta T_{BP} = mk_b$, where m is the molality of the solution and k_b is the molal boiling point constant for that particular solvent.

Vapor Pressure Lowering

Vapor pressure lowering is a colligative property of solutions that depends only on the number of particles in the solution, not on the identity of those particles. Adding a nonvolatile solute to a solution will lower the vapor pressure of that solution. Basically, the particles of the nonvolatile solute occupy space near the surface and block or inhibit the solvent particles from escaping from the surface of the solution. As fewer particles escape, the vapor pressure lowers. This decrease in vapor pressure causes an increase in the boiling point and a decrease in the freezing point.

Osmosis

Osmosis can be defined as diffusion through a **semipermeable membrane**. Typically, small solvent particles can pass through, but larger solute particles are too large to pass through. This means that osmosis is the net flow of solvent from a solution with a lower concentration to a solution with a higher concentration until a state of equilibrium is reached. The pressure that must be applied to the semipermeable membrane to stop the flow of solvent to reach this equilibrium state is called **osmotic pressure**. Osmotic pressure is a colligative property that depends on the number of nonvolatile solute particles, not the identity.

Review Video: Passive Transport: Diffusion and Osmosis
Visit mometrix.com/academy and enter code: 642038

Applications of Equilibrium in Ionic Solutions

Solubility of Ions in Water

Some general guidelines regarding solubility include the following:

- All nitrates and acetates are soluble.
- All chlorides, bromides, and iodides are soluble except those of silver, mercury(I), and lead(II).
- All sulfates are soluble except those of strontium, barium, mercury(I), and lead(II).
- All sulfides are insoluble except those of ammonium, the alkali metal cations, calcium, strontium, and barium.
- All carbonates are insoluble except those of ammonium and the alkali metal cations.
- All phosphates are insoluble except those of ammonium and the alkali metal cations.
- All hydroxides are insoluble except those of the alkali metal cations and calcium, strontium, and barium.

Solubility of Ionic Compounds in Water

If an ionic compound is soluble in water, the cations and anions will separate from each other when combined with water. In general, the rule for solubility is "like dissolves like." However, some ionic compounds are not soluble in water because the forces joining the ions are stronger than the intermolecular forces between the ions and the water molecules.

Soluble Ionic Compounds		Important Exceptions
Compounds containing	NO_3^-	None
	$C_2H_3O_2^-$	None
	Cl^-	Compounds of Ag^+, Hg_2^{2+}, Pb^{2+}
	Br^-	Compounds of Ag^+, Hg_2^{2+}, Pb^{2+}
	I^-	Compounds of Ag^+, Hg_2^{2+}, Pb^{2+}
	SO_4^{2-}	Compounds of Sr^{2+}, Ba^{2+}, Hg_2^{2+}, Pb^{2+}

Insoluble Ionic Compounds		Important Exceptions
Compounds containing	S^{2-}	Compounds of NH_4^+, the alkali metal cations, and Ca^{2+}, Sr^{2+}, and Ba^{2+}
	CO_3^{2-}	Compounds of NH_4^+, the alkali metal cations
	PO_4^{3-}	Compounds of NH_4^+, the alkali metal cations
	OH^-	Compounds of the alkali metal cations, and Ca^{2+}, Sr^{2+}, and Ba^{2+}

CALCULATING K_{sp} AND PERCENT DISSOCIATION

The solubility product constant, K_{sp}, is the equilibrium constant for a solution equilibrium. The general chemical equation for an ionic solution equilibrium is given by:

$$\text{ionic compound(s)} \leftrightarrow \text{cation(aq)} + \text{anion(aq)}$$

For this, the solubility product constant is $K_{sp} = [\text{cation}][\text{anion}]$. The percent dissociation for each ion is calculated by the following formula: $\frac{\text{amount dissociated}}{\text{initial concentration}} \times 100\%$, where the amount dissociated is the molarity of the ion in solution and the initial concentration is the molarity of the original compound. In general, the more dilute a solution, the greater the percent dissociation.

CALCULATE THE SOLUBILITY OF $AgBr$ IF THE SOLUBILITY PRODUCT CONSTANT, K_{sp}, FOR $AgBr$ IS 4.9×10^{-13} AT 25 °C.

The dissociation reaction for AgBr can be written as $AgBr(s) \leftrightarrow Ag^+(aq) + Br^-(aq)$. Because the dissociation of AgBr produces equal moles of Ag^+ and Br^- ions, the solubility is simply the concentration of the Ag^+ ions, $[Ag^+]$, or the concentration of the Br^- ions, $[Br^-]$. The solubility product constant for this reaction is given by $K_{sp} = [Ag^+][Br^-]$, but because $[Ag^+] = [Br^-]$, this can be written as $K_{sp} = [Ag^+]^2$. Substituting in the given value for K_{sp} yields $4.9 \times 10^{-13} = [Ag^+]^2$. Therefore, $[Ag^+] = 7.0 \times 10^{-7}$ M. Finally, the solubility of AgBr is 7.0×10^{-7} M.

COMMON ION EFFECT

The common ion effect is the decrease in the solubility of a salt in an electrolyte when that electrolyte solution already has an ion in common with that salt. An example of the common ion effect is when sodium chloride, NaCl, is dissolved in an aqueous solution of hydrochloric acid, HCl. The ions of the NaCl are Na^+ and Cl^-, and the ions of the HCl solution are H^+ and Cl^-. Therefore, the solute NaCl and the aqueous solution HCl share a common Cl^- ion. The equilibrium of the aqueous HCl solution can be represented by the following equation:

$$HCl(g) + H_2O(l) \leftrightarrow H_3O^+(aq) + Cl^-(aq)$$

According to Le Châtelier's principle, when a stressor is applied to this equilibrium, the system will respond in such a way to at least partially offset the stressor. Adding the NaCl to this equilibrium increases the concentration of the Cl^- ions in solution, which would shift the equilibrium to the left. The overall effect is that less Cl^- goes into solution. Therefore, because the solute and the solution share a common ion, the common ion effect is shown as the decrease in the solubility of the Cl^- ions.

Review Video: Common Ion Effect
Visit mometrix.com/academy and enter code: 311611

ELECTROLYTES AND NONELECTROLYTES

Electrolytes are substances that dissociate in solution to form ions. Strong electrolytes ionize essentially completely. Weak electrolytes only ionize partially and form only a few ions in solution. Nonelectrolytes do not dissociate or form ions in solution. Strong electrolytes such as salt water ($NaCl(aq)$) or hydrochloric acid ($HCl(aq)$) are good conductors of electricity. Weak electrolytes such as acetic acid ($HC_2H_2O_2(aq)$) and ammonia ($NH_3(aq)$) are poor conductors of electricity. **Nonelectrolytes** such as sugar water ($C_{12}H_{22}O_{11}(aq)$) and ethanol ($C_2H_5OH(aq)$) do not conduct electricity.

Chapter Quiz

Ready to see how well you retained what you just read? Scan the QR code to go directly to the chapter quiz interface for this study guide. If you're using a computer, simply visit the online resources page at **mometrix.com/resources719/texesphysc6-12** and click the Chapter Quizzes link.

Science Learning, Instruction, and Assessment

The Role of Pedagogy and Scientific Inquiry in Science Education

Developing Scientific Understanding

Scientific understanding involves not merely the knowledge of scientific theories and equations, but a comprehension of how science is done, how we come to know these theories (and how confident we are in them), and how the different domains of science fit together. Students are unlikely to develop a good scientific understanding merely by being presented with isolated facts. Rather, research suggests that a scientific understanding is best fostered by **inquiry** and by **problem-based learning** approaches, which help students develop their own critical thinking and reasoning skills. In these methods, students are not just provided with facts and theories to memorize but are led to "discover" principles on their own, through experimentation and analogy. The instructor must still provide guidance in the process; if students are completely left to their own devices they may be confused or arrive at incorrect conclusions that may do more harm than good. Furthermore, assessments used in the classroom should promote **higher-order learning**, focusing not just on repetition of facts but on reasoning and evaluation of claims. It is critical that students understand that science is a process and a way of knowing, not a collection of facts.

Prior Knowledge

Students vary in their prior knowledge and capabilities, and science instruction is not a one-size-fits-all process. Sometimes prior knowledge helps student, in that they already have some knowledge about the subject in question, but sometimes prior knowledge may seem to conflict with the new information being taught—a dilemma sometimes called the "**paradox of continuity**." Learning therefore can require a **conceptual change**, in a way that allows the students to reformulate their understanding to fit new information.

Students' experience and developmental characteristics can also affect their science learning. Some students learn more effectively through different **learning styles**, or modalities: some learn best from what they see (**visual learners**), others from what they hear (**auditory learners**), still others from handling objects (**tactile learners**), and others from active participation (**kinesthetic learners**). **Abstract thinking** develops during adolescence and may develop more rapidly in some students than others; students who have not fully developed this capability may benefit from more structured teaching methods. Adolescents tend to be at a stage in their social development in which they learn well in cooperative group activities.

Planning Activities

Instructors should be aware of and sensitive to students' different preferred styles of learning and prepare lessons that engage all these styles. The instructor should also try to tie lessons to students' individual interests in order to promote active engagement. A **positive learning environment** is one that adapts to students' individual needs and that often involves students working cooperatively.

In science in particular it's important for instructors not to exclude women and minorities, since they have been excluded so much in the past that it's easy to do so unconsciously. The instructor should make an effort to mention scientists of different ethnicities and genders and make it clear that women and minorities can be and are capable scientists.

Students currently learning English have their own needs that must be addressed. The instructor can help English learners, for instance, by speaking slowly and clearly, by writing down and providing definitions of key terms, by using visual aids and graphic organizers (which also may help visual learners who are not English language learners), and by giving access to translating devices if necessary. English learners can also benefit from working in groups with capable English speakers who can help explain instructions and procedures they don't understand.

Motivation and Engagement

Regardless of how clearly and accurately an instructor explains the topic, the students may not learn if they're unengaged and not paying attention. Therefore, it's important for the teacher to engage the students' interest and keep their attention. One of the advantages of inquiry-based learning is that it actively involves the students and keeps them more engaged by relating the topic to their interests and goals and finding ways to tie the topics in to the students' own experiences, prior knowledge, and daily lives. This requires the teacher to get to know the students and their interests, but this has other benefits as well: the students are also more engaged when there is a good relationship between the teachers and students.

Students also tend to be more engaged by collaborative group activities than by working on their own. Adolescents are at a stage in their social development in which they are increasingly driven to form social attachments with their peers. They are comfortable working in groups and benefit from collaborative learning environments.

Texts Used in the Classroom

Science instruction often involves the students acquiring information from textbooks and handouts, but not all students may be able to effectively use these texts without guidance. Most textbooks have various features designed to make it easier to locate information: an **index**, a **table of contents**, and often a **glossary** and/or a list of important variables and formulas. An instructor can explain how to use these features at the beginning of the year and perhaps even assign an activity that involves making use of them.

It may also be helpful to teach **active reading** techniques. One such technique is **pre-reading**—skimming and reading the headings before reading the text in depth, making predictions and building background knowledge. The instructor can also encourage active reading techniques through providing graphic organizers or techniques like **SQ3R**—a method that involves the student first Surveying the chapter, then formulating Questions about each section, then Reading the section, Reciting the main ideas (putting them in their own words), and Reviewing the material.

In the modern classroom, textbooks aren't the only kind of text that students can take advantage of. An effective teacher can also show students how to find information online, through web searches and reference sites.

Total School Program

While the science teachers plan the curriculum for their classes, they must also be aware of the **total school program**—the overall objectives for the students' learning in all subjects. The science teacher must be aware of school-wide objectives, and make sure that they are being adequately met in his or her class. The science instructor may also have a role in *setting* those objectives, in conjunction with other teachers and administrators; the science instructor in this case should work cooperatively with the rest of the team and ensure that any issues unique or important to the science classroom are properly addressed and incorporated into the objectives.

The science teacher must also be mindful of the statewide objectives. State standards lay out the curriculum requirements for the course and specify topics that must be covered. Students must master these topics to be ready not only for standardized exams, but to ensure that no gaps in understanding exist prior to advancing to the next grade-level.

Supportive Learning Environment

Creating a learning environment that supports student inquiries involves both setting certain procedures and expectations in the class and providing resources that lend themselves to inquiry-based learning. To encourage inquiry-based learning, the instructor should encourage students to ask questions, but try to guide them toward finding answers for themselves rather than giving direct answers to their questions. The instructor should pose questions that require higher-order thinking rather than rote recall or yes or no answers and include a time for reflection in each lesson. Lessons in inquiry-based classrooms are centered around projects and experiments rather than lectures—in fact, one increasingly popular technique is to "**flip the classroom**," having the students read the lesson or watch video lectures you provide as their homework and freeing up class time for discussion and analysis.

An inquiry-centered classroom environment should put a priority on student collaboration. The instructor should give the students assignments that involve their working together as much as practical. It is helpful to have some online resources that facilitate collaboration and sharing of information, such as a class website, and perhaps a class blog and wiki. Many online resources allow students to share documents and work on them together.

Participation in Scientific Investigation

Scientific investigations are an important part of science teaching, and it is vital that all students are given the opportunity to participate. Ideally, there will be enough space and equipment for the students to work in small groups on an experiment, but in practice this may not be possible. In this case, one solution is to have rotating stations in the classroom, where for one day or for part of the period one group works on one experiment, while another group works on a different activity that uses different equipment; as they rotate through the different stations, all the students will have the opportunity to do every activity, just not in the same order.

Another important part of making it possible for all students to participate in scientific investigations is to ensure that they all have the means to understand and carry out the instructions. Going over the procedure in a lecture may not be enough; it may be better to have a written handout and/or a screencast that the students can watch and refer back to as needed. Students with special needs must also be accommodated; for instance, English language learners can be given definitions of key terms.

Active Learning, Inquiry, and Reflection

Active learning and inquiry-based learning are two related pedagogical techniques that have been shown by research to be effective in teaching science. **Active learning** refers to teaching by making the student an active participant in the learning process. A class in which the instructor lectures, the students take notes, and the students later demonstrate their learning of the topic by taking a written exam is *not* engaged in active learning, and is not likely to be as effective. Active learning can include experiments that the students perform, interactive online simulations of processes that they can't physically experience in the classroom, and having the students create presentations and projects rather than have exams and worksheets as the main assessments.

Inquiry-based learning is a form of teaching by asking questions, having discussions, and helping students do their own research rather than just presenting them with lists of facts and formulas to be learned. Inquiry-based learning is effective not only because it involves the students directly, but because allowing them to formulate their own questions engages their curiosity and critical thinking. **Reflection** is also an important part of inquiry-based learning, having students think back on what they learned and how they learned it.

Modeling Scientific Thought

Modeling, in a pedagogical context, refers to *showing* the students what they should do, rather than telling them. This doesn't mean just demonstrating an activity at the front of the classroom while the students watch passively; effective modeling also involves the students as active participants. The important thing is that the teacher sets an example of the principles he or she wants to convey.

To model scientific attitudes, therefore, means to demonstrate and embody those attitudes. To instill curiosity and skepticism in students, the teacher should display those attributes. If the teacher doesn't know the answer to a question, the teacher should not be afraid to say "I don't know"—but should follow that by trying to find the answer, by looking it up online or by performing an experiment. When discussing a topic and coming up with questions about it, the instructor should come up with questions as well—ideally questions the instructor honestly doesn't know the answer to. On the other hand, the instructor should not be too quick to accept answers—not, for instance, immediately latching onto the first answer found online, but looking for multiple sources of information and analyzing their credibility.

Inquiry-Based Scientific Investigation

An **inquiry-based scientific investigation** is one that follows the **scientific method**. While the scientific method is often formalized in different ways, there are some essential aspects. The investigator formulates a specific **question** that the investigation will answer. Usually this question is based on an **observation** that the investigation is intended to explain. The investigator then does some background **research**, reviewing previously published information on the subject in question. For a professional scientist, this will usually involve reading articles in scientific journals; in a classroom setting, a web search may suffice. The investigator may formulate a **hypothesis**—a proposed possible answer to the question.

The investigator decides how to **gather evidence** to find an answer to the question and prove or disprove the hypothesis, designing an **experiment** that will test the hypothesis, and selecting the proper tools to carry it out. The investigator makes **predictions** as to what will happen in the experiment if the hypothesis is true or if it is not. The investigator then carries out the experiment, gathers data, and analyzes the results, drawing **conclusions** based on the data.

There remain other important steps: **communication** of the results to others, defending the results, and possibly formulating further questions.

Formulating Scientific Questions

Formulating scientific questions is an important part of an inquiry-based investigation; an investigation starts with a specific question, and then an experiment is designed to answer that question. The question usually is based on an observation: the student observes a phenomenon and then formulates a question about what was observed. The question should be as concrete, objective, quantitative, and measurable as possible. "Why did this object move?" is a vague and abstract question that cannot be easily answered. "Did this object move because of this force?" is more concrete. "What is the relationship between this force and the motion of this object?" is a good quantitative question that can potentially be answered by experiment.

To help the student to formulate a question, the instructor can first guide students through an observation, encouraging the students to think of anything about the observation they're curious about or that they don't understand. The instructor can then help the students come up with questions addressing the subject of their curiosity, and then gradually guide the students into making the questions more specific and measurable.

Hypotheses

The **hypothesis** is an educated guess as to the answer to the central question of a scientific investigation. It is an important part of the investigation because it helps guide the inquiry and suggest specific lines of investigation that can prove or disprove the hypothesis: the experiment at the heart of the investigation should be designed such that it will have different results depending on whether or not the hypothesis is correct.

It is important that the hypothesis is an *educated* guess; the student may not know the answer to the question, but there should be some basis for choosing the hypothesis—by extrapolation from known cases, or by analogy with similar scenarios. If the student has trouble coming up with a hypothesis, the instructor might prompt the student to think of similar situations the student understands better, or to research such situations that have been investigated before, and then to consider what those situations imply about the present question. Even a very loose analogy can be enough to make a hypothesis—for the purposes of the investigation, it doesn't matter that the student chooses a hypothesis that turns out to be *right*, only that it relates to the question.

Scientific Results

There are many methods that can be used to analyze and evaluate scientific results. Often **graphs** help investigators and readers visualize data better. If one variable is plotted against another and the points seem to form a straight line, that is evidence that a linear relationship may exist between these variables; if they form a parabola, they may have a quadratic relationship; and so on. In more advanced classes, **statistical methods** may be useful, from methods as simple as taking the **mean** of multiple measurements and comparing the means of sets of data rather than the individual points, to methods as complex as calculating **standard deviations** and **correlation coefficients**. All of these methods help show the relationships between quantities and can help to evaluate possible explanations of a result.

Error analysis is another important part of evaluating results. Students should have an idea of what possible sources of error exist in the experiment, and whether they are **random** or **systematic**. Random error can be identified by taking repeated measurements and seeing how close they are; identifying systematic error involves a more thoughtful consideration of what could lead results to be off in one direction or the other.

Higher-Level Thinking Skills

Students should be encouraged to engage in not just rote memorization and learning of procedures, but in higher-order thinking as well that involves putting together what they've learned in constructive ways. The most commonly used model of different levels of thinking in education is **Bloom's taxonomy**, which divides cognitive processes into six categories or levels. The lowest level, **Remember**, involves simple recall of data. The next, **Understand**, requires students to be able to explain or discuss concepts in their own words. Then come **Apply**, using the concepts in practice; **Analyze**, drawing connections and comparisons between ideas; **Evaluate**, judging and justifying ideas; and **Create**, synthesizing something new from the concepts.

It's easy to design activities that utilize the lower levels of Bloom's Taxonomy. Engaging the higher orders of thinking is more difficult, but it is important for developing a more thorough understanding of a topic. Some verbs commonly associated with each level of Bloom's Taxonomy give clues as to how to promote them. "Create", for example, is associated with the verbs "construct," "plan," and "design" (among others)—certainly designing an experiment to answer a specific question fits here. "Evaluate" is associated with "appraise," "argue," and "justify"—students could be asked to assess a scientific claim and argue for or against it.

Systematic Observations and Measurements

In a scientific investigation, observations are not haphazard; there are certain systematic principles that must be followed for useful observations. As far as possible, the observations should be **quantitative**; there should be some measured value recorded, and not simply a qualitative observation such as "it is longer". Measurements should be taken by a consistent method and recorded with proper units—and with an estimate of their **uncertainty**. A measurement taken with a meter stick with markings every millimeter, for instance, has an uncertainty of ±0.5 mm.

It is also important when making observations to vary only one quantity at a time. If you want to measure how a plant's growth is affected by temperature and by amount of light, it isn't useful to change both factors for each measurement—that would make it impossible to see how much of the effect was produced by each change. Rather, it is better to do at least one set of measurements in which the temperature is held constant and the amount of light is changed, and another where the reverse is true, so that the effects of each factor can be isolated. In many cases, an **experimental control** is also desirable.

Students' Prior Knowledge

Prior knowledge refers to the knowledge the student has about the subject matter before it's covered in class. This may come from previous classes, from books and television, from peers or parents, from experience, or from other sources. It's useful to know what prior knowledge students possess before the lesson begins, and there are a number of ways of finding out. One way is through **formative assessments**, assessments that are designed not to test what the student has learned but to test what the students already know in order to guide lesson planning. Another popular way of testing prior knowledge is a **K-W-L chart**, in which students write down what they *know* about the topic, what they *want* to know, and, after the lesson, what they *learned*.

The instructor can use the students' prior knowledge as a starting point for the lesson; having the students share what they already know can help introduce the topic. Prior knowledge may also guide the instructor's approach to the topic, since it may carry some assumptions or preconceptions that will affect the way the student might react to different presentations. In some cases, prior knowledge may even lead to misconceptions that must be overcome.

Performance in Inquiry-Based Investigations

The stereotypical classroom assessment may be a multiple-choice quiz, but this is not generally the most effective way of assessing student learning in an inquiry-based classroom. There may be a place for written exams as summative assessments, but more effective assessment methods will engage students' higher-order thinking processes and may involve collaboration and active participation.

For example, in a science class, a lab report can be a useful assessment; after performing an experiment, students may be asked to turn in a written account of the procedure and results. Along similar lines, a laboratory journal that students keep during an experiment can also be used for assessment, or a field journal for longer-term projects. The instructor may require students to compile all their work in a portfolio, to be turned in at the end of the semester or at shorter intervals; this can serve as a summative assessment in lieu of or in addition to a traditional exam. To assess the student's participation in a classroom activity as objectively as possible, rather than make a subjective judgment call the instructor can use checklists or a detailed rubric prepared ahead of time.

Assessment and Instruction

An **assessment** is an activity designed to measure students' knowledge, learning, or abilities, such as an exam. Assessments are not limited to testing how much the student has learned after a lesson; there are also formative assessments used before or during a lesson to test the student's prior knowledge and how well they are learning the topic.

There are important relationships between assessment and instruction, and the two must be designed together. Formative assessments guide instruction, since the instructor should take into account students' prior knowledge in planning a lesson, and if a formative assessment shows that students are not learning what the instructor expects, the instructor should use that information to try a different pedagogical approach. As for summative assessments, they should be designed to match the learning objectives; the instructor should make sure that the summative assessment is designed to test that the students have met the specific instructional goals of the lessons.

Ongoing Assessment

Ongoing assessment is vital in science instruction for several reasons. For one thing, formative assessments are important so that the instructor can be informed of the students' prior knowledge and plan the lesson accordingly. If the instructor learns from a formative assessment that the students lack some prior knowledge necessary to the lesson, then the instructor will have to be sure to cover that first; if the instructor learns that the students have a significant misconception about the topic, then the instructor may have to plan for a conceptual change. During the lesson, further formative assessments can monitor students' learning and inform the instructor whether the students are absorbing the information and methodologies that the instructor intends them to absorb, or whether the pace of the lesson should be changed or different pedagogical methods adopted.

Ongoing assessments can also benefit the students by reinforcing the subject matter. The assessments give the students another opportunity to put what they have learned to use, and may help them better retain it. They also give the students an idea of how well they are learning, and what topics they might need to review or about which they should ask more questions.

Types of Assessments

Assessments are divided into two main categories: **summative assessments** that measure how well students have learned the subject matter at the end of a unit, and **formative assessments** that are used before or during a lesson to test the student's prior knowledge and how well they are learning the topic. Both these types of assessment are important, and both can be carried out in a number of ways. Assessments can also be **formal**—data-driven, standardized assessments the results of which can be compared against preset benchmarks—or **informal**—less structured assessments based around performance and content. An effective science classroom utilizes a variety of different assessment methods.

For example, a **performance assessment** is an assessment that requires the student to demonstrate skills by completing a task, rather than by selecting a pre-set answer or filling in a blank. A **self-assessment** is an activity in which the student assesses his or her own work, perhaps using a rubric provided by the instructor; these are often not graded and serve to inform the student of his or her own learning. A **peer assessment** is an activity in which the student's work is assessed not by the instructor, but by a fellow student.

Review Video: Formative and Summative Assessments
Visit mometrix.com/academy and enter code: 804991

Combatting Misconceptions

One of the reasons it's important to gauge students' prior knowledge of a topic is because some of that prior knowledge may be incorrect or misleading, and the student may have misconceptions about the topic that must be overcome. Simply telling the students that their prior beliefs were incorrect is unlikely to be effective, and it may in fact be counterproductive, leading to their misconceptions being reinforced instead of removed. Rather, a better goal is to bring about a **conceptual change**, a gradual revision and rearrangement of prior knowledge to accommodate new ideas, in which the student is an active participant.

There are several research-based methods of bringing about conceptual change. One method is to promote **cognitive conflict**: presenting data or demonstrations that contradict the students' prior conceptions, and guiding the students into finding a resolution to the conflict. Another is the use of **refutational texts** that discuss and refute various views on the topic. Other methods include **collaborative argumentation**, in which students are encouraged to discuss, defend, and evaluate their positions; and **persuasive pedagogy**, applying methods of persuasion such as response shaping and reinforcing.

Reliability and Validity

Two measurements of the soundness of an assessment are reliability and validity. An assessment is **reliable** if it yields consistent results; students' scores on the assessment should not depend on external circumstances and should be similar for different questions that test the same skill. An assessment is **valid** if it measures what it is meant to measure. These two qualities can vary independently; it is possible for an exam to have a high reliability but a low validity, or vice versa.

The reliability of an assessment can be affected by many factors. Longer tests tend to be more reliable; tests with a short time limit so that many students cannot complete all the questions, or must rush to do so, tend to be less reliable. Reliability is also affected by difficulty; a test is most reliable when the questions are not so easy that almost every student answers the questions correctly, but not so hard that almost none do. It requires finding a suitable middle ground of difficulty. An assessment will tend to be more valid if it is designed to cover all the material that it is supposed to cover, but only that material. It will be less valid if it has hidden biases against certain categories of student.

Assessment as a Learning Experience

Though an obvious purpose of assessments is to allow the instructor to assign students a grade in the class, the assessments themselves can provide learning experiences. For one thing, as the students see what questions on the assessment they are unable to answer, or do not answer correctly, this helps them see what topics they have not fully learned and may need to further review. On the other hand, the questions that the students got right will help build their confidence and perhaps help them better remember in the future what they learned about those topics. Assessments also give students further practice with the methods and concepts they are testing, which may further work to reinforce them. They may also help students to learn new problem-solving strategies; as students go over the assessment after the fact and discuss how they were supposed to solve a particular problem, the answer might give them information about a strategy they were previously unaware of or underutilizing.

Equitable Use of Assessments

One important consideration that must be kept in mind in designing assessments is that they must be **equitable**—they must not be biased toward or against any part of the student population. Every student must have an adequate opportunity to demonstrate his or her skills and knowledge. There are many biases that may carelessly enter into assessments: cultural biases, language biases, biases against students with special needs.

There are a number of steps that instructors can take to ensure that assessments are equitable. Questions should not rely on "common knowledge" that may not be common to students of different cultures. Students with special needs must be provided with adequate accommodations. English language learners should be given definitions or paraphrases of difficult words and sentences. Other steps that can be taken toward making assessments more equitable include clearly laying out learning outcomes and grading rubrics, using many different methods of assessment that allow students to show their accomplishments in different ways, and ensuring that the subject matter covered in assessments is closely matched to what the instructor teaches in class.

Sharing Criteria and Results

It's important to share the evaluation criteria of assessments with students so that the students will know what to expect from the assessments and prepare accordingly, and so that during the assessment they will know where to best focus their time and attention. If the students have no idea how an assessment will be graded, then the assessment is not fair or equitable; students will not know what aspects of the assessment they should focus on the most and doing well on the assessment may be largely a matter of luck. Sharing the rubric for the assessment ahead of time makes the instructor's expectations clear and ensures that the students know what specifically they will be tested on and can prepare accordingly.

It is also important to share the results of assessments with the students. If the students know the results of their assessments, they can gauge their own progress and learning, and decide where they need to focus in the future and what topics they may need to revisit. Knowing their assessment results may also help students evaluate their study strategies and judge whether or not they are working and how or if they might need to be revised.

Scientific Inquiry Skills for Elementary Students

The six abilities that **grades K-4 students** should acquire are as follows:

- They should be able to ask questions about objects, organisms, and events in the environment.
- They should be able to devise a simple investigation to answer a question.
- They should be able to use tools such as magnifying glasses, rulers, and balances to gather data and make observations.
- They should be able to use the gathered data and observations to provide an explanation.
- They should be able to talk about, draw pictures, or use another method to communicate the results of an investigation and what they learned.

- With respect to the nature of scientific inquiry and scientists, students should understand that investigations involve formulating questions and answers, using different methods of discovering and disclosing answers, using basic tools, observing, sharing answers, and looking at and understanding others' work.

Scientific Inquiry Skills for Middle Grade Students

The five abilities that **grades 5–8 students** should acquire are as follows:

- They should be able to reformulate and clarify questions until they can be answered through scientific investigation.
- They should be able to create and carry out a scientific investigation, interpret the data to provide explanations, and use further data to revise explanations.
- They should be able to identify the tools necessary to gather and analyze data. They should be able to use computer hardware and software to store, organize, and gather data.
- They should be able to provide descriptions and explanations, create models, and make predictions based on the body of knowledge they possess.
- They should be able to explain cause and effect relationships using explanations and data from experiments.

Scientific Inquiry Skills for Older Students

The six abilities that **grades 9–12 students** should acquire are as follows:

- They should be able to identify questions and concepts that guide scientific investigation. In other words, they should be able to create a hypothesis and an appropriate experiment to test that hypothesis.
- They should be able to design and conduct a scientific investigation from start to finish. This includes being able to guide the inquiry by choosing the proper technologies and methods, determining variables, selecting an appropriate method for presenting data, and conducting peer review.
- They should be able to use technology and mathematics in investigations.
- They should be able to formulate and revise scientific explanations and models.
- They should be able to recognize and analyze alternative explanations. In other words, they should be able to devise other possibilities based on the current body of knowledge.
- They should be able to communicate and defend a scientific argument in both written and oral form.

Chapter Quiz

Ready to see how well you retained what you just read? Scan the QR code to go directly to the chapter quiz interface for this study guide. If you're using a computer, simply visit the online resources page at **mometrix.com/resources719/texesphysc6-12** and click the Chapter Quizzes link.

TExES Practice Test

Want to take this practice test in an online interactive format?
Check out the online resources page, which includes interactive practice questions and much more: **mometrix.com/resources719/texesphysc6-12**

1. Review the graph below. Which statement correctly describes what is happening to the object?

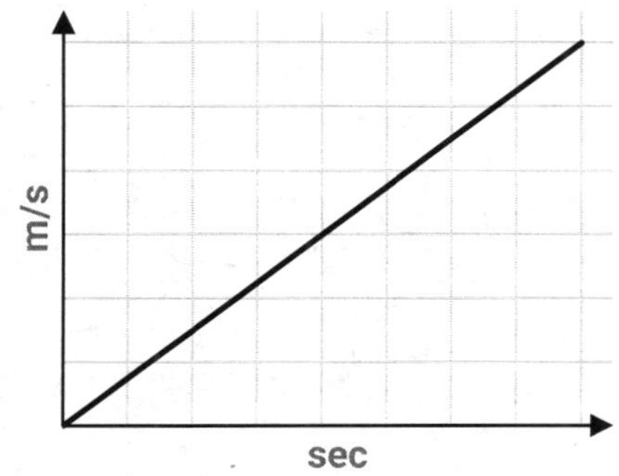

a. The object has constant velocity.
b. The object has constant acceleration.
c. The object is at rest. It is not moving.
d. The object has increasing acceleration.
e. The object has increasing inertia.

2. An object begins its motion at $(0, 0)$. It moves +5 units on the x-axis and then –3 units on the y-axis. Which vector represents the displacement of the object?

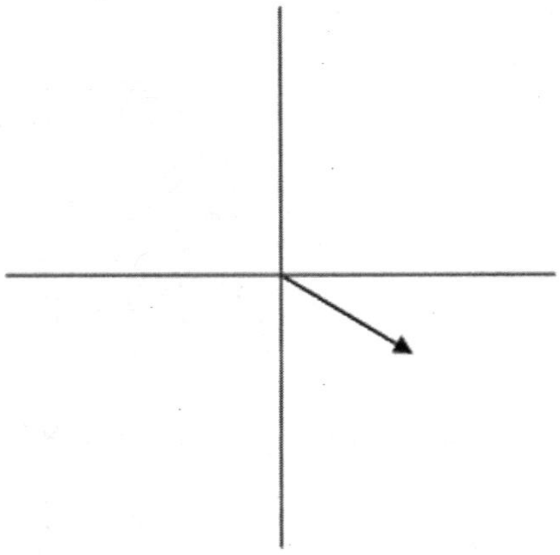

a.

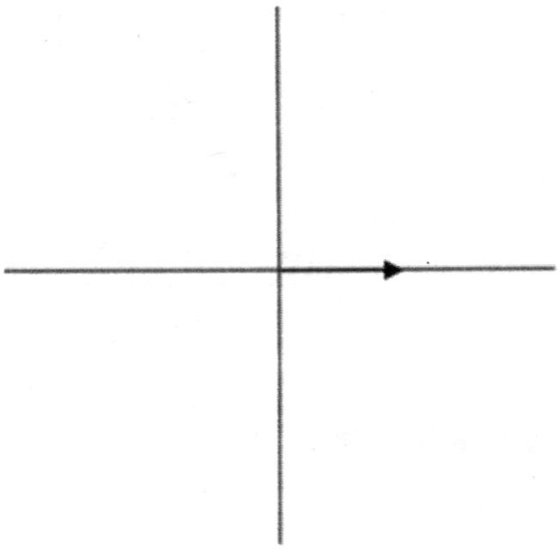

c.

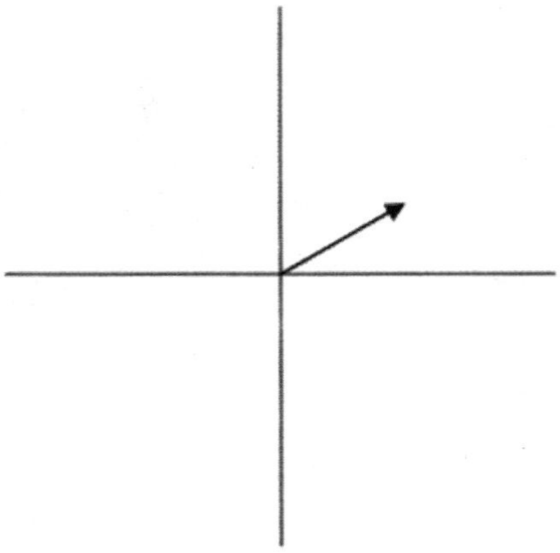

b.

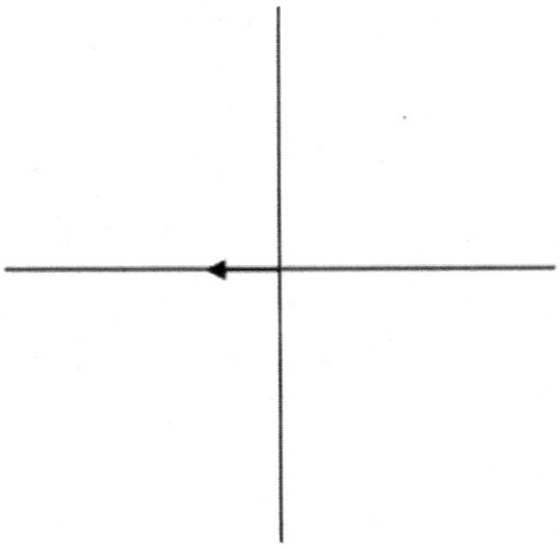

d.

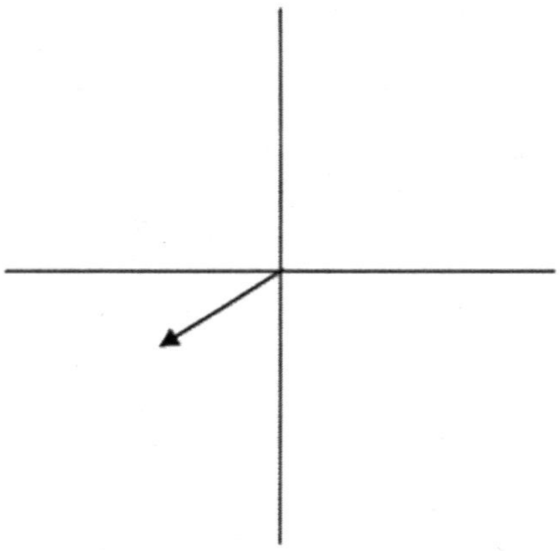

e.

Refer to the following for questions 3–4:

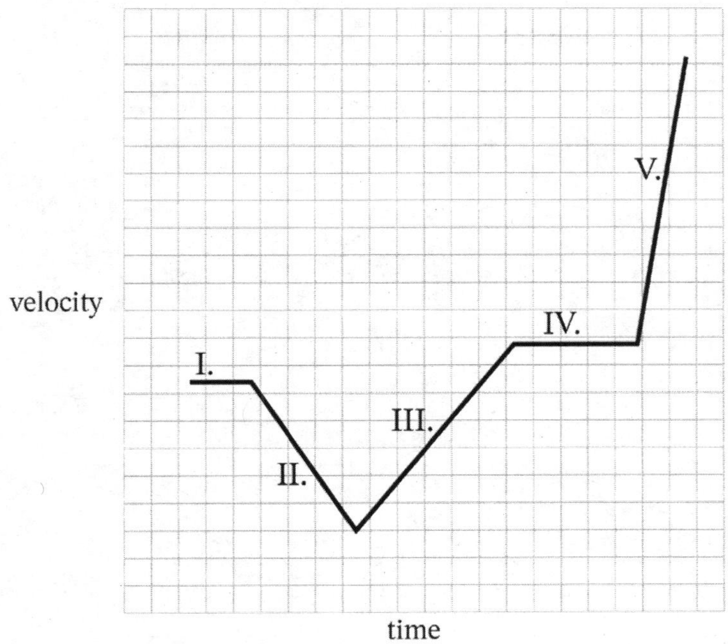

3. Which graph segments represent constant speed?

a. I and IV
b. III and V
c. II, III, and V
d. II and III
e. II and V

4. Which graph segment(s) show(s) the GREATEST acceleration?

a. II
b. III
c. V
d. III and V
e. I and IV

5. A bicyclist travels 10 miles in one hour, rests for an hour, and then travels 14 miles in two hours. What is the bicyclist's average speed for the trip?

a. 6 mph
b. 8 mph
c. 9.5 mph
d. 12 mph
e. 12.67 mph

6. Which two vectors when summed produce the following displacement vector?

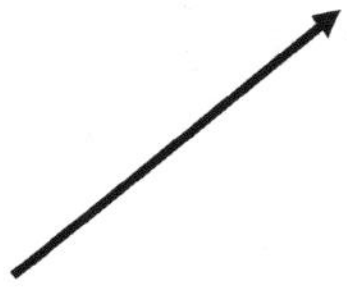

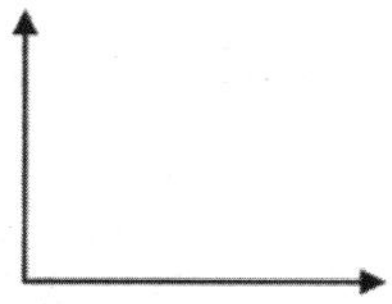

a.

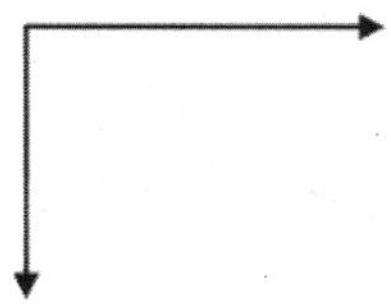

b.

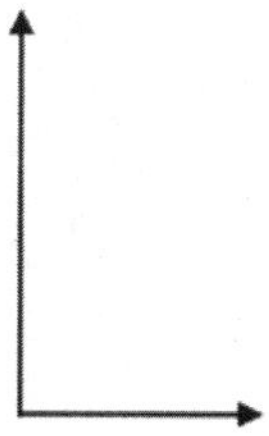

c.

d.

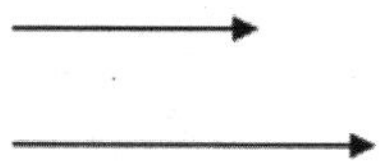

e.

7. Which of the following creates a magnetic field?

a. Spin and rotation of electrons in atoms
b. Separation of charged particles in atoms
c. Vibration and translation of atoms
d. Loosely held valence electrons surrounding an atom
e. a neutron to proton ratio greater than one

8. Which of the following creates an electromagnet?

a. Rapidly spinning and rotating electrons inside an iron bar
b. An iron bar inside a coil of wire that contains a current
c. The movement of electrons through a complete circuit
d. Convection currents within the liquid core of Earth's interior
e. Translational and vibrational motion of atoms

9. What is the definition of work?

a. The amount of energy used to accomplish a job
b. The force used to move a mass over a distance
c. The amount of work done per unit of time
d. Energy stored in an object due to its position
e. Force multiplied by the time over which the force acts

10. How many calories of heat are absorbed by 100g of water as it heats up from 50 °C to 55 °C?

a. 5 calories
b. 50 calories
c. 500 calories
d. 550 calories
e. 5,000 calories

11. What property of light explains why a pencil in a glass of water appears to be bent?

a. Reflection
b. Refraction
c. Angle of incidence = angle of reflection
d. Constructive interference
e. Destructive interference

12. Which of the following statements is explained by quantum physics?

a. Light exhibits properties that are both wavelike and particle-like.
b. Matter and energy cannot be created or destroyed, only transformed.
c. All energy transformations result in a more disordered state.
d. Temperature can be thought of as the average kinetic energy of molecules.
e. The actual mechanical advantage of a machine cannot exceed 100 percent.

13. The force of gravity on Earth's moon is $\frac{1}{6}$ the force of gravity on the Earth. The force due to gravity on Earth is $9.81\ m/s^2$. What is the weight of a 5 kg mass on the moon?

a. 0.833 N
b. 8.175 N
c. 30.00 N
d. 49.05 N
e. 294.30 N

14. 10 N of force are exerted on a sphere at an angle of 30°. An additional 10 N of force are exerted at an angle of 210°. Which statement about the sphere is correct?

a. The sphere is in a state of equilibrium and not moving.
b. The sphere is in a state of accelerating velocity.
c. The sphere is moving along a line at a 120° angle.
d. The sphere is experiencing additional g-force.
e. The sphere is moving in a circular path with a radius of 10N.

Refer to the following for question 15:

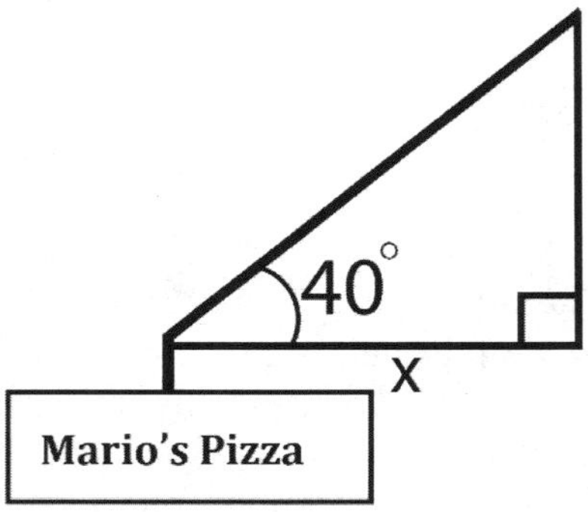

15. The Mario's Pizza sign shown above has a mass of 40 kg. Which mathematical expression could be used to correctly calculate the tension in Newtons exerted on the building by the sign?

a. $F = \frac{40 \times 9.8}{\sin(40°)}$
b. $F = \frac{40}{\sin(40°) \times 9.8}$
c. $F = \frac{40 \times \sin(40°)}{9.8}$
d. $F = \frac{40 \times 40°}{\sin(9.8)}$
e. $F = \frac{\sin(40) \times 9.8}{40°}$

Refer to the following for question 16:

Mass of the Moon (M_m)	7.36×10^{22} kg
Mass of Earth (M_e)	5.97×10^{24} kg
Gravitational constant (G)	$6.67 \times 10^{-11} \frac{N-m^2}{kg^2}$
Distance between Earth and the Moon (d)	3.84×10^5 km
Force of gravity on Earth (g)	9.81 m/s^2

16. Use the information in the table above to identify the mathematical expression that could be used to correctly calculate the force of gravity in Newtons between Earth and its moon.

a. $F = \frac{(6.67\times10^{-11})\times(7.36\times10^{22})\times(5.97\times10^{24})}{(3.84\times10^{8})^2}$
b. $F = \frac{(6.67\times10^{-11})\times(7.36\times10^{22})\times(5.97\times10^{24})}{(3.84\times10^{5})^2}$
c. $F = \frac{(6.67\times10^{-11})\times(3.84\times10^{5})}{(7.36\times10^{22})\times(5.97\times10^{24})}$
d. $F = \frac{(6.67\times10^{-11})\times(7.36\times10^{22})\times(5.97\times10^{24})}{(9.81)\times(3.84\times10^{5})}$
e. $F = \frac{(6.67\times10^{-11})\times(3.84\times10^{5})}{(9.81)\times(7.36\times10^{22})\times(5.97\times10^{24})}$

17. Which of the following materials has randomly aligned dipoles?

a. A non-magnetic substance
b. An electromagnet
c. A permanent magnet
d. A horseshoe magnet

18. Which of the following equations for sound waves correctly relates frequency to wavelength and speed of sound?

a. $f \times \lambda = v$
b. $f = \lambda \times v$
c. $f = \lambda + v$
d. $f \times \lambda \times v = 1$
e. $\frac{1}{f} = \frac{1}{\lambda \times v}$

19. What wave characteristic is related to the loudness of a sound?

a. Frequency
b. Amplitude
c. Wavelength
d. Speed of sound
e. Period

20. What wave characteristic determines if visible light is red or blue?

a. Frequency
b. Amplitude
c. Wavelength
d. Speed of sound
e. Period

21. What characteristic of electromagnetic radiation determines if it is classified as a radio wave or an x-ray?

a. Intensity
b. Phase angle
c. Wavelength
d. Speed of light
e. Period

22. What unit describes the loudness of a sound?

a. Hertz (Hz)
b. Decibels (dB)
c. Meters (m)
d. Meters per second (m/s)
e. Meters per second squared (m/s^2)

23. What unit describes the frequency of a wave?

a. Hertz (Hz)
b. Decibels (dB)
c. Meters (m)
d. Meters per second (m/s)
e. Meters per second squared (m/s^2)

Refer to the following for question 24:

Material	Coefficient of linear thermal expansion	Coefficient of volume thermal expansion	Specific heat	Density
Tin	$2.3 \times 10^{-5}\ °C^{-1}$	$6.9 \times 10^{-5}\ °C^{-1}$	$0.2\ cal \cdot g^{-1} \cdot °C^{-1}$	$2.5\ g \cdot cm^{-3}$

24. A 20 in tin rod is heated from 25 °C to 75 °C. Which equation could be used to correctly calculate the expansion of the rod?

a. $(2.3 \times 10^{-5})(20)(75 - 25)$
b. $(6.9 \times 10^{-5})(20)(75 - 25)$
c. $(20)^3(2.54)^3(2.5)(75 - 25)$
d. $(20)^3(2.54)^3(75 - 25)(K + 273)$
e. $(2.3 \times 10^{-5})(3 \times 20)(75 - 25)$

25. Any given temperature can be represented using three different temperature scales. Which temperature scale below yields a sequence of numbers from *lowest to highest* for the temperature of boiling water?

a. °C, °F, K
b. °F, °C, K
c. °F, K, °C
d. K, °C, °F
e. K, °F, °C

26. A pulley lifts a 10-kg object 10 m into the air in 5 minutes. Using this information you can calculate:

a. Mechanical advantage
b. Efficiency
c. Frictional resistance
d. Power
e. Energy conservation

27. A pulley lifts a 1 kg object 10 m into the air in 5 seconds. How much work is done?

a. 9.81 N
b. 10 J
c. 10 W
d. 98.1 N
e. 98.1 J

28. A pulley lifts a 5 kg object 10 m into the air in 5 seconds. How much power is used?

a. 50 J
b. 50 N
c. 98.1 J
d. 98.1 W
e. 250 W

29. What class of material increases in conductivity with increased vibrational motion within the material?

a. LASERS
b. MASERS
c. Photoelectric sensors
d. Semiconductors
e. Superconductors

30. The two waves shown below meet.

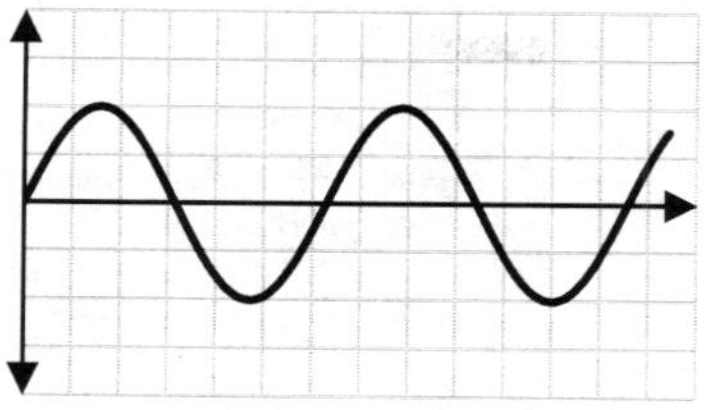

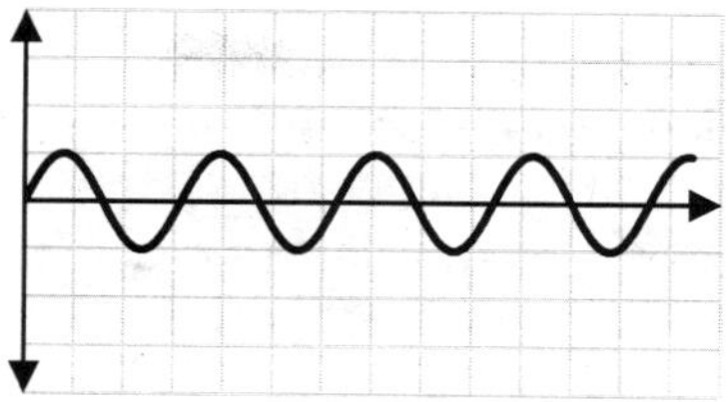

What is the shape of the resulting wave?

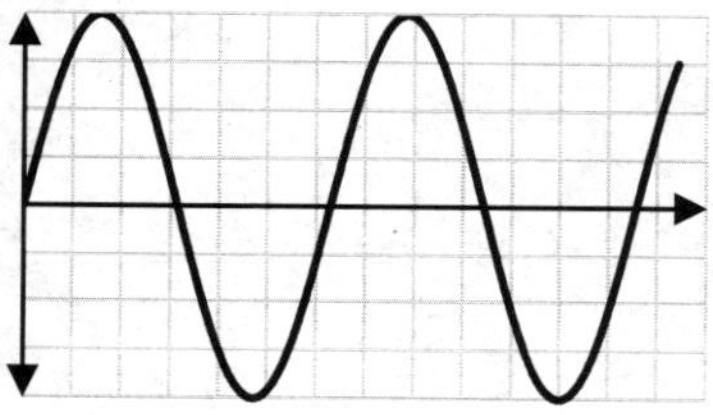

a.

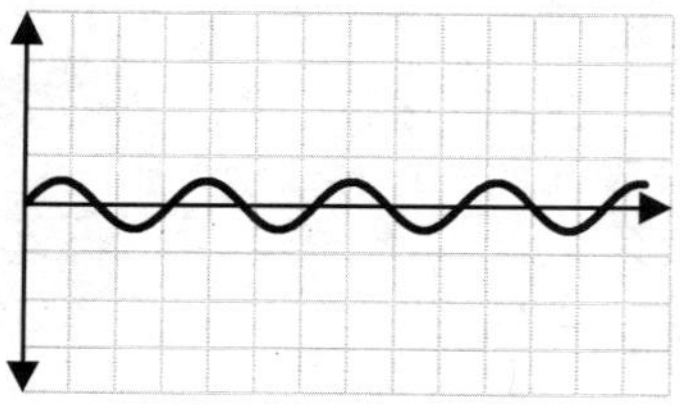

b.

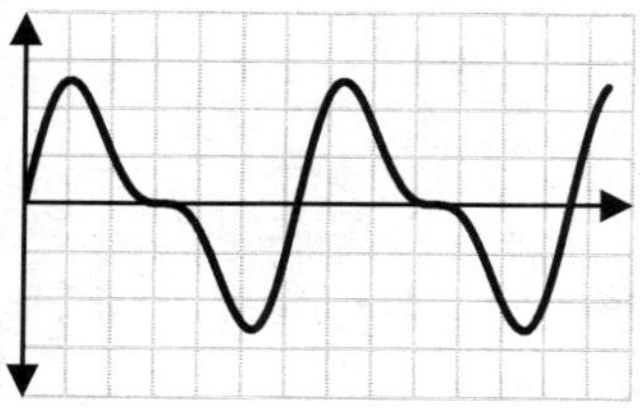

c.

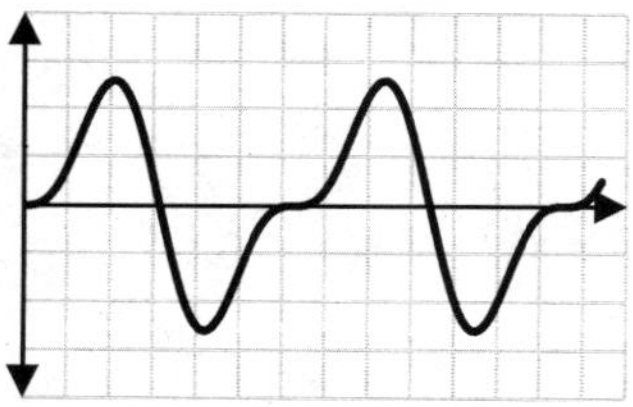

d.

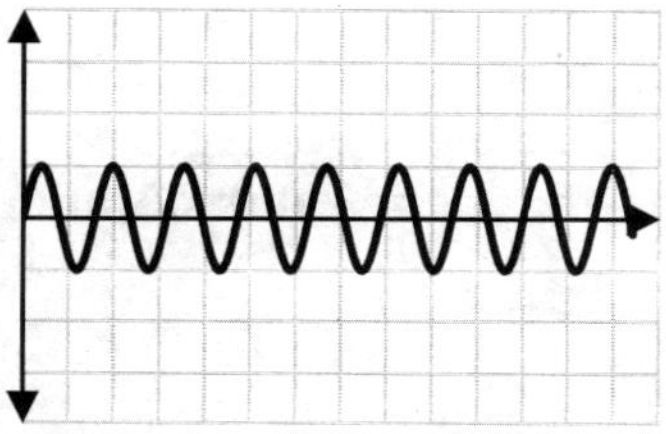

e.

31. Which of the following statements about electromagnetic waves with wavelengths in the range of 10^{-3} to 10^{5} m and frequencies in the range of 10^{3} to 10^{11} Hz is TRUE?

a. They can be used to transmit data.
b. They can be used to deliver Wi-Fi service.
c. They are absorbed by Earth's ozone layer.
d. They can be used in medical imaging.
e. They trigger cells in the human retina.

32. Which mathematical expression can be used to calculate the *total* resistance in a series circuit?

a. $R_{eq} = R_1 + R_2 + \cdots + R_n$
b. $\frac{1}{R_{eq}} = \frac{1}{R_1} + \frac{1}{R_2} + \cdots + \frac{1}{R_n}$
c. $R = \frac{\rho l}{A}$
d. $C = \frac{Q}{V}$
e. $C_{eq} = C_1 + C_2 + \cdots + C_n$

33. The electrolysis of water is an example of ____.

a. an adiabatic process
b. a chemical change
c. a synthesis reaction
d. reverse osmosis
e. neutralization

34. What type of change occurs when a liquid transitions to a gas?

a. A phase change
b. A chemical change
c. Sublimation
d. Condensation
e. Single replacement

35. A teaspoon of sugar is dissolved in a glass of water. The solution in the glass is ____.

a. an atom
b. a compound
c. an element
d. a mixture
e. a molecule

36. The center of an atom is called the ____. It is composed of ____.

a. nucleus; protons and neutrons
b. nucleus; protons and electrons
c. electron cloud; electrons and protons
d. electron cloud; electrons and neutrons
e. electron cloud; electrons only

37. Isotopes are two atoms of the same element that have different ____. They have the same number of ____, but a different number of ____.

a. mass; protons; neutrons
b. ionization number; protons; electrons
c. charge; protons; electrons
d. mass; protons; electrons
e. charge; electrons; protons

38. Which set of subatomic particles correctly describes an uncharged atom of carbon-13?

	# of protons	# of neutrons	# of electrons
a.	6	7	6
b.	7	6	7
c.	13	13	13
d.	6	7	7
e.	7	7	6

a. Set A
b. Set B
c. Set C
d. Set D
e. Set E

39. What is the electron configuration for an atom of nitrogen?

a. $1s^2 2s^2 2p^3$
b. $1K^2 2L^5$
c. Nucleus $= 7p + 7n$, electron cloud $= 7e^-$
d. $1s^2 2p^5$
e. $2L^7$

40. What information about the atom does the arrow point to?

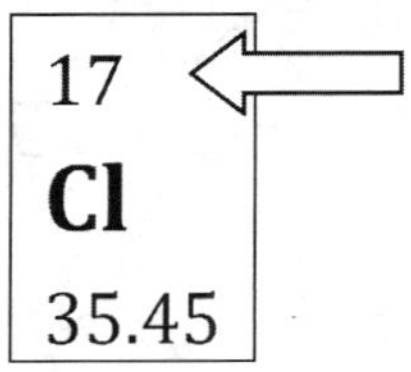

a. The atomic number or the number of protons
b. The average atomic mass in atomic mass units
c. The density of the element in g/mL
d. The number of stable isotopes of the element
e. The number of subatomic particles in the nucleus

41. Semiconductors belong to what group of elements?

a. Alkaline earth metals
b. Halogens
c. Metalloids
d. Noble gases
e. Transition metals

42. Which group of elements is highly reactive, need only one electron to fill their outer shells, and is known as the halogens?

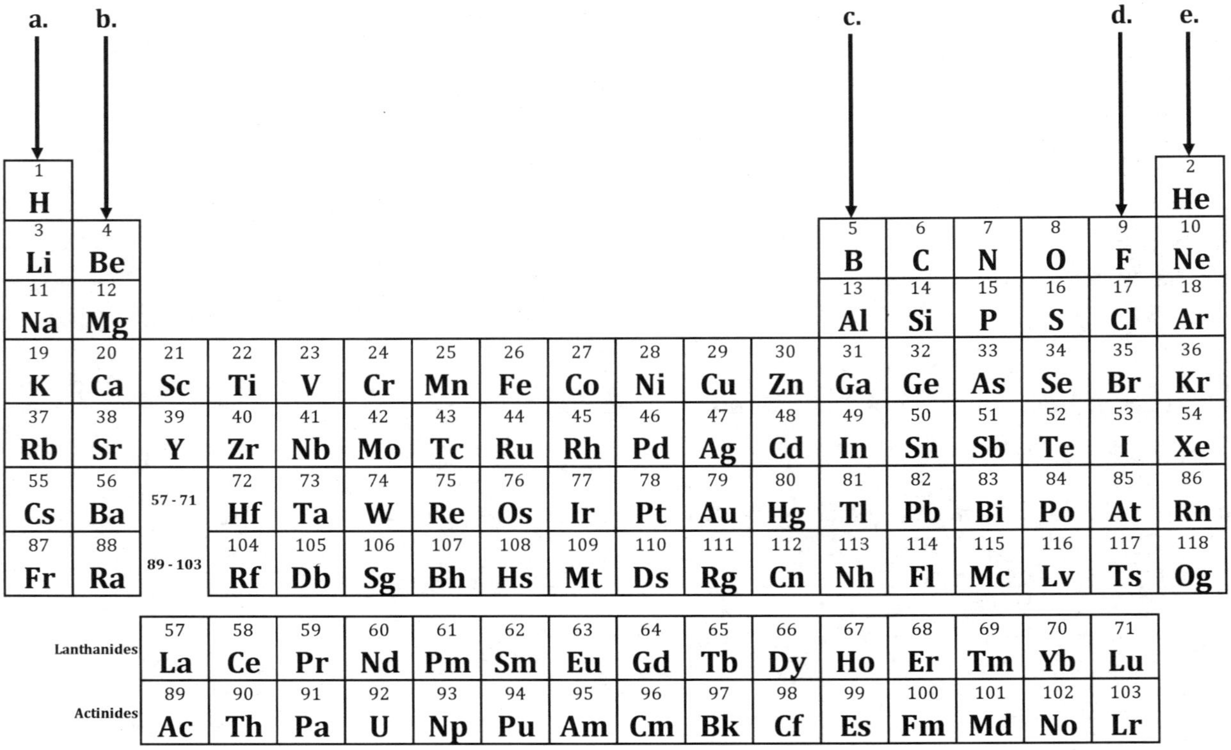

a. Group A
b. Group B
c. Group C
d. Group D
e. Group E

43. What mathematical expression can be used to calculate the volume in liters of two moles of an ideal gas at STP? $R = 8.314\frac{\text{L·kPa}}{\text{K·mol}}$

a. $V = \frac{(2)(8.314)(273)}{100}$
b. $V = (100)(2)(8.314)(273)$
c. $V = \frac{(2)(8.314)(0)}{100}$
d. $V = \frac{(2)(8.314)(0)}{1}$
e. $V = \frac{(100)}{(2)(8.314)(273)}$

44. What happens to gas particles as temperature increases?

a. The average kinetic energy decreases while the intermolecular forces increase.
b. The average kinetic energy increases while the intermolecular forces decrease.
c. Both the average kinetic energy and the intermolecular forces decrease.
d. Both the average kinetic energy and the intermolecular forces increase.
e. Temperature does not affect the average kinetic energy or the intermolecular forces.

45. Which group of elements has a stable electron configuration?

a. Alkali metals
b. Alkaline earth metals
c. Transition metals
d. Halogens
e. Noble gases

46. A sample of gas occupies 22.4 L at 10 °C and 1.00 atm. What is the new volume of the gas if the temperature increases to 100 °C and the pressure increases to 2.00 atm?

a. 8.97×10^{-4} L
b. 8.93×10^{-3} L
c. 7.51×10^{0} L
d. 1.48×10^{1} L
e. 1.12×10^{2} L

47. What kind of bond is formed between the two atoms shown in the periodic table below?

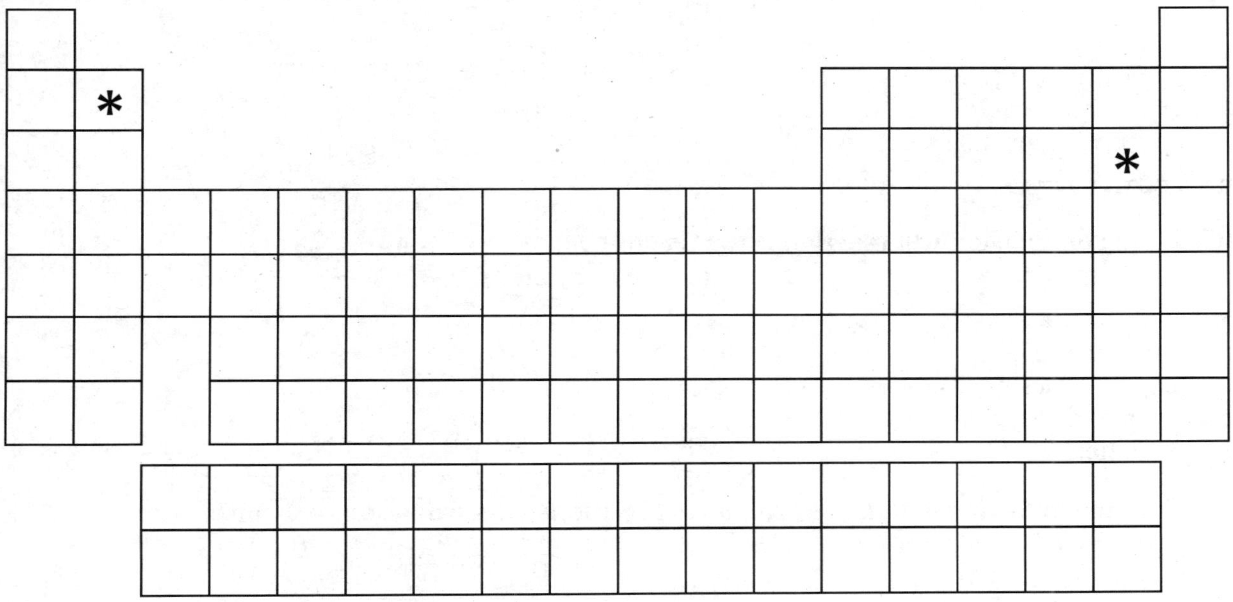

a. A covalent bond
b. An ionic bond
c. A metallic bond
d. A non-metallic bond
e. A Van der Waals bond

48. Which element will most likely form a covalently bonded compound when it bonds with sulfur?

a. Argon (Ar)
b. Iron (Fe)
c. Lithium (Li)
d. Oxygen (O)
e. Magnesium (Mg)

49. What is the chemical formula for a compound that forms when sodium ions interact with phosphate ions?

a. NaPO
b. NaPHO
c. $NaPO_4$
d. Na_3PO_4
e. Na_4PO

50. What is the chemical formula for aluminum sulfate?

a. AlS
b. $AlSO_4$
c. $Al_2(SO_4)_3$
d. $2Al_3SO_4$
e. $Al_3(SO_4)_2$

51. Which of the following ratios shows a balanced chemical equation for this reaction?

$$P_4 + O_2 \rightarrow P_2O_5$$

a. $P_4 + O_2 \rightarrow P_2O_5$
b. $2P_4 + 5O_2 \rightarrow P_2O_5$
c. $2P_4 + 5O_2 \rightarrow 7P_2O_5$
d. $P_4 + 5O_2 \rightarrow 2P_2O_5$
e. $5P_4 + 2O_2 \rightarrow P_2O_5$

52. What category of chemical reaction is the reaction below?

$$P_4 + O_2 \rightarrow P_2O_5$$

a. Synthesis
b. Decomposition
c. Single replacement
d. Double replacement
e. Oxidation

53. Which of the following *unbalanced* chemical equations is an oxidation reaction?

a. $NaCl + H_2O \rightarrow NaClO_3 + H_2$
b. $Hg_2(NO_3)_2 + K_2SO_4 \rightarrow Hg_2SO_4 + KNO_3$
c. $C_7H_{17} + O_2 \rightarrow CO_2 + H_2O$
d. $HgO \rightarrow Hg + O_2$
e. $SnO_2 + H_2 \rightarrow Sn + H_2O$

54. What is the percent composition of each element in $C_6H_{12}O_6$?

a. 6% carbon; 12% hydrogen; 6% oxygen
b. 25% carbon; 50% hydrogen; 25% oxygen
c. 40% carbon; 6.7% hydrogen; 53.5% oxygen
d. 37.5% carbon; 12.5% hydrogen; 50% oxygen
e. 41.4% carbon; 6.9% hydrogen; 51.7% oxygen

55. Hydrochloric acid and calcium carbonate react according to this balanced chemical reaction:

$$2HCl + CaCO_3 \rightarrow CaCl_2 + CO_2 + H_2O$$

What volume of carbon dioxide (CO_2) gas is produced when this reaction goes to completion at standard temperature and pressure?

a. 1 liter
b. 1 mole
c. 3 liters
d. 22.4 liters
e. 44 grams

56. Which combination of household chemicals produces a toxic gas?

a. Baking soda and vinegar
b. Bleach and ammonia
c. Water and sugar
d. Vinegar and antacid tablets
e. Rubbing alcohol and table salt

57. According to the solubility curves below, the solubility of which substance is *least* affected by a temperature change?

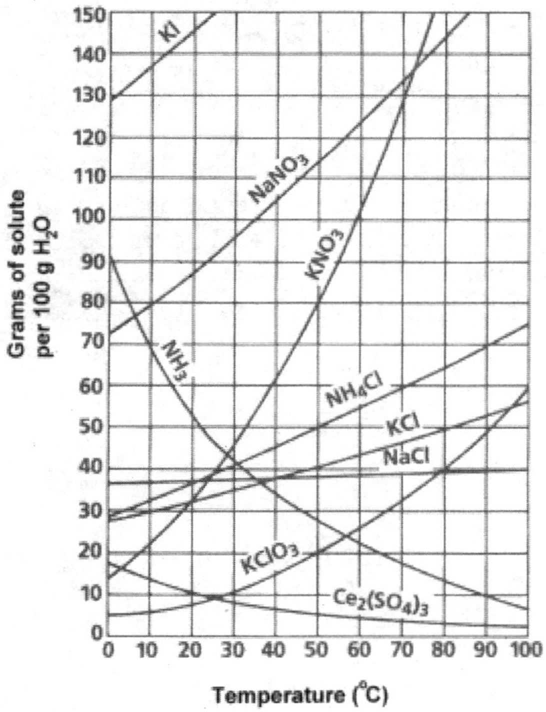

a. KI
b. NH_3
c. KNO_3
d. NaCl
e. $Ce_2(SO_4)_3$

58. A solution is made by dissolving 87.75 grams of NaCl into 500 mL of water. What is the final concentration of the NaCl?

a. 0.176 molar
b. 0.33 molar
c. 3 molar
d. 3.16 molar
e. 5.7 molar

59. A solution is made by dissolving 87.75 grams of NaCl into 500 mL of water. What is the weight percent of the NaCl in the solution?

a. 5.69%
b. 8.76%
c. 14.93%
d. 17.55%
e. 21.29%

60. Use the information in the solubility table below to identify the compound that is soluble in water.

Ion	Solubility	Exceptions
NO_3^-	Soluble	none
ClO_4^-	Soluble	none
Cl^-	Soluble	except Ag^+, Hg_2^{2+}, * Pb^{2+}
I^-	soluble	except Ag^+, Hg_2^{2+}, * Pb^{2+}
SO_4^{2-}	soluble	except Ca^{2+}, Ba^{2+}, Sr^{2+}, Hg^{2+}, Pb^{2+}, Ag^+
CO_3^{2-}	insoluble	except Group IA and NH_4^+
PO_4^{3-}	insoluble	except Group IA and NH_4^+
OH^-	insoluble	except Group IA, * Ca^{2+}, Ba^{2+}, Sr^{2+}
S^{2-}	insoluble	except Group IA, IIA and NH_4^+
Na^+	soluble	None
NH_4^+	soluble	None

a. FeS
b. KOH
c. $Al_2(CO_3)_3$
d. $CaSO_4$
e. HgI_2

61. The specific heat of aluminum is 0.215 cal/g°C. How much energy is required to change the temperature of 10 grams of aluminum from 25 °C to 75 °C?

a. 10.04 cal
b. 51.29 cal
c. 107.5 cal
d. 118.6 cal
e. 232.5 cal

62. When heat is removed from water during condensation, new ____ form.

a. atoms
b. covalent bonds
c. intermolecular bonds
d. ionic bonds
e. molecules

63. Which of the following would have the *most* massive radioactive decay?

a. An alpha particle
b. A beta ray
c. Gamma rays
d. X-rays
e. Ultraviolet light

64. Which of the following equations shows what happens when lead-210 decays through beta emission?

a. ${}^{210}_{82}Pb \rightarrow e^- + {}^{210}_{83}Bi$
b. ${}^{210}_{82}Pb \rightarrow e^- + {}^{210}_{83}Pb$
c. ${}^{210}_{82}Pb \rightarrow {}^{4}_{2}He + {}^{214}_{84}Po$
d. ${}^{210}_{82}Pb \rightarrow {}^{4}_{2}He + {}^{206}_{80}Po$
e. ${}^{210}_{82}Pb + e^- \rightarrow {}^{210}_{83}Bi$

65. Radon-222 is a radioactive gas. It has a half-life of 3.82 days. How much of a 1g sample of Radon-222 remains after 38.2 days?

a. 1/1,024 of a gram
b. 1/38.2 of a gram
c. 1/10 of a gram
d. 1/3.82 of a gram
e. 1/2 of a gram

66. Which of the following is an example of nuclear fission?

a. The formation of helium in our sun
b. The atomic bombs used at the end of WWII
c. The hydrogen bombs tested during the Cold War
d. Particles created in the Large Hadron Collider (LHC)
e. Particles created in the Stanford Linear Accelerator Center (SLAC)

67. Which of the following is NOT an example of an oxidation-reduction reaction?

a. A volcano eruption can be modeled using vinegar and baking soda.
b. Steel cans are electroplated with tin to produce grocery store food cans.
c. Blood catalyzes the decomposition of hydrogen peroxide on a cut.
d. Bread dough rises from the production of carbon dioxide gas by yeast.
e. Rust forms on a steel fence that is exposed to wind and rain.

68. The concentration of hydronium ions (H_3O^+) in a solution is 1.0×10^{-3} M. What is the pH of the solution?

a. -3
b. 0.001
c. 1.0
d. 3
e. 10

69. Which of the following conditions and chemical pairs is an example of a buffer?

a. Homeostasis; H_2CO_3/HCO_3^-
b. Water has a neutral pH; $(H_3O)^+/OH^-$
c. Copper can be electroplated onto tin; Cu^+/Sn^{2+}
d. Aluminum hydroxide is not soluble; Al^{3+}/OH^-
e. Sodium is more reactive than silver; Na^+/Ag^+

70. Which of the following laboratory safety devices is recommended but not required by state law?

a. Containers for broken glassware
b. Eye protection for every student
c. Emergency showers
d. Fire blankets
e. ABC fire extinguishers

71. Which of these signs shows the information contained on the Safety Data Sheet (SDS)?

a.

b.

c.

d.

e.

72. What information is contained in the safety icon below?

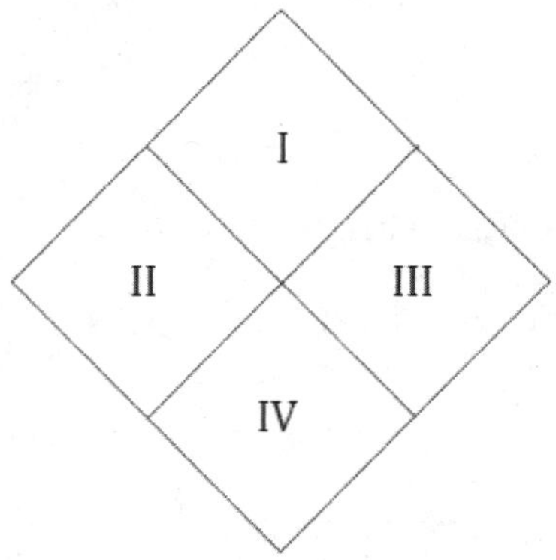

a. I = name of chemical, II = chemical formula, III = structural formula, IV = molecular weight
b. I = # of protons, II = # of neutrons, III = # of electrons, IV = atomic weight
c. I = chemical safety, II = biological safety, III = radiation safety, IV = emergency preparedness
d. I = flammability, II = health, III = reactivity, IV = special hazards
e. I = SDS master ID #, II = OSHA ID #, III = poison control #, IV = fire department #

73. Which unit represents $\frac{1}{1{,}000}$ of the basic metric unit of volume?

a. Milliliter
b. Centigram
c. Kilogallon
d. Deciquart
e. Hectometer

74. Which of the following measurements is equal to 25.4 centimeters?

a. 10 inches
b. 2.1 feet
c. 2.54 meters
d. 2,540 millimeters
e. 15.2 miles

75. What laboratory practice can increase the accuracy of a measurement?

a. Repeating the measurement several times
b. Calibrating the equipment each time you use it
c. Using metric measuring devices
d. Following SDS information
e. Reading the laboratory instructions before the lab

76. How can a computer aided design (CAD) program be used in the laboratory setting?

a. To collect and analyze digital data
b. To write up a lab report
c. To design a set of lab instructions
d. To generate graphical models
e. To reduce statistical error

77. Which of the following is usually the first form of study in a new area of scientific inquiry?

a. Descriptive studies
b. Controlled experiments
c. Comparative data analysis
d. Choosing a method and design
e. identifying dependent and independent variables

78. Which of the following is an example of a descriptive study?

a. Correlational studies of populations
b. Identifying a control
c. Statistical data analysis
d. Identifying dependent and independent variables
e. Drawing a valid conclusion

79. What is the purpose of conducting an experiment?

a. to test a hypothesis
b. to collect data
c. to identify a control state
d. to choose variables
e. to make a valid conclusion

80. Which of the following is needed for an experiment to be considered successful?

a. A reasonable hypothesis
b. A well-written lab report
c. Data that others can reproduce
d. Computer-aided statistical analysis
e. Graphs and tables

81. Which of the following is a characteristic of a reputable scientific journal?

a. Peer review of the quality of research
b. Famous scientists on the editorial board
c. Use of color graphics to represent data
d. Statistical analysis of all research data
e. Only government sponsored research is included

82. Which set of scientific thinkers is related to the study of chemistry?

a. Newton, Einstein, Feynman, and Hawking
b. Hooke, Pasteur, Watson & Crick, and Jacob & Monod
c. Ibn Hayyan, Lavoisier, Mendeleev, and Curie
d. Hutton, Darwin, Cuvier, and Wegener
e. Copernicus, Galileo, Kepler, and Hubble

83. When students are taught science, the information needs to be:

a. Correct, contextualized, and explained
b. Diverse, multicultural, and functional
c. Demonstrated, teacher-prepared, and manipulative
d. Theoretical, practical, and researched
e. Experimental, commercially available, and translated

84. Which of the following is a mnemonic strategy used in teaching science?

a. Memorizing the phrase King Phillip Came Over From Greece Saturday to help remember the biological classifications: Kingdom, Phylum, Class, Order, Family, Genus, Species
b. A guided reading strategy that involves summarizing, generating questions, clarifying, and predicting
c. Think, write, discuss lectures
d. Student-generated experimental procedures to answer a student-generated question
e. Lab reports that include: measurement, error analysis, more measurements, inductive reasoning

85. Broadly speaking, learning can be divided into what two categories?

a. Active and passive
b. Theoretical and practical
c. Hands-on and minds-on
d. Inquiry-based and book-based
e. Manipulating and reading

86. The scientific method is a series of steps to ____.

a. solve a problem
b. gather information
c. ask a scientific question
d. formulate a hypothesis
e. understand science

87. How long does an ideal high school science experiment last?

a. About half of the class period
b. 5 minutes less than the class period
c. 1 to 3 class periods
d. 3 to 5 class periods
e. 12 to 14 class periods

88. Which of the following assessment activities is a *formative assessment*?

a. College entrance exams (SAT or ACT)
b. A second semester final chemistry exam
c. Statewide testing
d. The National Assessment of Educational Progress (NAEP)
e. A chapter test on oxidation and reduction reactions

89. What is the purpose of assessing students' prior knowledge?

a. To plan appropriate activities to dispel student misconceptions and further students' conceptual understanding
b. To identify remedial, grade-level appropriate, and gifted/talented students
c. To meet school, district, and state requirements for IEPs
d. To collect student information that is reliable, valid, and without bias
e. To confirm student grades from previous years, semesters, or chapters

90. Which of the following is an example of engaging students in meaningful self-assessment?

a. Ask students to exchange papers and score each other's answers.
b. Ask students to score their own work using a teacher-provided rubric.
c. Ask students to write five questions to be included on the next exam.
d. Ask students to write a set of laboratory procedures to answer a question.
e. Ask students to bring in household items to be used in an experiment.

Answer Key and Explanations

1. B: The line on the velocity time graph represents acceleration. The slope indicates a constant rate of acceleration.

2. A: Vector addition involves the "head to tail" rule. The starting point is (0,0). Moving five units to the right and three units down will bring you to the end point. When these two points are connected the resulting vector is the one pictured in answer choice A.

3. A: Since change in velocity divided by change in time equals acceleration, the slope of each line segment on this graph represents acceleration. Line segments I and IV both have zero slope, meaning there is no change in velocity over the time represented. No change in velocity means the velocity is constant. Therefore, lines I and IV represent constant speed.

4. C: All lines on this graph represent acceleration since the slope of each line segment is equal to its acceleration. The line with the steepest slope therefore represents the greatest acceleration. The steepest line is V, so option C is the correct answer.

5. A: The bicyclist traveled a total of 24 miles (10 miles + 14 miles) in 4 hours. Therefore, the bicyclist's average speed is 6 miles/hour (24 ÷ 4).

6. A: Vector addition involves aligning the individual vectors "head" to "tail" and then drawing a line that connects the remaining "tail" to the "head."

7. A: A magnetic field is created by a spin magnetic dipole moment and the orbital magnetic dipole moment of the electrons in atoms. Therefore, it is the spinning and rotating of electrons in atoms that creates a magnetic field. Choice B describes the nucleus and electron clouds within an atom. Choice C creates thermal energy. Choice D creates a good electrical conductor. Choice E creates a radioactive atom.

8. B: An iron bar moving inside a coil of wire that contains a current would create an electromagnet. Choice A creates a magnetic field. Choice C creates an electric current. Choice D creates the Earth's magnetic field. Choice E creates thermal energy.

9. B: Work is defined as the force used to move a mass over a distance. Choice A may be a non-scientific definition of work. Choice C is the definition of power. Choice D is the definition of potential energy. Choice E is the definition of impulse.

10. C: One calorie is the amount of heat energy required to increase the temperature of 1 gram of water by 1 degree C. It is important to remember that the specific heat of water is 1 cal/g °C. The correct calculation to solve this problem is:

$$(\text{amount of water}) \times (\text{specific heat of water}) \times (\text{temperature change of water})$$

$$(100\text{ g}) \times (1\text{ cal/g °C}) \times (55\text{ °C} - 50\text{ °C}) = 500\text{ calories}$$

11. B: Light travels in straight lines. As light moves from one substance to another, the light rays bend according to the refractive index of each substance. As the light travels through the air, it hits the non-submerged portion of the pencil. The light is reflected from the pencil and this is what we see. However, as the light travels *into* the water, the light waves are bent (refracted), and that light is subsequently reflected and travels to our eyes. What we perceive is a pencil that is no longer whole and straight, but broken and bent. It is refraction (choice B) that causes this perception.

12. A: A fundamental concept of quantum physics is wave-particle duality. The remaining choices, while fundamental concepts in physics, can be explained by Newtonian physics. Choice B is the Law of Conservation of Matter and Energy. Distractor C is the 2nd Law of Thermodynamics. Choice D is the Kinetic Molecular Theory. Choice E is an application of the 2nd Law of Thermodynamics.

13. B: Weight is the force of gravity acting on a mass. The combination of Newton's 1st and 2nd Laws of Motion yields the mathematical formula $F = ma$. Applied to weight, this relationship can also be expressed as $F = mg$. To arrive at the correct answer, first multiply Earth's gravity by 1/6 to calculate the gravity on the moon ($g = 9.81\text{ m/s}^2 \times 1/6 = 1.635\text{ m/s}^2$). The second step is to multiply this value by the mass of the object ($F = 5\text{ kg} \times 1.635\text{ m/s}^2$; $F = 8.175\text{ N}$).

14. A: The two forces described in the item stem are equal in magnitude and opposite in direction. This creates a state of equilibrium and the sphere is not moving. The conditions necessary for the sphere to accelerate (B) are a change in direction or a change in velocity. The equal and opposite forces described in the item stem will not create either condition. The conditions necessary for the sphere to move along a line at a 120° angle (C) are two *unequal* forces acting at 30° and 210°. G-force is a measure of acceleration. The conditions necessary for the sphere to experience additional g-force (D) are freefall or increasing acceleration. The equal and opposite forces described in the item stem will not create either condition. A centripetal force on the sphere is required for the sphere to move in a circular path. 10 N is a unit of force, not a unit of distance. Choice E is therefore incorrect.

15. A: Choosing the correct answer requires an understanding of the following concepts:

- The sign system is at equilibrium.
- The weight of the sign is the downward force that must be balanced by the upward force since the sign system is at equilibrium.
- The weight of the sign is equal to the mass of the sign multiplied by the force of gravity.
- The upward force is acting through a 40° angle.

The only answer choice that correctly combines the concepts is A.

16. A: This correctly combines the information in the table. Note that the distance given is in units of kilometers while the other values use meters, and Newtons are based on meters as well. Once converted, the values can be substituted directly to get the expression. The Universal Law of Gravitation is an inverse square law that relates the mass of the two bodies, the square of the distance between them, and the gravitational constant (G):

$$F = \frac{G(m_1 \times m_2)}{r^2}$$

17. A: Magnetic poles occur in pairs known as magnetic dipoles. Individual atoms can be considered magnetic dipoles due to the spin and rotation of the electrons in the atoms. When the dipoles are aligned, the material is magnetic. Choices B, C, and D are all magnetic materials. Therefore, the magnetic dipoles in these materials are not randomly aligned. Only choice A has randomly aligned dipoles.

18. A: The relationship between wavelength and frequency is inversely proportional and, in general, the speed of sound is constant for almost all frequencies. So, the relationship between all three is defined to be: frequency times wavelength is equal to the speed of sound, in a given medium, or $f \times \lambda = v$.

19. B: The loudness of a sound depends on the amplitude of the sound wave.

20. C: Wavelength determines the color of the visible light spectrum.

21. C: Either wavelength or frequency can determine the classification of an electromagnetic wave (i.e., radio waves, microwaves, infrared radiation, visible light, ultraviolet radiation, x-rays, gamma rays). The intensity of an electromagnetic wave is independent from its classification. The speed of light is a constant and as such is what allows either wavelength or frequency to describe the wave.

22. B: The loudness of a sound is related to the amplitude of the wave and is measured in decibels (dB).

23. A: Hertz (Hz) is a unit of measure of wave frequency.

24. A: The mathematical formula for linear expansion is: $\Delta L = \alpha L_0 \Delta T$. Choice A correctly inserts the values provided in the table into this equation. Choice B is incorrect because it uses the coefficient of *volume* expansion. Choice C is incorrect because it uses density and then cubes the length of the rod in an attempt to rectify mismatched units. Choice D is incorrect because it cubes the length of the rod, converts from inches to centimeters, and converts from Kelvin to °C. Choice E is incorrect because it triples the length of the rod. This is an understandable mistake because the rule of thumb says that the coefficient of volume thermal expansion is three times the coefficient of linear thermal expansion.

25. A: The magnitude of the temperature on the Fahrenheit scale is calculated using the mathematical expression $°\text{F} = \frac{9}{5}°\text{C} + 32$. At the boiling point of water, 100 °C, the temperature in Fahrenheit is calculated to be 212 °F. Kelvin (absolute temperature) is calculated using the mathematical expression $\text{K} = °\text{C} + 273$. At 100 °C, the temperature in Kelvin is 373 K. Thus, the order from least to greatest is 100 °C, 212 °F, 373 K.

26. D: Power $= \frac{\text{work}}{\text{time}}$. The mass of the object (10 kg) and the distance (10 m) can be used to calculate work. The value for time is also provided.

27. E: The unit for work is J or $\frac{\text{kg·m}^2}{\text{s}^2}$. This eliminates answer choices A, C, and D. Work = force × distance. Lifting the 1 kg object requires a force to overcome the downward pull of gravity (1 kg × 9.81 $\frac{\text{m}}{\text{s}^2}$ = 9.81 $\frac{\text{kg·m}}{\text{s}^2}$). Multiplying this force by the distance of 10 meters gives 98.1 $\frac{\text{kg·m}^2}{\text{s}^2}$, or 98.1 J.

28. D: The unit of power is watts (W). The mathematical formula used to calculate power is power $= \frac{\text{work}}{\text{time}} = \frac{[(\text{mass}\times\text{gravity})\times(\text{distance})]}{\text{time}}$. Using the values in the question, this equation gives $\frac{[(5\text{ kg}\times 9.81\text{ m/s}^2)\times(10\text{ m})]}{5\text{s}} = 98.1\ \frac{\text{kg·m}^2}{\text{s}^3}$ OR 98.1 $\frac{\text{J}}{\text{s}}$ OR 98.1 W.

29. D: The conductivity of a material *decreases* with increased vibrational motion of the atoms. The exception is semiconductive materials. Superconductive materials have increased conductivity when the vibrational motion of the atoms decreases. LASERS, MASERS, and photoelectric sensors are all applications of quantum physics that are related to atomic emissions, not changes in the vibrational motion of atoms.

30. C: According to the principles of constructive and destructive interference, the two wave forms shown in the item stem will create waveform C.

31. A: The wavelength and frequency ranges are characteristic of waves at the lowest end of the electromagnetic spectrum—radio waves. These can be used to transmit data. Wi-Fi service is delivered by microwaves. Earth's ozone layer absorbs most ultraviolet waves. Medical imaging uses X-rays. Cells in the human retina are sensitive to visible light.

32. A: This expression can be used to calculate the total resistance in a series circuit. Choice B is the mathematical expression for total resistance in a parallel series. Choice C is the mathematical expression for resistance in a uniformly shaped material. Choice D is the mathematical expression for capacitance (stored electric charge). Choice E is the mathematical expression for capacitance in a parallel circuit.

33. B: The electrolysis of water is a chemical change that transforms water into hydrogen and oxygen gases. Synthesis reactions are those that combine reactants to form a product, which is the opposite of what happens when electrolyzing water. Reverse osmosis is a technique often used to purify water by forcing impure water through a semi-permeable membrane using a pressure differential.

34. A: The addition of energy causes a phase change. Phase changes are physical changes, not chemical changes. While sublimation is an example of a phase change, it occurs when a solid turns directly to a gas without passing through the liquid state. Condensation, another phase change, occurs when a gas turns to liquid. Single replacement reactions are one category of chemical change.

35. D: Sugar water is a mixture. The solution can be separated into its component parts. Evaporation will remove the water and leave the sugar in the glass.

36. A: The center of an atom is known as the nucleus. It is composed of protons and neutrons.

37. A: Isotopes are two atoms of the same element that have different mass. They have the same number of protons but a different number of neutrons. Choice C accurately describes ions. The other choices are incorrect.

38. A: All neutral (non-charged) carbon atoms have 6 protons and 6 electrons. The mass of carbon-13 is attributed to its 6 protons and 7 neutrons. Choice B, with 7 protons, is an atom of nitrogen. Choice C is an atom of aluminum. Choice D is a carbon ion with a 1- charge. Choice E is a nitrogen ion with a 1+ charge.

39. A: The correct electron configuration for an atom of nitrogen is $1s^2 2s^2 2p^3$.

40. A: The arrow is pointing to the atomic number, which also indicates the number of protons the element contains.

41. C: Metalloids have some properties of metals and some properties of nonmetals. A good semiconductor has the conductive properties of metals and a stability at high temperatures that is characteristic of nonmetals.

42. D: This is the group containing halogens, which are highly reactive and need only one electron to fill their outer shells. Group A are the alkali metals, which are highly reactive but have only 1 electron in their outer shells. Group B are the alkaline earth metals, which have 2 electrons in their outer shells. Group C consists of elements with 3 electrons in their outer shells. Group E are the noble gases, which are inert and have full outer electron shells.

43. A: Finding the correct answer to this item requires an awareness of and use of the following pieces of information:

- The mathematical expression known as the Ideal Gas Law is $PV = nRT$, where P is the pressure of the gas, V is the volume of the gas, n is the number of moles of the gas, R is the gas constant, and T is the temperature of the gas measured in Kelvin.
- The algebraic rearrangement of the expression yields the formula $V = \frac{nRT}{P}$.
- STP = 273 K and 100 kPa

Answer choices B and E incorrectly solve for V in the Ideal Gas Law. Answer choice C fails to convert from °C to K. Answer choice D interprets STP as 1 atm and fails to convert the pressure to kPa.

44. B: Temperature is a measure of the kinetic energy of particles. As temperature increases the average kinetic energy also increases. As the gas particles move more rapidly they occupy a larger volume. The increase in speed of the individual particles combined with the greater distance over which any intermolecular forces must act results in a decrease in the intermolecular forces.

45. E: The noble gases (inert gases) have full electron shells, which makes them chemically stable atoms.

46. D: The combined gas law is mathematically expressed as $\frac{P_1V_1}{T_1} = \frac{P_2V_2}{T_2}$ OR $V_2 = \frac{P_1V_1T_2}{T_1P_2}$. The temperatures need to be converted to Kelvin to complete the calculation:

$$T_1 = (273 + 10)\text{ K} = 283\text{ K}$$

$$T_2 = (273 + 100)\text{ K} = 373\text{ K}$$

$$V_2 = \frac{(1\text{ atm})(22.4\text{ L})(373\text{ K})}{(283\text{ K})(2\text{ atm})} \approx 14.8\text{ L} = 1.48 \times 10^1\text{ L}$$

47. B: Ionic bonds form between metals and nonmetals. Beryllium is an alkaline earth metal, and chlorine is a halogen, a non-metal.

48. D: Covalent bonds form when two nonmetals bond. Oxygen (O) is the only nonmetal in the answer choices. Iron (Fe) is a transition metal. Lithium (Li) is an alkali metal. Argon (Ar) is a noble gas and does not react with other elements.

49. D: The sodium ion has a 1+ charge (Na^+). The phosphate ion has a 3– charge $\left(PO_4{}^{3-}\right)$. Using the crisscross rule, it can be determined that three sodiums will balance the charge on one phosphate. Na_3PO_4 is correct.

50. C: An aluminum ion has a 3+ charge (Al^{3+}). A sulfate ion has a 2– charge $\left(SO_4{}^{2-}\right)$. Using the crisscross rule, two aluminums will balance the charge on three sulfates. Therefore, $Al_2(SO_4)_3$ is the correct answer.

51. D: When balancing a chemical reaction, the goal is to get an equal number of each type of atom on both sides of the reaction. The atoms that are there to begin with (reactants) must also be present at the end of the reaction (products). Answer choice D has 4 phosphorus atoms and 10 oxygen atoms on both sides.

52. A: In a synthesis reaction, simpler compounds are combined to form a more complex compound.

53. C: $C_7H_{17} + O_2 \rightarrow CO_2 + H_2O$ is an example of an oxidation reaction. Answer choice A is a hydrolysis reaction. Answer choice B is a double replacement reaction. Answer choice D is a decomposition reaction. Answer choice E is a single replacement reaction.

54. C: The percent composition of each element in $C_6H_{12}O_6$ is 40% carbon, 6.7% hydrogen, and 53.5% oxygen. Answer choice A is incorrect because it simply converts the subscripts to a percent. Answer choice B is incorrect because it looks at the number of atoms in the molecule instead of the mass of each element in the molecule. Answer choice D is incorrect because the percent is based on the atomic number of each element instead of the atomic mass. Answer choice E is incorrect because the atomic mass of oxygen was rounded to 15 instead of 16 to calculate the answer.

55. D: According to the balanced equation, 1 mole of carbon dioxide gas is produced. At the standard temperature and pressure conditions for the stated reaction, one mole of gas occupies 22.4 liters.

56. B: When combined, bleach and ammonia can release chlorine gas under certain conditions. Baking soda and vinegar (A) release carbon dioxide gas bubbles. Sugar simply dissolves in water (C). Vinegar (acetic acid) reacts with antacid tablets, producing salt, water, and non-toxic carbon dioxide gas (D). Nothing happens when table salt and rubbing alcohol are mixed (E)—there is no chemical reaction, and the salt does not dissolve.

57. D: The solubility curve for NaCl is nearly horizontal. Answer choice A is the substance with the *greatest* solubility. Answer choice B is the substance whose solubility *decreases* as temperature increases. Answer choice C is the substance whose solubility is *most* sensitive to changes in temperature. Answer choice E is the substance with the *lowest* solubility at any temperature.

58. C: Concentration is defined as the number of moles per liter of volume. Therefore, 87.75 g of NaCl = 1.5 moles of NaCl; $\frac{1.5 \text{ mol of NaCl}}{0.5 \text{ L of } H_2O} = 3$ molar.

59. C: Weight percent is calculated using the following mathematical expression:

$$\left(\frac{\text{mass of component}}{\text{total mass of solution}}\right) \times 100$$

Therefore, $\left(\frac{87.75 \text{ g}}{500 \text{ g}+87.75 \text{ g}}\right) \times 100 \approx 14.93\%$.

60. B: Hydroxides are insoluble. The exception is hydroxides formed by combining with group IA elements such as K. FeS (A) is insoluble because all sulfides are insoluble unless they combine with Group IA or IIA compounds or NH_4. $Al_2(CO_3)_3$ (C) is insoluble because all carbonates are insoluble unless they combine with Group IA elements. Al does not belong to Group IA. $CaSO_4$ (D) is one of the insoluble sulfate compounds. HgI_2 (E) is one of the insoluble iodide compounds.

61. C: The formula used to answer this problem is $Q = mc\Delta T$. Using the values provided in the question, $Q = (10 \text{ g}) \times (0.215 \frac{\text{cal}}{\text{g °C}}) \times (50 \text{ °C})$. Therefore, Q = 107.5 cal.

62. C: A physical change occurs when water condenses. The only thing formed during condensation is new intermolecular bonds. Therefore, no new molecules form (E) and no new covalent bonds form (B). The only time new atoms form is during a nuclear reaction (A). The water molecule is not ionizing, so no new ionic bonds form (D).

63. A: Alpha particles are essentially helium nuclei with a mass of 4 amu. When a neutron decomposes to a proton and releases an electron, the released electron is called a beta ray (B). The mass of an electron is approximately $\frac{1}{2{,}000}$ amu. Gamma rays (C) and x-rays (D) are high-energy, short-wavelength, high-frequency electromagnetic waves. As such, they are massless.

64. A: Lead-210 has a mass of 210 amu and an atomic number of 82. The starting material in the equation is $^{210}_{82}Pb$; beta emission is represented by e^- on the right side of the arrow. The mass of the final product does not change. However, the proton number increases by one. Answer B is incorrect because an atom with 83 protons is not Pb, but Bi. Answers C and D are incorrect because they contain an alpha particle instead of a beta ray. Answer E is incorrect because it shows lead-210 absorbing instead of emitting a beta ray.

65. A: After 38.2 days, 10 half-lives have occurred. This means that 1/210 remains of the original sample. This is equivalent to 1/1,024 of a gram.

66. B: The only example of nuclear fission is answer choice B. The nuclear reaction in the stars, including our sun (A), is a nuclear fusion reaction. Hydrogen bombs (C) are also examples of nuclear fusion. The Large Hadron Collider (D) and the Stanford Linear Accelerator Center (E) do not operate by means of nuclear reactions.

67. A: A model volcano eruption using vinegar and baking soda is an acid-base reaction, not an oxidation-reduction reaction. Tin cans are steel cans with a tin coating. Applying this coating involves an oxidation-reduction reaction. Decomposition of hydrogen peroxide and dough rising through the production of CO2 by yeast are both redox reactions. Rust formation is a redox reaction of iron, oxygen, and water. While the wind and rain are physical factors, rust formation is a chemical process.

68. D: The pH of a solution is defined as $-\log[H^+]$. Because the concentration is raised to a power of −3, the pH is 3. Using the equation, $-\log(-3) = 3$.

69. A: Homeostasis involves the balancing of many biochemical systems and process. Several of them include buffers as a means of expanding the range of stable conditions. In this instance, part of blood pH maintenance is controlled with the carbonic acid, H_2CO_3, and bicarbonate ion, HCO_3^-, buffer. While water, even when neutral, has a small amount of hydronium ions $(H_3O)^+$and hydroxide ions, OH^-, present, they do not act as a buffer (B). Electroplating copper onto tin is a redox reaction (C). The lack of solubility of aluminum hydroxide does not make it a buffer (D).

70. A: Using containers for broken glassware is recommended but not required by law. The other safety requirements listed are required by state law.

71. A: This sign shows the material contained on a Safety Data Sheet (SDS). The graphic in B is a generic *do not mix chemicals* warning. The graphic in C is a sign denoting the *location of the emergency exit*. The graphic in D is a sign denoting the *location of the fire extinguisher*. The graphic in E is the universal *reduce, reuse, recycle* emblem.

72. D: The information contained in the safety icon is as follows: I = flammability, II = health, III = reactivity, and IV = special hazards.

73. A: The prefix *milli-* means $\frac{1}{1{,}000}$ and liter is the basic metric unit of volume. Answer choice B is incorrect because the prefix *centi-* means $\frac{1}{100}$ and the gram is the basic unit of mass. Answer choice C is incorrect because the prefix *kilo-* means 1,000 and the gallon is not a metric unit of volume. Answer choice D is incorrect because the prefix *deci-* means $\frac{1}{10}$ and the quart is not a metric unit of volume. Answer choice E is incorrect because the prefix *hecto-* means 100 and the meter is the basic metric unit of length.

74. A: The conversion is done as follows: $(25.4\text{ cm}) \times \left(\frac{1\text{ in}}{2.54\text{ cm}}\right) = 10\text{ in.}$

75. A: Repeating a measurement several times can increase the accuracy of the measurement. Calibrating the equipment should only be done once for a whole set of measurements. Calibrating for each use will add a source of error and prevent measurements from being able to be compared. None of the other choices are useful strategies to increase the accuracy of a measurement.

76. D: A CAD program can be used in a laboratory setting to generate graphical models. Collecting digital data (A) requires the use of computer probes. Lab reports (B) are written up using a word processing program. Creating lab instructions (C) and reducing statistical error are not applications of a CAD program.

77. A: Descriptive studies are usually the first form of study in a new area of scientific inquiry. Others are also forms of scientific study, but are completed after initial descriptive studies.

78. A: A correlational study of a population is an example of a descriptive study. Answer choices B, C, and E are examples of the controlled experimentation type of scientific investigation. Identifying dependent and independent variables (D) is an example of the comparative data analysis type of scientific investigation.

79. A: The purpose of conducting an experiment is to test a hypothesis. The other choices are all steps in conducting an experiment designed to test a hypothesis.

80. C: For an experiment to be considered successful, it must yield data that others can reproduce. Answer choice A may be considered part of a well-designed experiment. Answer choices B, D, and E may be considered part of an experiment that is reported on by individuals with expertise.

81. A: A characteristic of a reputable scientific journal is that there is peer review of the quality of the research. The other choices may be characteristics of scientific journals, but these do not necessarily mean a journal is reputable.

82. C: Ibn Hayyan, Lavoisier, Mendeleev, and Curie are associated with the study of chemistry. The scientists listed in choice A are associated with the study of physics. The scientists listed in choice B are associated with the study of biology. The scientists listed in choice D are associated with the study of geology. The scientists listed in choice E are associated with the study of astronomy.

83. A: When students are taught science, the information needs to be correct, contextualized, and explained.

84. A: Memorizing the phrase **K**ing **P**hillip **C**ame **O**ver **F**rom **G**reece **S**aturday to help remember the biological classifications is an example of a mnemonic strategy. Answer choice B is a description of the ReQuest reading strategy. Answer choice C is a lecture variation. Answer choice D is an example of an active student inquiry activity. Answer choice E is a mnemonic for "mnemonic."

85. A: Active and passive learning are the two general categories of learning.

86. A: The scientific method is a series of steps to solve a problem. Answer choices B, C, D, and E are all parts of the scientific method.

87. E: According to the Teacher Certification Guidelines, an ideal high school science experiment should last 12 to 14 class periods.

88. E: A chapter test on oxidation and reduction reactions is an example of a formative assessment. Answer choices A, B, C, and D are all examples of summative assessments.

89. A: The purpose of assessing students' prior knowledge is to plan appropriate activities to dispel student misconceptions and further students' conceptual understanding.

90. B: An example of engaging students in meaningful self-assessment is asking them to score their own work using a teacher-provided rubric. Answer choice A does not provide students with an opportunity to constructively critique the work of another student. Answer choice D is an example of an appropriate inquiry technique to use in a scientific investigation. Choices C and E are not examples of assessment strategies.

Online Resources

Due to our efforts to try to keep this book to a manageable length, we've created a link that will give you access to all of your online resources:

mometrix.com/resources719/texesphysc6-12

It's Your Moment, Let's Celebrate It!

Share your story @mometrixtestpreparation